THOMAS ALVA EDISON

SIXTY YEARS OF AN INVENTOR'S LIFE

Thomas Alva Edison
(February 11, 1847 – October 18, 1931)

FRANCIS ARTHUR JONES

Would you like to buy a copy of
THOMAS ALVA EDISON ?

Please visit:
http://www.diamondbooks.ca/books

THOMAS ALVA EDISON

SIXTY YEARS OF AN INVENTOR'S LIFE

BY

FRANCIS ARTHUR JONES

English writer and journalist (b. 3/15 May 1871 in Chester), born
Francis Arthur Launcelot Jones; also known as
Francis Arthur Jameson.

TORONTO, CANADA – 2017

DIAMOND BOOKS - CANADA

Toronto, ON, CANADA
http://www.diamondbooks.ca

Copyright © 2017 – DIAMOND BOOKS. All rights reserved.

BIBLIOGRAPHIC INFORMATION

' THOMAS ALVA EDISON '
was first published in 1907,
by: THOMAS Y. CROWELL & CO.,
New York.

PUBLISHED IN CANADA

Published in Canada by DIAMOND BOOKS - CANADA, an imprint of
DIAMOND PUBLISHERS - http://www.diamondpublishers.com

Published Edition: July, 2017.

PAPERBACK EDITION : ISBN: 978-1-988942-04-9
E-BOOK EDITION : ISBN: 978-1-988942-05-6

PRINTED IN CANADA

Thomas Alva Edison
(February 11, 1847 – October 18, 1931)

PREFACE

IN the preparation of this book the author has received, and here acknowledges, the invaluable co-operation of many persons who knew Mr. Edison in his younger days, and who cheerfully placed at his service the result of their acquaintance and association with the inventor. To the American Press generally the writer is indebted for much valued assistance, and especially grateful does he feel towards the following: to the Editor of the *Electrical Review* for permission to incorporate Edison's own account of the circumstances under which he erected the first power-house for the distribution of the electric light; to Mr. W. K. L. Dickson, the consulting electrician; to Mr. J. R. Randolph, private secretary to Mr. Edison, Mr. Frank L. Dyer, chief of the Legal Department, and the late Dr. Wangemann, phonographic expert, for much interesting "inside" information; and also to the Cassier Magazine Company, holders of the copyright, for courteous permission to use certain pictures and to quote from Dickson's "Life of Edison," now out of print.

To the inventor himself the writer is grateful for all the time he spent away from his experimental laboratory to give, with his customary cheerfulness and good-nature, much of the personal history which is here recorded. To Mrs. Edison acknowledgment should be made for the loan of various portraits of her distinguished husband taken in his younger days;

for a copy of the paper (the only one believed to be in existence) which Edison printed and published on the train at the age of fourteen; and for a lecture written by Mr. Edison many years ago recounting the results of experiments made in connection with platinum wire during his invention of the incandescent electric light.

This book is in no sense an exhaustive "Life" of Edison, and, indeed, could not be, seeing that the inventor is still young in heart and enthusiasm, and that there are probably many years of his brilliant career still to run. His grandfather and great-grandfather lived to be centenarians, and their noted descendant gives every indication of coming into healthy competition with them in the matter of a long life. And although Mr. Edison avers that he has "quit the inventing business" and is now devoting himself almost exclusively to pure science, there is every reason to hope that by his investigations many scientific problems will yet be solved, and that some of the secrets which Nature still holds will be revealed through him.

FRANCIS ARTHUR JONES.

CONTENTS

CHAPTER		PAGE
I.	BIRTHPLACE AND EARLY LIFE	1
II.	BOYHOOD AND YOUTH	10
III.	NEWS AGENT AND TELEGRAPHER	29
IV.	IN SEARCH OF EMPLOYMENT	38
V.	HIS FIRST WORKSHOP	48
VI.	EARLY TELEGRAPHIC INVENTIONS	61
VII.	THE TELEPHONE	71
VIII.	THE ELECTRIC LIGHT	94
IX.	EXPERIMENTS WITH PLATINUM WIRE	126
X.	THE PHONOGRAPH	134
XI.	THE KINETOSCOPE, MAGNETIC ORE SEPARATOR, AND OTHER INVENTIONS	165
XII.	SOME LESSER INVENTIONS	176
XIII.	WAR MACHINES	192
XIV.	ELECTROCUTION	203
XV.	THE STORAGE BATTERY	213
XVI.	THE LABORATORY AT ORANGE	221
XVII.	NOTION BOOKS	249
XVIII.	BANQUETS	254
XIX.	IN EUROPE	267
XX.	HOME LIFE	279

CONTENTS

CHAPTER		PAGE
XXI.	HIS PERSONALITY	290
XXII.	PHOTOGRAPHING THE WIZARD	313
XXIII.	SOME ANECDOTES	317
XXIV.	HIS OPINIONS	334
INDEX		351

ILLUSTRATIONS

THOMAS ALVA EDISON . . . . . *Frontispiece*	
	PAGE
EDISON'S BIRTHPLACE, MILAN, OHIO	4
EDISON AT THE AGE OF FOUR	10
EDISON WHEN A NEWSBOY ON THE GRAND TRUNK .	10
EDISON'S RAILWAY NEWSPAPER, "THE GRAND TRUNK WEEKLY HERALD"	18
EDISON AT THE AGE OF NINETEEN	40
EDISON AT FORTY	40
EDISON'S FIRST INVENTION, THE VOTE RECORDER .	54
EDISON'S UNIVERSAL STOCK PRINTER	64
EDISON AT THE AGE OF TWENTY-FOUR	72
EDISON AT THE AGE OF TWENTY-EIGHT . . .	72
MOTOGRAPH RECEIVING AND TRANSMITTING TELEPHONE	80
EDISON'S FIRST INCANDESCENT LAMP	106
EDISON DYNAMO OF 1880	116
EDISON DRIVING HIS FIRST ELECTRIC LOCOMOTIVE .	124
EDISON'S FIRST SKETCH OF THE PHONOGRAPH . .	134
EDISON'S ORIGINAL TIN-FOIL PHONOGRAPH . . .	138
EDISON LISTENING TO A PHONOGRAPHIC RECORD . .	142
TESTING A PHONOGRAPHIC RECORD IN THE EXPERIMENTAL ROOM	150
THE EDISON BAND MAKING A PHONOGRAPHIC RECORD .	158
KINETOSCOPE RECORD OF CARMENCITA'S DANCE . .	168
EDISON MAGNETIC ORE SEPARATOR	172
EDISON EXPERIMENTING IN HIS PRIVATE LABORATORY .	184
EDISON REPLYING TO SOME PUZZLING QUESTIONS . .	194

	PAGE
CHARGING AN EDISON STORAGE BATTERY IN THE GARAGE ATTACHED TO THE LABORATORY	214
LIBRARY AT THE EDISON LABORATORY, ORANGE, N.J.	222
EDISON IN HIS CHEMICAL LABORATORY, ORANGE, N.J.	228
LEGAL DEPARTMENT, EDISON LABORATORY, ORANGE, N.J.	234
EDISON EXAMINING A STATEMENT RENDERED BY ONE OF HIS WORKPEOPLE	252
EDISON'S "DEN," IN HIS HOME AT LLEWELLYN PARK, N.J.	282
MR. AND MRS. EDISON AND FAMILY ON THE PORCH OF THEIR HOME AT LLEWELLYN PARK, N.J.	290
MR. AND MRS. EDISON IN THE CHEMICAL LABORATORY	316

CHAPTER I

BIRTHPLACE AND EARLY LIFE

It was a cold day in February, 1847, and the little town of Milan, Ohio, was noisy with the rumble of farm wagons carrying wheat to the canal for shipment to Lake Erie; the wharf was crowded with farmers, shippers, laborers, and idlers, all gathered together to assist or retard the weighing and loading of the grain; everywhere appeared bustle and movement save, perhaps, in the Edison homestead, where the advent of a new life was awaited.

The Edison home was built on elevated ground, and from the windows an excellent view of the canal and the Huron River could be obtained. Mr. Samuel Edison was not down on the wharf — where every other male member of the community appeared to have assembled — having preferred to remain indoors until the birth of his child was safely accomplished. He was a tall man, over six feet in height, somewhat thin though indicating giant strength. His bearded face was full of resolution tempered with good-nature, while the eyes were kindly. As he stood looking on the busy scene below he little thought that the event he was awaiting was one which would have a direct bearing on future generations.

Presently the nurse who had been looking after Mrs. Edison — a good-hearted neighbor — entered the room and informed Mr. Edison that he was the father of a fine, sturdy boy. "A pretty child," said the nurse, "fair, with gray eyes — the very image of his mother." Mr. Edison received the news philosophically, and a little later, when allowed to see the child, he regarded it with great interest. The boy certainly was like his mother, that was a fact, and the father expressed his pleasure at the resemblance, and remarked that if he grew like her in disposition as well as feature then he would indeed prove a blessing to them. His mother adored him from the moment he was placed in her arms, and there was from the first an affection between them which increased as the child grew.

Samuel Edison had emigrated to Milan in 1838, having fled thither from Canada, where he had fallen into disgrace through taking too active a part in the Papineau Rebellion. He owned land in the Dominion which he had received as a gift from the British Government, and when it became known that he also was among the rebels the grant was forfeited, and Mr. Samuel Edison found it wise to make hasty tracks for the St. Clair River. In his flight from Canadian territory he walked one hundred and eighty-two miles without sleep, for his powers of endurance were no less remarkable than those which afterwards characterized his son.

On reaching Milan, Samuel Edison found that it was a town which would serve him well as a retreat, and he thereupon decided to adopt it as his future place of residence, eschew rebellions, and live in harmony both with Government and neighbor. A few years later he married a pretty school teacher named Nancy Elliot, whom he had known in his Canadian days, rented the small house already mentioned, busied himself in various enterprises, and settled down to a peaceful, industrious, and contented life. He had seen Milan in her prosperous days, but the time was coming when she would rank no higher than a pretty suburban village, and the various vicissitudes through which the town passed are, perhaps, best described in a letter written a short time since by a resident.

"Seventy years ago," says this correspondent, "before the railroads had penetrated the Western Reserve, it became necessary to establish an outlet for the great amount of grain requiring shipment to Eastern ports from Central and Northern Ohio. The Huron River, emptying into Lake Erie, was navigable only a few miles from its mouth, and so a landing was chosen about three miles below the beautiful village of Milan, then in its infancy. Warehouses for the storage of grain were built there, and vessels came up the river from Huron to receive their cargoes. The business proved so profitable that in a short time a few capitalists conceived the idea of digging a canal from 'Lockwood Landing' to Milan, thus bringing navigation to their village.

"The project was carried out, and soon Milan became a prosperous grain market. A dozen warehouses were built on the bank of the canal, and my earliest recollections are associated with the wagon-loads of grain in bags standing in front of my father's warehouse, having been drawn by oxen or horses from all sections of the surrounding country; and in the busy season the line would extend from one to two miles out on the main road, each awaiting its turn for the slow process of loading and weighing the grain.

"It was a glorious prospect for Milan. Shipbuilding soon became a prominent industry, and many fine vessels, including six revenue cutters, were launched in the waters of the canal. The village now had a thriving population of independent, refined people. A Presbyterian church was established with a 'Huron Institute' as an outgrowth which became famous through all sections of the State. Other churches were organized and houses of worship erected — Episcopal, Methodist, and, some years later, Roman Catholic. Graded schools were established, and in every direction the progress was marked.

"But, alas for Milan's brilliant future! An enterprising railroad made overtures to pass through the village, but the canal capitalists could see no avenue leading to prosperity more swiftly than the ditch they had dug, and they awoke one day to the knowledge that Norwalk and Wakeman had cut them off from railroad communication, and their trade soon became as stagnant as the waters of their beloved canal. Oh, the bitter irony of fate that one should be born in their village who was destined to create an entire revolution in the mode of rapid transit, that a child born in a house on a bluff overlooking the canal should be endowed with wonderful perceptions of chained lightning!

"And soon the exodus of our business men to other States began. You will find throughout the Union to-day men of ability, prominent in professional and commercial circles, who once claimed Milan as their home. The old 'Huron Institute' was converted into the 'Western Reserve Normal School,' and proved a noted and beloved resort of learning for hundreds of teachers now scattered throughout the length and breadth of the land, and the old brick building still stands, a monument of pleasant memories.

"If you would view the birthplace of Edison to-day, take passage on the electric railway from Norwalk to Sandusky, and you will be borne swiftly along through a section of rich farm lands and a beautiful hilly country that presents a succession of picturesque scenery, especially along the banks of the Huron River. At Milan you can leave the car and wander at will through the little village nestling among the

EDISON'S BIRTHPLACE, MILAN, OHIO

hills. There are few attractions for the stranger. The old-time Sabbath-like stillness pervades the air, broken only at stated times when the echo of the locomotive wheels from two railroads sounds over the hills.

"There is a public square in the centre of the business portion of the town surrounding a handsome monument erected to the memory of the volunteers from that vicinity who enlisted in the Fifty-fifth and Sixty-seventh O.V.I. There are green-shaded trees, comfortable homes, some fine residences, and a cultured Law-and-Gospel-loving community; and there is a cemetery, so tastefully inviting that people who ever lived in Milan ask to be taken back there for their last abiding rest. You will not find any canal, but perhaps the oldest inhabitant can point out to you a slight depression in the ground which might be traced for a few miles as the bed of the old channel, now mostly under cultivation as vegetable gardens."

And here it was, when Milan revelled in her prosperity, that Thomas Alva Edison was born and passed the first seven years of his life. In infancy he was what mothers and nurses would call a "good" child, for he seldom cried, and his temper, from the moment when he could distinguish between pleasure and pain, was an angelic one. He is said to have cracked jokes when a baby, and from the time when he began to "take notice" he was quite conscious of the humorous side of a situation. This characteristic he probably inherited from his father, who, like Lincoln, enjoyed a good story. The serious side of his nature came from his mother, not so much as an inheritance perhaps, but because during his early years he was constantly with her. To him his mother was something more than a fond parent, and his love for her was of that superlative quality which ever remained one of the strongest attributes of his nature. Many years later — long after her death, when fame and fortune had come to him — interviewers would ask the inventor to tell them something about his mother. But her loss had been so great a grief to him that he never could speak of her to strangers — only to those who had known her and appreciated her goodness, and who could realize a fraction of all that she had been to him. Once, however, he broke down this reserve, and to a writer in the New York *World* he spoke of her in words which indicated something of the strength of those ties which had bound them together.

"I did not have my mother very long," he said on this occasion, "but in that length of time she cast over me an influence which has lasted all my life. The good effects of her early training I can never lose. If it had not been for her appreciation and her faith in me at a critical time in my experience, I should very likely never have become an inventor. You see, my mother was a Canadian girl who used to teach school in Nova Scotia. She believed that many of the boys who turned out badly by the time they grew to manhood would have become valuable citizens if they had been handled in the right way when they were young. Her years of experience as a school teacher taught her many things about human nature, and especially about boys. After she married my father and became a mother, she applied that same theory to me.

"I was always a careless boy, and with a mother of different mental caliber I should have probably turned out badly. But her firmness, her sweetness, her goodness, were potent powers to keep me in the right path. I remember I used never to be able to get along at school. I don't know now what it was, but I was always at the foot of the class. I used to feel that the teachers never sympathized with me and that my father thought that I was stupid, and at last I almost decided that I must really be a dunce. My mother was always kind, always sympathetic, and she never misunderstood or misjudged me. But I was afraid to tell her all my difficulties at school, for fear she too might lose her confidence in me.

"One day I overheard the teacher tell the inspector that I was 'addled' and it would not be worth while keeping me in school any longer. I was so hurt by this last straw that I burst out crying and went home and told my mother about it. Then I found out what a good thing a good mother was. She came out as my strong defender. Mother love was aroused, mother pride wounded to the quick. She brought me back to the school and angrily told the teacher that he didn't know what he was talking about, that I had more brains than he himself, and a lot more talk like that. In fact, she was the most enthusiastic champion a boy ever had, and I determined right then that I would be worthy of her and show her that her confidence was not misplaced. My mother was the making of me. She was so true, so sure of me; and I felt that I had some one to live for, some one I must not disappoint. The memory of her will always be a blessing to me."

When "Al," as his mother always called him, emerged from baby clothes and was able to walk and talk, neighbors soon made the discovery that he was rather a remarkable-looking child. He had a fine, large, well-shaped head, of which his mother was very proud. But his hair was a terrible trial to her. It would not curl, it would not part, it would not lie down like other boys'. He was always rumpling it with his baby fingers, and so the only thing to be done was to keep it "close," a plan which was advocated by his father and adopted, after a mental struggle, by his mother. He had a broad, smooth forehead, deep-set eyes, almost straight brows, and the sweetest, most amiable, and lovable mouth ever seen in a baby. His high forehead was usually unruffled and serene, except when he asked those innumerable questions which came to his lips almost as soon as he could talk. Being greatly puzzled over any matter in which he happened to take an especial interest, he would scowl a little. "When this occurred," writes some one who knew him when a child, "his lips went tight together, his brows contracted, and as he got busy with his infant schemes he would go fast and with a walk that showed all kinds of determination."

At four years of age he was friendly with all the neighboring children — especially boys — and every one liked him. He was ready to take part in any escapade suggested, and when his mother's back was turned for a moment he would slip out of the house, take a short cut to the canal by scrambling down the bluff, and a few minutes later his anxious parent would detect him from one of the windows running along the tow-path as fast as his sturdy legs would carry him. From there he would make his way to the shipbuilding yards, pick up and examine every tool he could find, ask a hundred questions of the busy workmen, get under their feet and in their path, and bother them generally. But they liked him nevertheless; though with that lack of instinct which is sometimes so hard to understand they often thought his questions foolish, and, as a consequence, the boy anything but bright. Even his father, forty years later, said that many folk considered he was a little lacking in ordinary intelligence, probably because they could not always give him satisfactory replies to the puzzling questions which he put to them. He was forever asking his father the reason for this and that, and when, in very desperation and thinking frankness the better policy, the unhappy parent would answer, "I don't know," the boy would reduce him to still deeper depths of distraction by instantly demanding, "Why don't you know?"

There are many people in Milan to-day who remember little Al Edison, and they will tell you how on one occasion he chased the old goose off her nest and tried to hatch out the eggs himself by sitting on them, just to satisfy a natural desire to know how it was done. A little later on he evinced his first interest in avian flight by endeavoring to persuade the "hired girl" to swallow some fearful concoction, with the promise that if she did so she would certainly be able to fly. The young woman firmly declined to try the experiment, but Al, who in all probability thoroughly believed what he had undoubtedly been told, was so persistent in his entreaties that she would try even a little, that at last she swallowed a small dose, and immediately became so ill that the doctor had to be summoned. The boy expressed regret that she was sick, but appeared to think that her inability to fly lay with herself and not with the liquid.

CHAPTER II

BOYHOOD AND YOUTH

WHEN Al was seven years of age his father decided that the time had come when it would be wise to leave Milan. Even at that period the town had begun to lose prestige and work of every kind commenced to suffer in consequence. Mr. Edison was a man who believed in having an eye to the future, and the reduction of tariff on the canal having already started, owing to the construction of the Lake Shore Railroad, he foresaw that the end of Milan as a commercial centre was in sight. He had many consultations with his wife regarding the advisability of moving, and she, sensible woman that she was, stifled the longing to remain in their pretty, peaceful home, and declared her readiness to make any change that might result in advantage to the family.

Discussions regarding the best place to settle in were many, and at last it was decided to begin life anew in Port Huron, Michigan, a prosperous town whose chief characteristics were bustle and enterprise. Thither Mr. Edison made several trips in advance, inspected many homes which he thought might prove suitable for him and his small family, and eventually chose one which was large and comfortable, a fine, roomy house located in the centre of an extensive grove containing several apple and pear trees. It was, in fact, one of the best residences in the locality, situated amid country surroundings, yet within easy distance of the town.

EDISON AT THE AGE OF FOUR

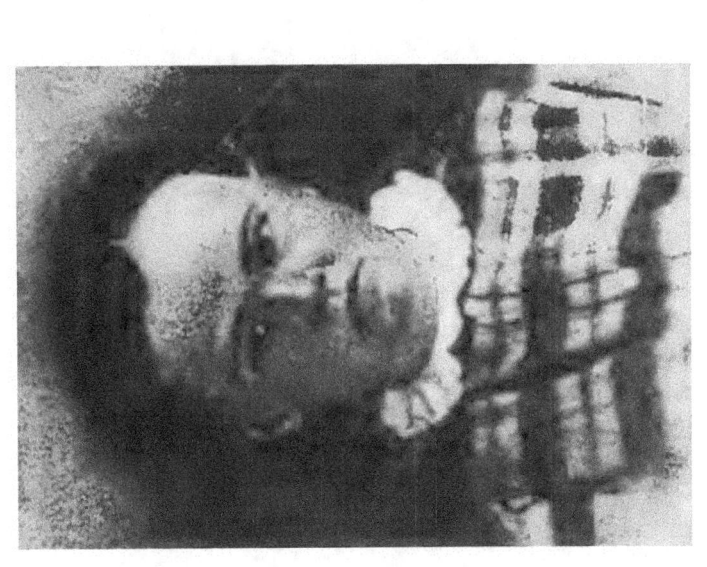
EDISON WHEN A NEWSBOY ON THE GRAND TRUNK

Here the family arrived one evening in the fall of 1854, and were soon comfortably installed in their new home.

Their residence in Port Huron proved no less happy than the years they had spent in Milan. Al, now a sturdy boy "going on eight," was the same cheerful little lad he had been in the Ohio home, good-tempered, fond of fun, and as sharp as a needle; just as curious regarding the meaning of everything and rather more determined than before to strip his relations and friends of all the knowledge they possessed. He was as passionately devoted to his mother as in the Milan days, and there was also a link of affection forging between him and his father which no years of separation were to sever.

Al received all his instruction from his mother, with the exception of about three months when he went to the Huron Public School and left on account of the incident already narrated. Mrs. Edison was very fond of children even if they were not her own, and soon the little ones who passed the house every morning on their way to school began to look upon her as a friend. One of these very children — now a woman of sixty-five — whose acquaintance with the Edison family began in these early days, recently said:

"I well remember the old homestead, surrounded by the orchard, and frequently saw Mrs. Edison and her son sitting on the porch reading or conversing. Sometimes I noticed that she was instructing him in his lessons and I often wondered why he never went to school. I remember how much alike I thought them at the time. The boy was essentially his mother's son, every characteristic and every feature were hers, and I think now that it is to her that he is indebted for his genius. He had the same deep-set eyes, the smooth, broad brow, and the strong chin. Their mouths were very similar and each had the same kindly and, at times, humorous smile hovering about the lips. Mrs. Edison loved every child in the neighborhood and used to meet us at the gate as we passed on our way to school with her hands full of apples, doughnuts, and other goodies that she knew we liked."

Mr. Edison had not been many months in the new house before he conceived the idea that it might be improved by the addition of an observatory, and, being a handy man and able to carry out most plans which his brain suggested, he started to erect a tower from designs which he had himself drawn up. It was built behind the house, was about eighty feet high, and commanded a glorious view over the broad river and the distant hills. This observatory became so popular that the builder decided to make a small charge to strangers who desired to view the surrounding country from its summit, and in a neat handbill announced that only on payment of the modest sum of ten cents might the prospect of Lake Huron and the St. Clair River be enjoyed from the Edison Tower.

The investment, however, did not prove a very profitable one, for people soon discovered that the ten cents somewhat detracted from the beauty of the scenery, and the tower was left to the sole enjoyment of Mr. Edison and his family. But apart from the charge it is just possible that visitors found the ascent of the observatory a little too much for their nerves. The structure was not a very substantial one, and when the wind was fresh it certainly rocked a good deal. Some nervous women, when they got about halfway up and felt the building shake and tremble beneath their feet, became so frightened that they would turn back and decline to proceed further. But Al and his mother spent many pleasant hours on the summit of the tower, and they were never tired of gazing over the magnificent stretch of land and water mapped out beneath them. Mr. Edison possessed an old telescope, which he sometimes loaned to Al, and the boy would "sweep" the sky-line with all the skill of an old explorer.

At Port Huron the family lived for several years, united and happy. Mrs. Edison continued to conduct the education of her son with that rigid observance of punctuality and other rules which she would have exercised had she been holding a class in the public schools. And Al repaid her well by his seriousness, his wonderful gift for absorbing knowledge, and his ability to remember things. He had, indeed, a marvellous memory and never needed to be told twice regarding any matter which really interested him. He had learned his alphabet in a few lessons and his progress in reading, writing, geography, and arithmetic was equally rapid. At the age of nine he had read, or his mother had read to him, "The Penny Encyclopædia," Hume's "History of England," "History of the Reformation," Gibbon's "Rome," Sears's "History of the World," and several works on subjects which had a wonderful fascination for him even at that time — electricity and science.

He read these books seriously, too, never skipped the big paragraphs or passed over the uninteresting and difficult chapters. When he came to a particularly abstruse sentence he would get his mother to explain the facts to him and she could always satisfy his inquiring mind. Some of these books Mrs. Edison would read aloud, not to her son only but to her husband and other children as well. She was a beautiful reader, with a soft, clear, and finely modulated voice. Mr. Edison often declared in later years that he was sure Al understood a good deal more about what his wife read than he did, for at times the subject of the books chosen was not altogether to his taste. He himself did not take any great interest in electricity and science, though he was very fond of history and historical works.

When Al was about eleven years old the idea occurred to him that he might assist the family exchequer by engaging in some work during the time when he was not studying. He made the suggestion to his mother, but for a long time she was averse to his becoming a breadwinner at so early an age. At last, however, he coaxed her around to his way of thinking, and finally the two consulted as to what kind of work would be best suited to him. Al possessed opinions then very similar to those which he holds to-day, — that it does not matter much what you do so long as the work is honest and brings in the cash. And therefore he decided that for the time being he might do worse than sell newspapers. His idea, however, was not to shout the news-sheets through the streets, but to obtain a post where the work would be less precarious; and so with that excellent judgment which has characterized most of his business transactions he applied for the privilege of selling newspapers, books, magazines, fruits and candies on the trains of the Grand Trunk Railroad running between Port Huron and Detroit.

During the time that his application was being considered, for even then he believed in his own modernized version of the old proverb, "Everything comes to him who hustles while he waits," he managed to make a few nickels by selling newspapers on the streets. He had only been a short while at this work, however, when he received a letter informing him that he might have the job he had applied for and could commence business as soon as he pleased. He was very much elated, but his mother, ever fearful for his safety, was still somewhat worried. She had vivid visions of smash-ups with Al beneath the overturned engine, but he succeeded in laughing away her fears and a few days later entered on his duties with a light heart.

Some account of these days has come to us from Mr. Barney Maisonville, son of Captain Oliver Maisonville, who for over thirty years had charge of the Grand Trunk Transfer Steamers at Fort Gratiot and Detroit. Mr. Maisonville became acquainted with young Edison just prior to his going into business as a newsboy, but it was not until the war broke out that he was thrown into close friendship with the future inventor. "As near as I can make out," said Mr. Maisonville on one occasion when speaking of Edison, "young Al obtained the privilege of selling newspapers, books, and fruit on the trains running between Port Huron and Detroit as a favor or for very small pay and received all the profits himself. One day he came and asked my parents to let me go with him on Saturdays, when there was no school, and help him with his work. Consent was given and thereafter for more than a year I was a 'candy butcher' on the train. The war was going on and there was a big demand for newspapers.

"The train left Port Huron about 7 A.M., and arrived in Detroit at 10 A.M. Returning, it would leave Detroit at 4.30 P.M., and get back to Port Huron at 7.30 P.M. He instructed me regarding my duties on the first Saturday and then let me do all the business afterwards by myself, and while on the train I very seldom saw him. There was a car on the train divided into three compartments — one for baggage, one for United States Mail, and the other for express matter.

The express compartment was never used and Al employed it for a printing office and a chemical laboratory. In it were stored jars of chemicals to make electrical currents, telegraph instruments, a printing press, some type and a couple of ink-rollers.

"Al was very quiet and preoccupied in disposition. He was of ordinary size, well built, with a thick head of brown hair and quite neglectful of his personal appearance. His mother kept him supplied with clean shirts and he always washed his face and hands, but I think in those days he did not often comb his hair. He would buy a cheap suit of clothes and wear them until they were worn out, when he would buy another. He never by any chance blacked his boots. Most boys like to have money, but he never seemed to care for it himself. The receipts of his sales, when I sold for him, were from eight to ten dollars the day, of which about one-half was profit. But when I handed the money to him he would simply take it and put it into his pocket. One day I asked him to count it, but he said: 'Oh, never mind, I guess it's all right.'

"When we got to Detroit we would take dinner at the Cass House, for which he would pay. Some of our time in Detroit was spent in buying goods to sell on the train, and we would go to the stores and buy papers, stationery, prize packets, fruit, peanuts, oranges, and candies. We carried the stationery and papers down to the cars ourselves, and the fruit men generally sent their goods to the depot.

"Al was a curious but lovable fellow. I was rather high-spirited at that time, and I verily believe that I was one of the few persons who could make him laugh, though no one enjoyed a good story better than Al. He was always studying out something, and usually had a book dealing with some scientific subject in his pocket. If you spoke to him he would answer intelligently enough, but you could always see that he was thinking of something else when he was talking. Even when playing checkers he would move the pieces about carelessly as if he did it only to keep company, and not for any love of the game. His conversation was deliberate, and he was slow in his actions and carriage.

"Still, he showed sometimes that he knew how money could be made. When the papers containing the news of some big battle were published in Detroit he would telegraph to the station agents, who all liked him, and they would put up a bulletin board, and when the train arrived the papers would go off like hot cakes. I believe, however, that he would sooner have sat in his caboose studying than come out on the platform and sell newspapers.

"His own paper, the *Weekly Herald*, was a little bit of a thing about the size of a lady's handkerchief. Of course he did not set it up altogether on the train, because you cannot set type and have it stand up on a car, but it was printed there. Sometimes the stationmaster at Mt. Clemens, who was also a telegraph operator, would catch some country news on the wires, and he would write it down and hand it to Al when the train came in. This news, of course, would be later than that contained in the daily papers. He would immediately retire to his caboose, set it up, put it on the little form, and before the train reached Ridgeway he would have it printed off. I sold lots of these papers for three cents each."

Of the *Weekly Herald* there is, so far as is known, but one copy now in existence, and this is in the possession of Mrs. Edison, who treasures it beyond any other souvenir of her husband's early days. It hangs on the wall of the inventor's "den" at Glenmont,

Llewellyn Park, the present residence of the family, and is preserved between two sheets of glass, so that both sides of the interesting little journal may be read. It is in a very good condition, if rather seamed down the centre, evidently through being carried folded for some time in the owner's pocket. The date on this copy is February 3, 1862, so it must have been published before the editor had reached the patriarchal age of fifteen. The paper is the size of a large sheet of business "note," printed on both sides and unfolded. Single numbers were sold at three cents apiece, but monthly or yearly subscribers obtained the paper for eight cents per month. At the height of its popularity the paper had a regular subscription circulation of five hundred copies, while another couple of hundred were bought by chance passengers on the train. All the work — setting up, printing, and publishing — being performed by the proprietor himself, a clear profit of something like forty-five dollars a month accrued from this modest publication.

The copy of the *Weekly Herald* which was shown to the present writer by Mrs. Edison contains plenty of interesting news, and though the spelling and punctuation are not perfect, the "editing" generally reflects the greatest credit on the young proprietor. The paper is a three-column sheet, the first column being headed as follows:

THE WEEKLY HERALD.

Published by A. Edison.

TERMS.

The Weekly Eight Cents per Month.

EDISON'S RAILWAY NEWSPAPER, THE "GRAND TRUNK WEEKLY HERALD"

The first part of the paper is devoted to "Local Intelegence," and contains the following items of news and gossip:

"Premiums:—We believe that the Grand Trunk Railway, give premiums, every six months to their Engineers, who use the least Wood and Oil, running the usual journey. Now we have rode with Mr. E. L. Northrop, one of their Engineers, and we do not believe you could fall in with another Engineer, more careful, or attentive to his Engine, being the most steady driver that we have ever rode behind (and we consider ourselves some judge haveing been Railway riding for over two years constantly,) always kind, and obligeing, and ever at his post. His Engine we understand does not cost one fourth for repairs what the other Engines do. We would respectfully recommend him to the kindest consideration of the G. T. R. Offices.

"The more to do the more done:— We have observed along the line of railway at the different stations where there is only one Porter, such as at Utica, where he is fully engaged, from morning until late at night, that he has everything clean, and in first class order, even the platforms the snow does not lie for a week after it has fallen, but is swept off before it is almost down, at other stations where there is two Porters things are visa a versa.

"J. S. P. Hathaway runs a daily Stage from the station to New Baltimore in connection with all Passenger Trains.

"Professor ——— [name unreadable] has returned to Canada after entertaining delighted audiences at New Baltimore for the past two weeks listening to his comical lectures, etc.

"Did'nt succeed:— A Gentleman by the name of Watkins, agent for the Hayitan government, recently tried to swindle the Grand Trunk Railway company of sixty-seven dollars the price of a valise he claimed to have lost at Sarnia, and he was well night successful in the undertaking.

"But by the indominatable perseverance and energy of Mr. W. Smith, detective of the company, the case was cleared up in a very different style. It seems that the would be gentleman while crossing the river on the ferry boat, took the check off of his valise, and carried the valise in his hand, not forgetting to put the check in his pocket, the baggageman missed the baggage after leaving Port Huron, while looking over his book to see if he had every thing with him, but to his great surprise found he had lost one piece, he telegraphed back stateing so, but no baggage could be found. It was therefore given into the hands of Mr. Smith, to look after, in the meantime Mr. Watkins, wrote a letter to Mr. Tubman Agent at Detroit, asking to be satisfied for the loss he had sustained in consequence, and referring Mr. Tubman to Mr. W. A. Howard, Esq., of Detroit, and the Hon. Messrs. Brown and Wilson of Toronto for reference. We hardly know how such men are taken in with such traveling villians, but such is the case, meantime Mr. Smith, cleared up the whole mystery by finding the lost valice in his possession and the Haytian agent offered to pay ten dollars for the trouble he had put the company to, and to have the matter hushed up,

"Not so, we feel that the villian should have his name posted up in the various R. R. in the country, and then he wll be able to travel in his true colors.

"We have noticed of late, the large quantitys of men, taken by Leftenant Donohue, 14 regt. over the G. T. R. to their rendezvous at Ypsalanta and on inquiring find that he has recruited more men than any other man in the regiment. If his energy and perseverance in the field when he meets the enemy, is as good as it was in his recruiting on the line of the Grand Trunk R. he will make a mark that the enemy won't soon forget.

"Heavy Shipments at Baltimore — we were delayid the other day at New Baltimore Station, waiting for a friend, and while waiting, took upon ourselves to have a peep at things generly; we saw in the freight house of the GTR. 400 bls of flour and 150 hogs, waiting for shipment to Portland."

A certain section of the paper was devoted to announcements of births, deaths, and marriages likely to interest subscribers and their friends, and not infrequently the young editor would be handed an item of the kind by one of his many patrons. He took care to let all know that the columns of his publication were

BOYHOOD AND YOUTH

always open for such announcements — not for payment, but as a courtesy. The present copy of the paper has no death or marriage notice, but there is a birth chronicled in the following succinct language:

"BIRTH.

"At Detroit Junction G. T. R. Refreshment Rooms on the 29th inst., the wife of A. Little of a daughter."

It would be interesting to know if the lady is still living.

Two announcements of especial interest and encouragement to subscribers are printed, viz.:

"We expect to enlarge our paper in a few weeks."

"In a few weeks each subscriber will have his name printed on his paper."

Then comes a little bit of philosophy which appears to be somewhat profound for a boy of fifteen:

"Reason Justice and Equity, never had weight enough on the face of the earth to govern the councils of men."

Next are a number of "Notices," some of which, it may be presumed, were either paid for as advertisements or inserted in return for "courtesies received":

"NOTICE.

"A very large business is done at M. V. Milords Waggon and carriage shop, New Baltimore Station. All orders promptly attended to. Particular attention paid to repairing.

"RIDGEWAY STATION.

"A daily Stage leaves the above Station for St Clair, every day, Fare 75 cents.

"A Daily stage leaves the above named place for Utica and Romeo, Fare $1.00.

"ROSE & BURREL, proprietors.

"OPPISITION LINE.

"A Daily Stage leaves Ridgeway Station for Burkes Cor. Armada Cor. and Romeo.

"A Daily stage leaves Ridgeway Station on arrival of all passenger trains from Detroit for Memphis.

"R. QUICK, proprietor.

"UTICA STATION.

"A daily Stage leaves the above named Station, on arrival of Accommadation Train from Detroit for Utica, Disco, Washington and Romeo.

"S. A. Frink, driver. Mr. Frink is one of the oldest and most careful drivers known in the State. (Ed.)

"Mt. CLEMENS.

"A daily stage leaves the above named station, for Romeo, on arrival of the morning train from Detroit, our stage arrives at Romeo two hours before any other stage.

"HICKS & HAISY, prop."

Then comes "The News," which must have been somewhat scarce that week, for it is brief. Three items only, two of which scarcely appear to be in their right section, are recorded:

"THE NEWS.

"Cassius M. Clay will enter the army on his return home.

"The thousandth birthday of the Empire of Russia will be celebrated at Novgorod in august.

" 'Let me collect myself,' as the man said when he was blown up by a powder mill."

The fifth column contains the only illustration of

which the paper boasts. It is a woodcut of a railway train of a somewhat antique build, the engine, with steam up, emitting a great quantity of very black smoke. The cut appropriately heads the column devoted to the announcements of the "Grand Trunk Railroad," and is useful in the present number for the —

"CHANGES OF TIME.

"Going West.
"Express, leaves Port Huron, 7.05 P.M.
"Mixed for Detroit, leaves Pt. Huron at 7.40 A.M.

"Going East.
"Express leaves Detroit, for Toronto, at 6.15 A.M.
"Mixed for Pt. Huron leaves at 4.00 P.M.
"Two Freight Trains each way.
"C. R. CHRISTIE, Supt."

"Stages" played an important part in transportation during the days that the *Weekly Herald* flourished, and therefore it is not surprising to find that young Edison devoted considerable space to announcements in connection with them. In the column denoting changes of time on the Grand Trunk there are the following advertisements of —

"STAGES.

"New Baltimore Station.

"A tri-weekly stage leaves the above named station on every day for New Baltimore, Algonac, Swan Creek, and Newport.
"S. GRAVES, proprietor.

"MAIL EXPRESS.

"Daily Express leaves New Baltimore Station every morning

on arrival of the train from Detroit. For Baltimore, Algonac, Swan Creek and Newport.

"CURTIS & BENNETT, proprietors.

"Pt. HURON STATION.

"An omnibus leaves the station for Pt. Huron on the arrival of all trains."

When passengers lost property or left parcels on the trains Edison was often appealed to and asked to announce the fact in the columns of his paper. He was always obliging in this respect, and though he seldom got payment for these advertisements it was highly gratifying to him when lost property was returned through a notice inserted in his paper. One such announcement appears in the copy under inspection, and is printed in large type in order to attract special attention:

"LOST LOST LOST

"A small parcel of cloth was lost on the cars.
"The finder will be liberally rewarded."

Though no address is given indicating the person to whom the lost property was to be returned, subscribers always understood that if they found the mislaid parcel, or whatever it happened to be, they must communicate with the "Newsagent on the Mixed," which was the Editor himself.

Many of Edison's regular subscribers were interested in farm products, and for their especial benefit he always devoted a certain portion of his paper to the market prices ruling during that week. It may not be without interest, therefore, to give the quotations as printed in this number of the *Weekly Herald:*

"MARKETS.

"New Baltimore.

"Butter at 10 to 12 cents per lb.
"Eggs at 12 cents per dozen.
"Lard at 7 to 9 cents per lb.
"Dressed hogs at 3.00 to 3.25 per 100 lbs.
"Mutton at 4 to 5 cents per lb.
"Flour at 4.50 to 4.75 per 100 lbs.
"Beans at 1.00 to 1.20 per bush.
"Potatoes at 30 to 35 cts. per bushel.
"Corn at 30 to 35 cts. per bush.
"Turkeys at 50 to 65 cts. each.
"Chickens at 10 to 12 cts. each.
"Geese at 25 to 35 cents each.
"Ducks at 30 cents per pair."

The last half-column of the paper is devoted to

"ADVERTISEMENTS"

and contains the following notices:

"RAILWAY EXCHANGE.

"At Baltimore Station.

"The above named Hotel is now open for the reception of Travelers. The Bar will be supplied with the best of Liquors, and every attention will be paid to the comfort of the Guests.

"S. GRAVES, proprietor.

"SPLENDID PORTABLE COPYING
PRESSES FOR SALE AT
Mt. CLEMENS.

"ORDERS TAKEN BY

The Newsagent on the Mixed.

"Ridgeway Refreshment Rooms:— I would inform my friends that I have opened a Refreshment Room for the accommodation of the traveling public.

"R. ALLEN, proprietor.

"TO THE RAILWAY MEN.

"Railway men send in your orders for Butter, Eggs, Lard, Cheese, Turkeys, Chickens and Geese.
"W. C. HULCH, New Baltimore Station."

The *Weekly Herald* attracted the attention of the English engineer Stephenson, who happened to be travelling on the "Mixed" one day, and who purchased a copy. He complimented the young editor on his enterprise, said the paper was as good as many he had seen edited by men twice his age, and gave an order for a thousand copies. Even the *London Times* expressed interest in the paper, and unbent sufficiently to quote from its columns, and it is more than probable that if Edison had not followed the life of an inventor he would have continued his work as an editor, and, if he had, his name would, doubtless, have become equally famous in the newspaper world.

Mr. Maisonville, the gentleman already referred to, was on the train when the incident occurred which struck the death-knell of the *Weekly Herald*. The story has been repeatedly told, with various alterations and additions, but here is an authentic account of what actually happened. Young Maisonville was busily engaged in the front car selling papers and candies, while Edison was in the baggage van — or "Laboratory and Printing Shop," as the trainmen occasionally called it when in merry moods — engaged in one of his many experiments, when the train ran over a bit of rough road; there was a heavy lurch, and a bottle of phosphorus fell to the floor of the car and burst into flame. The woodwork caught fire, and Edison was finding considerable difficulty in stemming the progress of the fire when Alexander Stevenson, the conductor, made his appearance.

Stevenson was a Scotchman, an elderly man with iron-gray hair, a rubicund face, and an accent that would have been strong even in the heart of Midlothian. Moreover he had a temper, which may best be described as "hasty." He didn't waste any time talking while the fire was in progress, but quickly fetching some buckets of water, soon had the flames extinguished. Then he let out a flood of eloquence which sounded like a chapter from a Scott novel, and when the train arrived a few minutes later at Mt. Clemens Station, he pitched the young experimenter on to the platform, and hurled after him the type and printing press, the telegraph apparatus, the bottles of chemicals, and, in fact, the entire contents of the laboratory. Then he signalled the train to proceed, and left the future inventor forlornly standing among the ruins of his most cherished possessions.

Lest it may be supposed that Conductor Stevenson was utterly unfeeling and entirely lacking in all sympathy with searches after knowledge, a few words appear to be necessary. Stevenson had a good heart, and was by no means unfriendly towards Edison, but, like many other worthy Scotchmen, his temper was fiery, and when his wrath was aroused he usually acted with a good deal of haste. He considered that the limit of friendship was reached when the boy set the train — his train — on fire, and thereby jeopardized the lives of those committed to his care. He argued that at such times it was well to act quickly, and so he summarily kicked the young experimenter and his belongings off the train at the first stopping-place, and congratulated himself on having done his company good service. Soon afterwards he resigned his position, and removed to a small village near St. John's, Michigan, where he became an important and respected member of the community. There he was made a Justice of the Peace, and for some years sat on the bench, where he administered the law with much more leniency than he had shown when a conductor on the Grand Trunk Railroad.

The man who sold Edison the printing-press used by him in the publication of his paper was J. A. Roys, at that time the most prominent bookseller in Detroit. "I sold Edison that famous printing-press," he often told customers who questioned him regarding his friendship with the inventor, "and I have sometimes wondered what became of it. I suppose it was pretty well smashed up when Stevenson dumped it out on the platform. The press formerly belonged to the man who was landlord of the Cass House, at one time the best hotel in Detroit. He used the machine to print the bill of fare in that hotel, but he made a failure of the place and went to smash. He afterwards became tenant of a house that I owned, but after the first quarter he failed to pay the rent. To reimburse me he turned over, among other articles, the printing-press. Young Edison, who was a good boy and a favorite of mine, bought goods of me and had the run of the store, saw the press, and I suppose the idea of publishing a paper of his own immediately occurred to him, for he would catch on to anything new like lightning. He examined the machine, got me to show him exactly how it worked, and finally bought it from me for a small sum. Afterwards I saw many copies of the paper he printed, and for several years kept some as curiosities, but they got torn up or lost, and now I don't believe there is one to be had unless he owns it himself. He was a smart youngster, and I always prophesied great things of him."

CHAPTER III

NEWS AGENT AND TELEGRAPHER

HAVING lost his laboratory on the Grand Trunk, Edison immediately set about finding some other place where he could continue his experiments. He did not condescend to make overtures to Stevenson for a renewal of his tenancy of the baggage-wagon, but took his father into his confidence, explained matters, and begged for a room in the Port Huron house which he might fit up as a workshop. His father, however, on learning that the cause of his sudden exodus from the train was due to his setting fire to the car during his scientific investigations, at first declined to allow him to experiment in the house, but on his son promising not to store anything inflammable he relented, gave him a room near the roof, and told him he might "go ahead." So the boy bought more chemicals, some crude telegraph instruments, wire, and tools, and was soon more deeply absorbed in his scientific studies than ever.

He still continued to publish his paper, but it was set up and printed in his workshop at home from type which had been given to him by a friend connected with the *Detroit Free Press*. At this time he had over five hundred subscribers, so he had no desire to close down a concern which was founded on so sound a basis. But in an unlucky hour he was persuaded by a journalistic friend to discontinue the *Herald* in favor of another paper of a more personal character, which the youthful editors and proprietors called *Paul Pry*. This journal never was a real success. The editors were too outspoken, and some of the public characters of Port Huron and the surrounding towns whom they "guyed" were so sensitive that they took offence, and were not slow in expressing their disapproval of the paper's policy. Indeed, one gentleman was so annoyed at a certain "personal" reflecting somewhat upon himself, that on meeting Edison he wasted no time telling him what he thought of his paper, but seizing him by the coat collar and a certain baggy portion of his pants, threw him into the canal. The boy was a good swimmer, so that with the exception of a wetting he came to no harm. But he had learned his lesson. He argued that if others who took offence expressed themselves in a similar way, he would have little time to work out those ideas which were even then coursing through his brain. So he broke loose from *Paul Pry*, and the paper came to an inglorious end.

He still kept his job as "candy butcher" on the Grand Trunk, and the business continued to grow. Many stories have been written regarding these train days — perhaps the most interesting period of his early youth — and some of them have possibly been quite new to Edison. Here is one, however, which an anonymous writer declares was related to him by the inventor himself, and which, therefore, may be considered authentic. The occasion of its narration was a "reunion" at which were present Edison and a gentleman who happened also to have been at one time a candy seller on the Grand Trunk. The two immediately began to compare notes, and laughed together over the way they used to work the peanut trick on customers. Readers who know nothing of the American

NEWS AGENT AND TELEGRAPHER

"candy butcher" and his methods may be interested in learning the *modus operandi* of this famous deception. Briefly, it was a trick whereby an unsuspecting client paid for a measure of peanuts when he really obtained only half that quantity.

It was engineered in this way. The tin measures which the boys used were long and narrow, being smaller at the top than at the bottom. In filling a measure an adept at the trick would push it rapidly through the peanuts into the open basket. A few nuts would rattle inside, but almost immediately a dozen or two would jam or wedge in the narrow mouth of the measure. When lifted up the measure would appear to be full, and as the trick would be performed in view of the purchaser, the latter would suspect nothing, and innocently allow the boy to dump the contents of the half-empty can into his pocket, when, of course, all trace of the deception would be lost. Edison acknowledges that he sometimes worked this trick on customers, though on one occasion he received such a dressing from a client who had detected him in the act — and who went to the trouble of informing all in the car as to "how it was done" — that he ultimately came to the conclusion that honesty was the best policy even among candy butchers, and ever afterwards gave full measure and running over.

While laughing over the remembrance of these days, Edison said: "A funny thing occurred when I was newsboy on one of the old three-car trains. In my day, you know, they used to run trains made up of three coaches — a baggage-car, a smoking-car, and what we called a ladies' car. The ladies' car was always last in the string. Well, one day I was carrying my basket of nuts and apples through the ladies' car — I hadn't sold a thing so far — when I noticed two young fellows sitting near the rear end of the car. They were dandies, what might be called 'dudes,' but we called them 'stiffies' in those days. They were young Southerners up North on a lark, as I found out afterwards. Behind them sat a negro valet who had a large iron-bound box beside him on the seat. Probably he was an old slave. He was dressed in as many colors as an English flunkey, and looked mighty fine.

"As I passed the dudes one of them took the basket and threw the contents out of the window. Then he told the colored man to give me a dollar. The man grinned, and turning to the box beside him, he opened it. It was really full of money and valuables. He took out a dollar and gave it to me. I grabbed it and walked up the car. I was still surprised. At the door I looked back at them, and everybody laughed at me for some reason or other — all except the young men, they never even smiled during the whole performance.

"Well, I filled up my basket with prize packages and came back through the train. Nobody bought any of them. When I reached the Southerners, however, the same one said, 'Excuse me, sir,' grabbed the basket again, and sent the prize packages after the peanuts. He handed me my basket and sat back without a smile, but everybody else laughed again. This time I said, 'Look here, mister, do you know how much those were worth?' 'No,' he said — 'how much?' 'There were three dozen and four at ten cents each,' I replied, 'not to mention the prizes in some of them.'

"'Oh!' he said. Then turning to the colored man, 'Nicodemus, count how much the boy ought to have and give it to him.' The man opened his box and gave me four dollars, and again I went away with the empty

NEWS AGENT AND TELEGRAPHER 33

basket, while the passengers laughed. Next I brought in some morning papers, and nobody bought those either. Somehow the passengers had caught the spirit of the thing, and as it cost them nothing they apparently did not wish to deprive the Southerners of their fun. I was watchful when I came to the young bloods this time, and I carried the papers so that they could grab them easily. Sure enough, the nearest one threw them out of the window after the other things. I sat on the edge of a seat and laughed myself. 'Settle with Nicodemus,' he said, and Nicodemus settled up.

"Then I had an idea. I went into the baggage-car and got every paper I could find. I had a lot of that day's stock and over a hundred returns of the day before which I was going to turn in at the end of the run. The whole lot was so heavy that I could just manage to carry it on my shoulder. When I staggered into the ladies' car and called 'Paper!' in the usual drawl, the passengers fairly shrieked with laughter. I thought the Southerners would back down, but they never flinched. They both just grabbed those papers and hurled them out of the window by the armful. We could see them flying behind the train like great white birds — you know we had large blanket sheets then — and they spread themselves over the landscape in a way that must have startled the rural population of the district. I got over ten dollars for all my papers.

"The dandy was game. 'Look here, boy,' he said, when the passengers had seen the last of those papers floating around the curve, 'have you anything else on board?' 'Nothing except my basket and my box,' I replied. 'Well, bring in those too.' The box was a big three by four in which we kept the goods — a great, clumsy affair. But I put the basket in the box and turned it over and over down the aisle of the car to where the fellows sat. They threw the basket out of the window, but the box was too big to go that way. So they ordered Nicodemus to throw it off the rear platform. I charged them three dollars for that box. When it had gone one of them turned to me and said:

"'How much money have you made to-day?' I counted up over twenty-five dollars which Nicodemus had given me. 'Now,' he said, 'you are sure you have nothing more to sell?' I would have brought in the smoking-car stove if it hadn't been hot. But I was compelled to say that there was really nothing more. 'Very well,' and then with a change of tone he turned to the negro and said, 'Nicodemus, throw this boy out of the window.' The passengers yelled with laughter, but I got out of that car pretty quick, I can tell you."

During these days young Edison had not as much time as he desired for investigating the mysteries of electricity. His work on the train occupied him from seven in the morning until nearly nine at night, and his father, having been brought up on the old maxim that early to bed and early to rise would confer health, wealth, and wisdom on those who followed the advice, insisted on his son retiring at 9.30. This was a very great grievance, and the boy frequently expostulated, but Mr. Edison was gifted with an adamantine will, and he declined to budge from the 9.30 rule. So Al had again to set his wits to work to break down this barrier to his progress as an electrical experimenter. How he accomplished this is best told in his own words.

"While a newsboy on the railroad," he says, "I got very much interested in electricity, probably from visiting telegraph offices with a chum who had tastes similar to my own. We ran a telegraph line between our respective houses, supporting the wire on trees

NEWS AGENT AND TELEGRAPHER 35

and insulating it by the necks of bottles. We learned how to 'send' and 'take,' and got a lot of fun out of it when we were not on the run. But my spare time was limited, for just as soon as I commenced making experiments with the instruments each night I would hear my father's voice ordering me to bed. At that time what he said was law, and if I tried to sneak a few hours up in the workshop he would come in and take the light away. So I had to think of the best way to overcome his prejudice to late study.

"Each evening I would come in with a bunch of papers that I had not sold, and my father would start in to read them, and I had to go to bed, while he sat up till midnight reading the news. But he never became so absorbed that he failed to hear 9.30 chime, though frequently I gave him long, interesting articles to read, hoping that it would take his mind off the time. But it was no good; as the half-hour approached his eye would wander towards the clock, and at the tick I would hear his voice yelling to me to go to bed, and off I went. But one day on the train my chum and I concocted a plan whereby we hoped to break down this foolish rule. That night I didn't bring any papers home, and when my father asked me for one I said, 'Dick's got them all. He took them to his house. His folks wanted them.' That took him back a bit, but I didn't say any more until I was going to bed, and then I made a suggestion. 'Dick and I have a telegraph line working between our rooms,' I said; 'maybe I could call him up and get the news by wire.' Well, my father was quite agreeable, though probably a little dubious about our ability, but I went to work, and everything turned out all right.

"I called on Dick, and he sat at the other end of the wire with a paper in front of him sending the news, while I took it on slips of paper, handing them over to my father to read as fast as each item was finished. There I sat until after 11 o'clock, feeding my father the news in broken doses and getting a lot of amusement and telegraphic practice out of it. This went on every night for some time, until my father was quite persuaded that I could stay up late without serious harm. And then I began bringing papers home again and put my extra time allowance on my experiments."

This hobby of rigging up telegraph lines between his home and those of his boy friends was a favourite one with Edison, and he was sending and receiving messages at all hours of the day and night to and from half a dozen houses. One of the operators, who lived within a hundred yards of the Edison home, could not receive very well, and would come out, climb on the fence, and yell across to know what message Al had been sending. This always angered Edison, for he seemed to take it as a reflection on his telegraph line. The work of constructing workable wires between the various houses was not easy, and had it not been for Edison's perseverance the experiments would have been abandoned soon after they were started. At first the wires were run from tree to tree, but subsequently small poles were erected. This was a considerable advantage, and messages were despatched and received with remarkable smoothness.

One morning, however, Edison awoke to find his telegraph poles "down" and everything more or less in chaos. If a cyclone had struck the town the damage could not have been more complete, yet it was all due to nothing more terrible than a peace-loving but straying cow. The animal had wandered into the orchard during the night, knocked down one of the poles, and become so entangled in the wires that very soon she had the rest of the sticks lying useless. Her terror increased as she became the more hopelessly imprisoned in the coils, and it was not long before she proceeded to let the neighbors know some of her difficulties. Her mournful bellowing had the desired effect, and several people from the neighboring houses rushed to her rescue, cut away the wires and liberated the terrified animal, but not until she had irretrievably damaged the delicate instruments which had been adjusted at the cost of so much labor. The wires were never re-strung, for soon after Edison obtained a position where he was able to practise as a telegraph operator all he wanted without having to erect lines.

CHAPTER IV

IN SEARCH OF EMPLOYMENT

It was in 1862, when Edison was fifteen years of age, that an event occurred which considerably stimulated his interest in telegraphy. While following his occupation as "candy butcher" he dropped off the train one day at Mt. Clemens — the very station where he and his instruments had been so ignominiously ejected from the baggage-car by the incensed Stevenson a few months previously — to have a chat with the agent there, who was a particular friend of his. This man, J. U. Mackenzie, was a quiet, sympathetic, sensible individual, and between the two a friendship had formed which was broken only by the death of Mackenzie some years ago. He was telegraph operator as well as agent, and it was from him that Edison so often received items of news which came over the wire and which he published in his paper.

On the day referred to Edison and his friend were standing on the platform chatting over the events of the day when the latter's baby son ran out of the office and on to the track. Mackenzie did not observe him, but Edison, following the boy's progress, was dismayed to see him take up a position between the metals on which a freight train was running at an express clip. With a hasty word to Mackenzie, Edison dashed across the track and succeeded in pulling the child away just as the train tore by. He brought the boy back to his father, and the poor man was so overcome that he could only gasp out incoherent words of thankfulness and gratitude. Al, always cool, hastily bade the agent good-by and did not see him again for some days.

The next time they met, Mackenzie, who had been worrying his brains as to the best way of rewarding the lad who had really risked his life to save that of his child, offered to teach him how to become a telegraph operator. The offer was gladly accepted, and for three months, four days a week, after he had finished his work on the train, Edison dropped off at Mt. Clemens and received lessons from Mackenzie in the mysteries of telegraphy. At the end of that period he knew so much about telegraphic instruments, and had become so expert an operator, that his teacher informed him that he might now graduate.

"By this time," said Mackenzie in after years, "he knew as much about telegraphy as I did, and on my suggestion he applied for a position as night operator at Port Huron Station. He obtained it, and mighty proud he was when he informed me that his salary had been fixed at twenty-five dollars a month."

His duties were not very exhausting, for he had but to record the passing of trains; but Edison, unlike the majority of night operators, could seldom be persuaded to sleep during the day, and consequently he went on duty each night feeling drowsy and tired. He had, of course, resigned his position on the train, but it is a question whether he did not work just as hard in his workshop at home when he should have been resting. He was constantly thinking of and evolving new schemes, and, as a matter of fact, his mind was not always on his work. His telegraphic reports were meagre in the extreme, and though the train despatcher was a particular friend of his — like almost every one who came in contact with him — and had a real affection for the boy, he was always threatening to report him for inattention to duty.

Edison did not wish to give up his experimenting during the day, but it was absolutely necessary that he should obtain sleep somehow, so after consulting the railroad timetable with considerable care he purchased a clock furnished with a particularly aggressive alarm, carried it to his office one night, and set it to go off five minutes before the first train was scheduled to pass. Then he settled himself comfortably and proceeded to enjoy a nap. Punctual to the minute the clock roused him, when he would send his message, set the clock for the next train, and go to sleep again.

The plan worked excellently so long as the trains were on time, but — well, sometimes they were not, and then there was more trouble. The despatcher began to lose patience. He had a serious talk with Edison, and in very solemn tones informed him that the next time he slept on duty he would be reported to the company. Edison, very contrite, assured him that it should not happen again, and for a couple of nights his messages were all that could be desired. But it was impossible to keep the thing up long, for his experiments during the day still continued, and sleep he must have.

His brain soon became busy again. The train despatcher, distrustful of his promises and still fearing that he might drop off to sleep any moment while on duty, conceived a plan whereby he thought to guarantee Edison's remaining wakeful throughout the night. On his own initiative he ordered the sleepy operator to signal to him the letter "A" in the Morse alphabet every half-hour. Edison expressed the

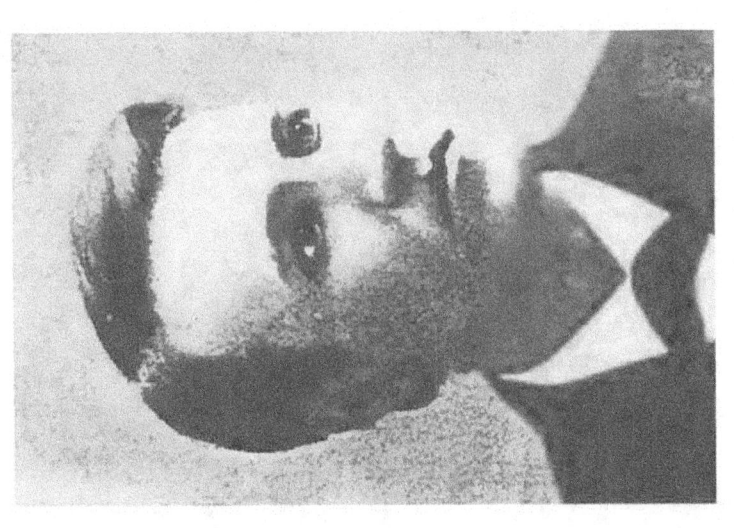

EDISON AT THE AGE OF NINETEEN   EDISON AT FORTY

greatest delight at the plan and cheerfully agreed to fall in with the train despatcher's wishes. The first night he diligently sent "A" over the wire every thirty minutes, but towards morning he felt so sleepy and worn out that he clearly saw that some means must be contrived whereby he might obtain sleep between signals.

The following day he experimented long but successfully in his workshop at home, and that evening when he reported for duty there was a bland expression on his countenance which might have revealed to the observant the fact that he had solved the difficulty. He carried a small box in his hand, and when he was alone in his office he opened this and took out various articles usually to be found in the kit of a line repairer, including some coils of wire. Then he spent half an hour or so putting the things together, and the result was an interesting-looking instrument which he connected by wire to the telegraph and the clock. Then he took a seat and waited.

This is what happened. Promptly at the half-hour a little wooden lever fell, sending an excellent imitation of the Morse "A" to the telegraph key, and immediately afterwards another lever closed the circuit. Edison was jubilant. He watched the instrument for another half-hour and when it again fulfilled its duty he gave a sigh of relief and went to sleep.

Every night the signal was faithfully flashed each half-hour and the train despatcher's confidence in Edison was becoming reestablished, when one of those circumstances over which the most ingenious has no control occurred and revealed the scheme in all its deceptions. The despatcher happened on his rounds one night to be only one station away from Edison, and after getting the usual signal he thought he would call up the operator and have a chat with him. So he opened the key, and on getting no reply became alarmed. He called for fifteen minutes, and then, feeling sure that something terrible had occurred, he rode to the next station on a hand-car.

Looking through the office window in considerable anxiety — for he half expected to find the operator murdered — he was astounded to see Edison quietly sleeping in a corner of the room, his steady breathing indicating the profoundness of his slumbers. He was about to arouse him angrily when his attention was attracted to a curious bit of mechanism which stood on the table near the telegraph instrument, and as it was close upon the half-hour the despatcher decided to wait and see what would happen. He expected something to occur which would arouse the sleeper, and was therefore the more astonished when Edison still remained locked in slumber as the hands of the clock pointed to the time when the prearranged signal should be sent. But his astonishment was increased a hundredfold when he discovered that the queer bit of mechanism he had noticed performed the duty for him. Before his very eyes — he afterwards declared that he would not have believed it otherwise — the instrument "got busy," and while one lever threw open the key the other sent the signal over the wire. Then the astonished train despatcher also "got busy," and arousing Edison with no gentle hands declared in forcible language that he was done with him, and the same day the Port Huron operator was looking for another job.

But in spite of his inattention to duty Edison had given evidence over and over again of his wonderful skill and quickness in grappling with a difficulty, and many stories illustrative of this trait in his character

IN SEARCH OF EMPLOYMENT

are told in Port Huron to-day. On one occasion, for instance, there was an interruption in the line to Detroit, and the day operator asked Edison to look out and try and ascertain where the trouble was. The boy immediately laid a wire from his father's house and strung it along the railway fence. Thence he tumbled down the bank by the swing bridge and fastened a wire to one end of the cable, which, as he suspected, had been parted by a passing vessel. Then he went back and was telling the day operator what he had done, when George Christie, a line repairer, came along, and, overhearing the conversation, dropped his kit and wanted to lick Edison for interfering with his work. But the day operators got between them and prevented a fight and Edison escaped. Christie was finally persuaded that the boy he was desirous of clubbing had really performed a far-sighted and commendable feat.

From Port Huron Edison went to Sarnia, where he remained some months as telegraph operator at the railroad station. And here again he got into a scrape which might have landed him in the State prison. While experimenting, he allowed a train to pass by his station when he should have stopped it, as there was another train immediately ahead. The instant it had flashed by, Edison realized the seriousness of the affair, and, in a fever, ran down the line, shouting as he went, and fervently praying that he might be in time to avert an accident. This, of course, was an insane hope, and a terrible calamity would have occurred had not the engine-drivers heard each other's whistles in time to realize their danger and thus prevent a rear-end collision. Edison was so relieved at the outcome of his carelessness that when he was summoned before the manager of the line he was almost light-hearted. But when he learned that there was a probability of his being prosecuted for his neglect of duty, he decided to take the matter into his own hands, and while the Board were consulting as to his fate, he packed his belongings and returned to Port Huron.

Here he obtained a position in the Western Union Office, for he was now a rapid operator, and his skill with the key was beginning to be recognized. But an unfortunate incident occurred a few months later which decided him to throw up his post and shake the dust of Port Huron from his feet. It appears that the leading local daily being extremely anxious to obtain a report of the Presidential message to Congress — which was hourly expected — offered the agent of the Western Union sixty dollars if he would secure it. The agent closed with the bargain, and knowing that Edison was the most skilled operator in his employ promised him a third of the sum as a bonus if he would receive the message. Edison gladly agreed, and took the message, but when he asked for his twenty dollars he was calmly assured by his chief that he did not intend to pay either the bonus promised or any additional sum for extra work. Edison, astounded at the man's barefaced dishonesty, but recognizing that he had no redress — the agent's word would, he knew, have greater weight than his — declined to serve any longer under him and went to consult his friend Mackenzie. Mackenzie, full of sympathy, wanted Edison to sue the agent, but, quickly coming to the conclusion that the game was hardly worth the candle, advised him instead to apply for the post of night operator on the railroad at Stratford, Canada, which was then vacant. Edison took his friend's advice, sent in his application, and was at once given the position at the modest remuneration of twenty-five dollars a month.

At Stratford he remained a few weeks only, for he saw there was little opportunity of advancement and the pay was scarcely sufficient to keep him in food and lodging. On the advice of a friend, therefore, he took train to Indianapolis, where he believed he would stand a fair chance of obtaining a good position. And here it may be remarked that it is a somewhat curious fact that in all his ups and downs during the early part of his life it never seemed to occur to Edison to try any profession other than that of a telegrapher. He was a born operator and at that time no other work had any attractions for him.

Edison arrived in Indianapolis before he was eighteen years of age, and in a private account-book of the agent of the Western Union in that city, there appears, entered monthly during the latter part of 1864 and the first part of 1865, the name "T. A. Edison." The first time it appears it is inscribed in rather bold characters, but in every other instance the signature is small and neat and of that peculiarity of form which he cultivated for the purposes of rapid penmanship. Edison went to live in Indianapolis about the 1st of November, 1864, and his office records show that at the end of that month he drew a full month's salary.

At that time the Superintendent of the Western Union Company in Indianapolis was John F. Wallick. This gentleman used to say that he distinctly remembered his first meeting with Edison. He was walking on one of the down-town streets, when a smooth-faced, boyish-looking young man stopped him. The young man was Edison. The Superintendent recollects nothing of his appearance to distinguish him from other young men, except, perhaps, a face somewhat more frank than the ordinary, and a manner that was rather hesitating. He had evidently learned before who Mr. Wallick was, for he stopped him and asked for a position. Mr. Wallick replied in the conventional way:

"Come around to-morrow and I will see what I can do for you."

The next day, bright and early, young Edison walked into the Superintendent's office. Mr. Wallick bade him sit down and asked him some questions which were evidently satisfactorily answered, and he was at once given a position. He was assigned to the Union Station, his duties being of ordinary responsibility and relating to the reception of messages as well as the flagging of trains. During the time he was in Indianapolis he drew seventy-five dollars a month, which was about the regulation salary paid in those days. While he was at the station Mr. Wallick saw very little of him, but one day while sitting in his office Edison entered. The Superintendent asked him what he wanted, and he replied eagerly:

"I just came to ask if you would give me some old instruments there are about the office."

The Superintendent told him that he was welcome to any that he could find if they were of use to him, and he went away highly pleased. A day or two after Mr. Wallick went down to the station to take a train. He stepped into the operator's room and there on a big rough board were spread out the instruments he had given to Edison. He did not think much of the circumstance at the time, but a few years later, when Edison was in the East, and the Superintendent saw notices of his discoveries and inventions, the thought occurred to him that the foundation, perhaps, for some of them might have been laid in Indianapolis. Mr. Wallick had no personal remembrance of the inventor after the incident at the depot, but twenty years later Edison, then a famous man, went back to Indianapolis on a holiday, hunted up Mr. Wallick, and the two men visited together the scenes of the boy-operator's labors at the Union Station.

CHAPTER V

HIS FIRST WORKSHOP

EDISON remained in Indianapolis until February, 1865, when he resigned his position and commenced a wandering life which carried him from state to state and from city to city. During this nomadic existence he arrived in Cincinnati, where he remained for several months as a telegraph operator, earning a fair salary, but devoting so much of it to the purchase of books and electrical instruments, that little was left to provide him with even the necessaries of life. He continued to combine his experimental work with hard reading, and through this devotion to literature he narrowly escaped death at the hands of an over-zealous policeman. Edison himself has often told the story of how he was shot at as a supposed thief, and the incident is worth recalling. It was all due, so he says, to his liking for reading.

"While a telegraph operator in Cincinnati," he says, "I was just as great a reader as in the old days, and my salary being small, I used to wander among the auction-rooms and pick up a bargain whenever I got the chance. One day there was put up to the highest bidder a stack of *North American Reviews*, and, after some desultory offers, I secured the lot for two dollars. I carried the parcel — which was heavy enough to put on a truck — to the telegraph office, arriving there just in time to report. At 3 A.M. I was

HIS FIRST WORKSHOP

free, and shouldering my package, I went down the dark street at a pretty lively pace, for I was not only anxious to get rid of my burden, but was also very desirous to start in reading the books as soon as possible.

"Presently I heard a pistol shot behind me and something whizzed past my ear, nearly grazing it, in fact. As I turned, a breathless policeman came up and ordered me in tones I didn't fail to hear that time to drop my parcel. Evidently hurrying along the dark alley-way with my bundle I did look rather a suspicious character, and the policeman had concluded that I was decamping with property not my own. I stopped and opened my package. The policeman looked disgusted. 'Why didn't you halt when I told you?' he said. 'If I'd been a better shot you might have got killed.' He apologized afterwards when I explained to him that it was owing to my deafness that I didn't obey his commands."

In connection with his telegraphic days in Cincinnati, Edison tells a story in support of his theory that there is no work so mechanical as that of a telegraph operator. "One night," he says, "I noticed an immense crowd gathering in the street outside a newspaper office. I called the attention of the other operators to the crowd and we sent a messenger boy out to find the cause of the excitement. He returned in a few minutes and shouted, 'Lincoln's shot!' Instinctively the operators looked from one face to the other to see which man had received the news. All the faces were blank and every man said he had not taken a word about the shooting. 'Look over your files,' said the boss to the man handling the press stuff. For a few minutes we waited in suspense, and then the man held up a sheet of paper containing a short account of the shooting of the President. The operator had worked so mechanically that he had handled the news without the slightest knowledge of its significance."[1]

From Cincinnati, Edison journeyed to Memphis and immediately started for the Western Union Office after work. His first appearance there has been described by a writer who claims to have been an operator with him in his Tennessee days, and the account is so humorous that I cannot refrain from quoting it.

"He came walking into the office one morning," says this unknown author, "looking like a veritable hay-seed. He wore a hickory shirt, a pair of butternut pants tucked into the tops of boots a size too large and guiltless of blacking. 'Where's the boss?' was his query, as he glanced around the office. No one replied at once and he repeated the question. The manager asked what he could do for him, and the future great one proceeded to strike him for a job. Business was rushing and the office was two men short, so almost any kind of a lightning-slinger was welcome. He was assigned to a desk and a fusillade of winks went the rounds of the room, for the new arrival had been put on the St. Louis wire, the hardest in the office. At the end of the line was an operator who was chain lightning and knew it.

"Edison had hardly got seated before St. Louis called. The newcomer responded, and St. Louis started on a long report, which he pumped in like a house afire. Edison threw his leg over the arm of the chair, leisurely transferred a wad of spruce gum from his pocket to his mouth, took up a pen, examined it critically, and started in about fifty words behind. He didn't stay there long though. St. Louis let out another link of speed and still another, and the instru-

[1] Dickson's "Edison."

HIS FIRST WORKSHOP

ment on Edison's table hummed like an old-style Singer sewing-machine. Every man in the office left his desk and gathered around the Jay to see what he was doing with that electric cyclone.

"Well, sir, he was right on the word and taking it down in the prettiest copper-plate hand you ever saw, even crossing his 't's' and dotting his 'i's,' and punctuating with as much care as a man editing telegraph for rat printers. St. Louis got tired by and by and began to slow down. Then Edison opened the key and said:

"'Hello, there! when are you going to get a hustle on? This is no primer class.'

"Well, sir," said the gentleman in conclusion, "that broke St. Louis all up. He had been rawhiding Memphis for a long time, and we were terribly sore, and to have a man in our office who could walk all over him made us feel like a man whose horse had won the Derby. I saw the Wizard not long ago. He doesn't wear a hickory shirt or put his pants in his boots, but he is very far from being a dude yet."

This account is, of course, exaggerated, and the narrator has taken the liberty of turning the incident into one of a humorous nature, though the main facts are correct. Edison at one time in his career was the fastest operator in the employ of the Western Union, and a constant source of astonishment to every one, from the manager down, was the way in which he would take the swiftest messages with ease almost amounting to indifference. His remarkably clear handwriting might be described as one of his first inventions, for he originated it expressly for the purpose of taking quick reports. He could, with no apparent effort, write forty-five words a minute, sufficient to take down messages from the speediest senders, and had it been necessary might have increased his capacity to fifty and fifty-five words, and with no decrease in neatness and legibility. As a sender he was no less remarkable, and there were few who could take his messages when Edison felt in good condition and his blood was up.

But Memphis did not enjoy the society of their champion operator for long. Again he lost his job, this time, according to Alexander Knapp, a fellow-worker, through an exuberance of spirits which scandalized the Memphis manager, a gentleman of the name of Baker. Knapp and Edison were firm friends and would occasionally visit the theatres and other places of amusement together. One evening they went to the "Zoo," a variety theatre on Washington Street, where they saw a performance of the "can-can" dance, which had just then been introduced to Memphis audiences. Both operators were delighted with the novel performance, and on reaching the office to begin the night's work they decided that the time and the place were convenient for a trial of the new dance. For the benefit of their co-workers they began to give the "can-can" with so much energy that several of the tables were knocked over and some of the instruments put out of business. In the midst of this scene Mr. Baker arrived, and, without asking for any explanation, he took Edison by one ear and Knapp by the other, led them to the door of the office, and turned them loose into the street, telling them that they might continue their performance there if they liked. Neither Edison nor Knapp returned to explain matters, but immediately sought fresh fields for the exercise of their apparently unappreciated talents. Subsequently Knapp eschewed telegraphy, and afterwards became a very prominent man in railroad circles.

Edison decided to try Boston. He had a friend

there named Milton Adams, and to him he wrote, begging him as a favor to find him a job. Adams was also a telegrapher, and connected with the Western Union office there, and he mentioned the matter to G. F. Milliken, the manager, showing him Edison's application. The curious handwriting immediately attracted Mr. Milliken's attention, and his interest being aroused, he inquired if the operator took messages from the line and put them down in that shape. Adams replied: "Yes, and there is no one who can stick him," whereupon Milliken told him to write to his friend, and tell him to call upon him, and he would see what could be done. Edison took train for Boston immediately after the receipt of Adams's hopeful letter, and a five minutes' interview sufficed for Milliken to size the young man up and give him a position. On entering the office his retiring manner and eccentricities of dress — he was just as untidy as ever — created some amusement, but he soon showed such remarkable gifts as an operator — no one could touch him even in Boston — that amusement turned to admiration, and he was looked upon with respect and even veneration.

Edison had no sooner settled in his new position than he opened a small workshop for the perfecting of many ideas which were germinating in his busy brain, and it was while here that he took out his first patent — perhaps the most unfortunate of the many hundreds with which his name is associated. This was a vote-recording machine, comprising a system whereby each member of a legislative body could, by moving a switch on his desk to right or left, register his name on a sheet of paper under the "ayes" or "noes." The paper was chemically prepared, and when the circuit was closed an iron roller passed over the paper, under which was the type signifying the member's name. The current passing through the chemically prepared paper caused its discoloration wherever the type came in contact with it, and the name was accordingly printed on the paper. At the same time the vote was counted by a dial indicator which was operated by the same current.

This ingenious instrument worked perfectly, and the young inventor was in high feather over his wonderfully simple yet adequate system for "purifying" the ballot. He had been used to handling press reports, and the time taken in counting votes as well as the ease with which they could be "manipulated" had suggested to him the idea for the invention. So he travelled to Washington, and after some little delay succeeded in exhibiting his instrument to the Chairman of Committees, who, after examining the machine very carefully, said: "Young man, it works all right and couldn't be better. With an instrument like that it would be difficult to monkey with the vote if you wanted to. But it won't do. In fact, it's the last thing on earth that we want here. Filibustering and delay in the counting of the votes are often the only means we have for defeating bad legislation. So, though I admire your genius and the spirit which prompted you to invent so excellent a machine, we shan't require it here. Take the thing away."

Whereupon Edison mournfully shouldered his vote-recorder and left the committee-room. "Of course I was very sorry," said Edison afterwards, "for I had banked on that machine bringing me in money. But it was a lesson to me. There and then I made a vow that I would never invent anything which was not wanted, or which was not necessary to the community at large. And so far I believe I have kept that vow."

A story which will stick to Edison has reference

EDISON'S FIRST INVENTION, THE VOTE RECORDER

HIS FIRST WORKSHOP

to the way in which he rid the office of cockroaches, and the inventor always smiles when the incident crops up — as it usually does — if in conversation with an interviewer interested in his early days. Says an operator who worked with him in Boston: "We were terribly bothered and disgusted by the vast army of cockroaches that each night formed an entire square, with the operators' lunches on the inside. These lunches were kept on an unused table, and promptly at half-past six each night the cockroach legions would march upon the old table, ascend the four legs that upheld it, and make a raid on sandwiches, apple-pie, and other eatables. One night while Edison was waiting for Washington to start the newspaper specials he conceived a plan to annihilate the entire cockroach horde.

"He said nothing, but when he reported for duty the next night he was supplied with a quantity of tin-foil and four or five yards of fine wire. Unrolling the tin-foil and cutting two narrow strips from the long sheet, he stretched them around the table, taking care to keep them as near together as possible without touching, and fastening them into position with some very small tacks. Then he connected the ribbons and foil with two heavy batteries and awaited the result.

"We were all deeply interested and little work was done until the advance guard of the cockroach army put in an appearance. Now to complete the circuit and set this unique little engine of death in operation it needed but a single cockroach to cross the dead line. One big fellow came up the post at the southeast corner of the room and stopped for a moment. Then he brushed his nose with his forelegs and started. He reached the first ribbon in safety, but as soon as his fore-creepers struck the opposite or parallel ribbon over he went as dead as a free message. From that time until after lunch the check boys were kept busy brushing the dead insects to the floor. At midnight the cordon of defunct beetles around the table looked like a square made out of an old rope."

While in Boston, Adams was Edison's constant companion, and the two lived and worked together more like brothers than friends. They would wander among the old second-hand book stores and pick up bargains which Edison would devour when he should have been resting. "One day," says Adams in Dickson's "Edison," "he bought the whole of Faraday's works on electricity, brought them home at four o'clock in the morning, and read steadily until I arose, when we made for Hanover Street, about a mile distant (where we took our meals) to secure breakfast. Edison's brain was on fire with what he had read, and he suddenly remarked to me: "Adams, I have got so much to do and life is so short that I am going to hustle," and with that he started on a run for breakfast.

Captain H. M. Anderson, of Kansas City, was an operator with Edison at this time, and often met the inventor at his little workshop in Wilson Street. Anderson was on day duty, but Edison had a night shift. "Where he slept," says Captain Anderson, "I don't know, for he worked most of the day down in that little machine shop. He never was in time to go on duty. He would get to working out some idea, and would not think about his job until half an hour after time to report. Often he got called over the coals by the manager, but though he always expressed sorrow he never repented, or if he did, he never reformed. He made some guncotton once from a formula of his own. He had been working for weeks on something, but we never ventured to ask him what it was. He would not have told us if we had. One day I heard him say, 'I don't believe it's any good,' and he laid something in a metal case and put it on the mantel, back of the stove. It lay there for weeks until they started a fire, and then there was an explosion which blew the front of the stove out. We all rushed from the room, Edison leading the bunch, and all he said was: 'Well, it was good after all.' So I suppose the cause of the explosion was his home-made gun-cotton.

"In the cloak-room, where the operators hung up their hats and coats, there was a large tank filled with ice-water for drinking. Opposite it hung a tin dipper on a nail in the wall. Edison, in one of his merry moods, connected this nail with a wire at the other end of which were 190 cells of Fuller battery. He then placed a sign below the dipper requesting all to 'Please return this dipper.' His request was heeded. The dipper was never taken down but there were a dozen or more wrenched arms in the office in less than an hour.

"I remember once when Edison bought a new suit of clothes. It was not often he spent much money on these luxuries, but that time he got a thirty-dollar suit. The next Sunday he was experimenting in his workshop with a bottle of sulphuric acid. Suddenly the bottle exploded and the new suit was ruined. 'What I get for putting so much money in a suit!' was Edison's only comment."

Edison himself, through the medium of W. K. L. Dickson, tells a story of his Boston days which I have permission to quote here. It is related at the expense of his friend Adams, who, much to his disgust, was the principal in the amusing incident. "One day," says the inventor, "Milton and I were passing along Tremont Row when we noticed a crowd collected in front of two dry-goods stores and stopped to see what was the matter. It happened that these were rival establishments and that each had received a consignment of stockings which they were eager to dispose of. Their methods were very entertaining. One would put out a sign stating that this vast commercial emporium had five thousand pairs of stockings to dispose of at the paralyzing price of twelve cents a pair, an announcement which wound up with: 'No connection with the firm next door.' In a moment the rival firm would follow suit, underbidding the other by one cent at a time, until the price was actually reduced to one cent for five pairs of stockings.

"The crowd had been steadily increasing all the time, contenting itself with jeering and making merry, but showing no avidity to take advantage of these tempting bargains. Milton and I had been agog, however, for some time and he now broke out with: 'Say, Edison, I can stand this no longer — give me a cent,' and on being supplied with this handsome financial basis he boldly entered the store, which was filled with lady clerks. Throwing down the cent, he demanded five pairs of stockings, while the crowd excitedly awaited the result. The young lady attendant surveyed the customer with magnificent disdain and handed him five pairs of baby stockings. 'Oh,' said my friend, in much discomfiture, 'I can't use these.' 'Can't help it, young man,' was the curt reply; 'we don't permit selections at that price.' The crowd roared and the commercial struggle soon afterwards ended."

Many stories have been written regarding Edison's first lecture, and it is generally supposed that he was so nervous when he found himself in front of his audience that all he could blurt out was: "Ladies and Gentle-

HIS FIRST WORKSHOP

men, — Mr. Adams will now lecture on electricity while I illustrate his remarks with the lantern." This is a little exaggeration of what actually happened. His first lecture, which took place while he was in Boston, was a success, though at the commencement he certainly was greatly embarrassed, as was also his partner, Mr. Milton Adams. His name as a scientist had become a well-known one by this time in Boston, and he bore so excellent a character that he was selected by a fashionable ladies' academy to lecture on telegraphy.

"Immersed in other projects," says Mr. Dickson, "he not only neglected to inquire into the sex of his audience but totally overlooked the appointment, and when summoned by his friend Mr. Adams was discovered on the top of a house performing certain acrobatic feats connected with the erection of a telegraph wire. Curiously enough, Adams shared his colleague's ignorance in regard to the expected ordeal, and possessed, like Edison, with the belief that the audience would be composed of boys, thought it unnecessary, in view of the late hour, to devote any time to personal adornment.

"Unsuspiciously they hurried through the streets and plunged into the scientific arena, where, to their horror and amazement, they found themselves confronted, not by a horde of undisciplined boys, but by an assembly of beautifully attired young ladies. Confusion descended upon them, their tongues clove to the roofs of their mouths, and the upturned sea of quizzical faces before them loomed faintly through a crimson maze. At last, Edison, possessed of the courage of despair, and seeing that Adams was absolutely *hors de combat*, plunged into an exposition of his subject and succeeded, in spite of certain catching sensations at the back of the throat, in conveying to the fair scientists a brief, pleasant, and lucid view of the subject. This diffidence, perhaps, served Edison's cause better than a bumptious and self-satisfied glibness would have done. From that day the sweet girl graduates made a point of recognizing Edison in public and bestowed upon him such smiles as made him a subject of envious admiration among his less favored associates."

CHAPTER VI

EARLY TELEGRAPHIC INVENTIONS

THROUGH all his wanderings Edison never lost sight of the one great object which he had in view, viz., to be a successful inventor, and during the time that he was working in the different offices of the Western Union his mind was busy with schemes connected with telegraphy or which had electricity as a basis. He worked alone and no one shared his confidences. Just as he is to-day, he never talked of his plans or boasted about what he was going to accomplish. Modesty and retirement were born with him and have stuck to him now for sixty years. It is a question whether his closest friend knew what he had in mind when tinkering with those sets of telegraph instruments and electrical apparatus on which he spent every cent of his hard-earned money. Certainly he confided to no one the principle of any invention prior to its being perfected, and, in fact, very seldom spoke of his own work. When he became famous, of course, it was different, but even then he rigidly forbore to make any statement regarding an invention which was still in the making. He never talks about a device until it is perfected, and then any one is quite at liberty to find out anything about it that they have a mind to.

Edison left Boston soon after patenting his vote-recorder and went to New York. He had no desire to continue his career as a telegraph operator, for it interfered too much with his work as an experimenter. What he aimed at was to have a laboratory of his own, where he could carry out those ideas which were gathering so thickly in his brain. But he had no money, and without capital it was impossible for him to make headway as an inventor. He arrived in New York with scarcely sufficient cash to rent a respectable lodging — all had gone either in books or apparatus.

Walking along lower Broadway one morning, soon after his arrival, and wondering whether the time would ever come when he would be able to put his schemes to a practical test, he turned into Wall Street and entered the head office of the Law Gold Indicator. These indicators, or "tickers," were distributed among five or six hundred brokerage offices and were regarded as rather wonderful instruments, though occasionally they went wrong and then a messenger from each subscriber would be sent down post-haste to the head office to inquire what the trouble was and when the machines would be working again. The memorable morning Edison happened to look in, for the express purpose of discovering whether there was any job in his particular line going begging, the indicators had struck work and messengers from all parts of the city were clamoring to know what was wrong. Excitement ran high, for gold was dear and moments were precious.

Mr. Law was in the office, together with a small army of workmen, but no one seemed capable of locating the trouble. Then Edison, who was standing by and seemed mildly interested in the commotion, remarked that he thought he could put things to rights, and Mr. Law told him to go ahead and see what he could do. Whereupon the young man quietly but deliberately removed a loose contact spring which had fallen between the wheels and immediately the instruments worked as chirpily as before. The repairers looked foolish and Mr. Law requested Edison to step into his office. After asking him a few questions, Mr. Law offered him the position of manager of the service at a salary of three hundred dollars a month. Edison says he nearly fainted when told what his remuneration was to be, but somehow he managed to keep a straight face and accepted the position with becoming gravity.

Now that he had an assured income of thirty-six hundred dollars a year, Edison immediately opened a workshop "down town," and every moment that he could spare was devoted to his beloved experimenting. His telegraph and electrical instruments were set out, bottles of chemicals lined the shelves, batteries were purchased, and soon the little shop really did begin to have the appearance of a *bonâ-fide* laboratory. Here Edison would work until the "small hours" and sometimes right through the night, for from his earliest years he seems to have been able to thrive on the minimum amount of sleep. He was busy on the duplex telegraph, but for a time he put this aside to see what he could do with the gold and stock ticker. It did not take him long to discover that in its then condition it was little better than useless; for in spite of his being manager, the system broke down again and again, causing endless trouble to the subscribers.

So he determined to improve the instrument and convert it into a reliable and trustworthy "ticker." As assistant he took into his workshop a man of the name of Callahan, a clever mechanic, and the two worked early and late to perfect the system. They finally succeeded in evolving many important improvements, and the president of the company,

General Marshall Lefferts, sent for Edison and asked him what he wanted for these. The inventor, modest in his demands, was about to mention five thousand dollars when good sense came to his aid, and he replied that he would rather the president made him an offer. Thereupon this gentleman mentioned forty thousand dollars. Edison opened his mouth to give voice to the astonishment he felt at the magnitude of the sum, when General Lefferts, misinterpreting his expression, added that it was as much as he cared to give, and so, like a wise man, Edison quietly accepted the handsome sum.

After a few preliminaries the inventor was subsequently handed a check for the amount agreed upon; and as this was the first piece of paper of the kind which had ever come into his possession, he was in some perplexity as to what he was to do with it. Finally, he went to the bank and tried to cash it, but the paying teller, knowing nothing of Edison, declined to pay out so large a sum until he had been "identified." Edison, firmly convinced that he had been "done," was moodily leaving the bank when he met an acquaintance, a man well known in commercial circles, to whom he told his trouble. This gentleman laughed heartily at Edison's embarrassment, returned with him to the bank, and "identified" him to the satisfaction of the cashier. He received the money, "a great stack of it" as he afterwards described the big bundle of bills, and then he was uncertain what to do with it. He carried it about with him for two days, afraid to trust it to a bank, and probably no one before or since has ever been so inconvenienced by an overplus of wealth. In the end a friend persuaded him to open an account at a reliable institution, where he eventually deposited his forty thousand.

EDISON'S UNIVERSAL STOCK PRINTER

This was Edison's first real start, though a greater triumph came to him when he gained the confidence of the president of the Western Union through a breakdown of the lines between New York and Albany. Dr. Norvin Green was president at that time, and he himself afterwards declared that it was entirely due to his stupidity and that of his associates that the corporation was so long in taking advantage of Edison's genius. The inventor had called on Dr. Green many times for the purpose of asking him to take up his improvements and inventions, but the president "turned him down" every time, believing that the schemes of so young a man could scarcely be worth serious consideration. But Edison did not give up. He knew that it was the Western Union that could best handle his inventions, and he was determined to exhaust every means in his power to persuade the company to give him a trial.

On the occasion of one of these many visits he found Dr. Green in a somewhat irascible state of mind, and in no mood to discuss inventions with him. As some excuse for his irritability he informed Edison that they were unable to get into communication with Albany, and that a considerable amount of business was being held up. "Perhaps," said Dr. Green, "as you know so much about telegraphy, you will come to our assistance and fix things up for us." His tones were not entirely confident, and some of his associates even smiled. But Edison saw his opportunity and was quick to make a bargain.

"Dr. Green," he said, "if I locate this trouble within two or three hours, will you take up my inventions and give them honest consideration?" The president instantly gave his word, and, seeing Edison's eagerness, added: "I will consider your inventions if you get us out of this fix within two days." Edison made a rush for the main office, and, as he was already well known there as an expert operator, every one was ready to assist him.

It was not until years after that Edison related how he went to work to find out where the trouble lay. Here is the story in his own words: "At the main office," he says, "I called up Pittsburg and asked for the best operator there. When I had got him I told him to call up the best man at Albany, and direct him to telegraph down the line toward New York as far as he could, and report back to me as soon as possible. Inside of an hour I received this telegram: 'I can telegraph all right down to within two miles of Poughkeepsie, and there is trouble with the wire there.' I then went back to the office of the president and told him that if a train should be sent to Poughkeepsie with materials for the work, they would find a break two miles on the other side of Poughkeepsie, and could repair it that afternoon." The break was located and repaired, and Dr. Green completed his part of the contract by considering every invention which Edison afterwards brought to him.

With his first check Edison was enabled to carry out a long-cherished plan. He gave up his little shop in New York, resigned his position as manager of the Gold and Stock Indicator, and opened up a factory in Newark, N.J., where he soon gathered around him a small army of assistants. Here he not only manufactured his improved "tickers" and sent them out in large numbers, but he also busied himself with many brilliant and new inventions which began to issue from his creative mind in bewildering profusion. He had already sold his duplex telegraph to the Western Union, and the company now had a contract with him by which they held an option on all his future telegraphic inventions.

The duplex was Edison's first important invention connected with electrical telegraphy, and embodied a method of multiple transmission which doubled the capacity of a single wire. "By this instrument," wrote the late Luther Stieringer in his descriptive catalogue of the Edison inventions exhibited at the Paris Exposition of 1889, "two messages can be sent in opposite directions at the same time over the same wire without any confusion or obstruction to each other. The attempt to run two trains on the same track in opposite directions at the same time is attended with results too familiar to need mention, but in duplex telegraphy a skilful adjustment of the apparatus at each end of the line enables a strictly analogous idea to be put into force with the most brilliant success.

"The principle or electrical fact from which the invention is built up is that currents of electricity split up and follow any number of paths that may be opened to them exactly in proportion to the resistance that the wire offers to their passage, just as water flowing through a set of pipes will fill them in exact proportion to their size. The apparatus at each end so embodies this principle that each set is unresponsive to the movements of its own transmitting key, although at the same time it responds to every movement of the key operated at the distant station. The great feature is the use of an artificial line furnished by a rheostat and supplemented by a condenser, and balancing the real line actually in service, so that the current is divided between the artificial line and the real line — in the one doing nothing, and in the other carrying the impulses that constitute the message."

Having perfected this invention, which Edison sold

outright to the Western Union, the inventor decided to go one better, and turned his attention to the now familiar quadruplex, which he devised in 1874. This not only doubled the capacity of a single wire, but made possible the simultaneous transmission of two messages each way. The principle involved is that of working over the line with two currents that differ from each other in strength or nature, so that they will only affect instruments adapted to respond to just such currents and no others. By combining instruments that respond only to variations in the strength of current with instruments that respond only to change in the direction of current, and by grouping a pair of such at each end of the line, the quadruplex was the result. With this invention there are two sending and two receiving operators at each end, or eight in all, kept busy upon a single wire.

The value of this invention it is impossible to gauge. It has saved the Western Union millions, which they would otherwise have had to expend in additional wires and their repairs. It has turned a hundred thousand miles of wire into four hundred thousand, and without any added cost. In other words, for every mile of actual wire the quadruplex adds three miles of "phantom" wire which perform their work just as reliably as though they really existed. For this invention Edison received thirty thousand dollars, the whole of which he spent in trying to invent a wire which would carry six messages. The attempt was not commercially successful, so that Edison derived little financial benefit from his quadruplex telegraph — perhaps the greatest invention ever conceived in connection with electrical telegraphy.

Another important invention of Edison's in connection with telegraphy was his automatic telegraph.

EARLY TELEGRAPHIC INVENTIONS 69

This instrument required that the message be prepared in advance. This was accomplished by perforating paper tape with Morse characters, the tapes being afterwards run through a transmitter at the highest possible rate of speed up to several thousand words a minute. In connection with this invention a characteristic story is told by his associate Charles Bachelor, who was for many years the inventor's right-hand man. "In the development of the automatic telegraph," Mr. Bachelor said on one occasion, "it became necessary to have a solution which would give a chemically prepared paper upon which the characters could be recorded at a speed greater than two hundred words a minute. There were numerous solutions in French books, but none of them enabled him to exceed that rate. But he had invented a machine that would exceed it, and must have the paper to match the machine. I came in one night, and there sat Edison with a pile of chemistries and chemical books that were five feet high when they stood on the floor and lay one upon the other. He had ordered them from New York, London, and Paris. He studied them night and day. He ate at his desk and slept in his chair. In six weeks he had gone through books, written a volume of abstracts, made two thousand experiments on the formulas, and had produced a solution (the only one in the world) which would do the very thing he wanted done — record over two hundred words a minute on a wire 250 miles long. He ultimately succeeded in recording 3100 words a minute."

Two other inventions occupied Edison's attention during his Newark days. These were the harmonic multiplex telegraph and the autographic telegraph. The former is a system by which the inventor employed tuning-forks, or "reeds" actuated by electro-magnets, each reed serving as a key to transmit impulses over the line, so that the tuning-fork at the other end vibrating at the same frequency will analyze the current, so to speak, separating and selecting so much of the current as belongs to it. A number of tuning-forks can be operated at the same time on this principle, and as many as sixteen messages have been sent at once, or eight each way, by means of this harmonic multiplex system.

The object of the autographic telegraph was to reproduce in one place the exact counterpart of a message written by the sender in another place. In the Edison autographic telegraph the message is written with a pencil on specially prepared paper. This paper is soft and spongy, and the pressure of the pencil makes a deep indentation in it. The next step is the transmission. The message is placed on a cylinder revolved by an electric motor, which is in synchronism with a similar motor and apparatus at the other end of the line, the cylinder of the latter, however, being of metal covered with a sheet of chemically prepared paper. A delicately adjusted spring is placed against the revolving drum at the sending end, and as the spring of wire passes over the paper and falls into the indentations produced in the messages it closes the circuit at the distant end of the line, where an iron spring or wire decomposes the solution in the chemically treated paper on the revolving drum at the exact moment of making the circuit. As the pens at each end of the line are caused to move downward a trifle at each revolution of the drum the entire message is accurately reproduced.

CHAPTER VII

THE TELEPHONE

Soon after locating in New York and perfecting the printing telegraph for gold and stock quotations, Edison established a factory at Newark for the making of his "tickers," and here he went in extensively for experimenting along different lines. His entire mind, however, seems to have been engrossed with telegraphy, and he soon brought out the sextuplex transmission of messages. As an inventor and patentee he was now so well known, and his "applications" at the Patent Office were so numerous, that the Commissioner on one occasion in an address spoke of Edison as "that young man in New Jersey who has made the path to the Patent Office hot with his footsteps." The public followed his work with the keenest interest, and there was scarcely a newspaper in the country but recorded from day to day some item of interest — either true or false — connected with the energetic inventor.

But Edison soon found that he could not very well combine the superintending of the manufacture of his various inventions with experimentation, and so he went to Menlo Park, and there devoted himself entirely to perfecting some of those wonderful schemes which were forever passing through his mind. He left the Newark factory in the hands of a capable manager, and henceforth became known as the "Wizard of Menlo Park" — a title which stuck to him for many years even after removing his laboratory to Orange.

Just about this time the possibility of employing electricity as a means of conveying speech great distances — or what was then considered great distances — attracted universal interest, and many scientists engaged in the work of solving the fascinating problem. The idea, however, was not altogether new, for a quarter of a century previously — somewhere about 1852 — Charles Boursel declared that the time would come when conversations would be carried on over a wire with no greater effort than that required in ordinary speech. "I have asked myself," he then wrote, "if the spoken word itself could not be transmitted by electricity, in a word, if what was spoken in Vienna could not be heard in Paris. Suppose that a man speaks near a movable disk, sufficiently flexible to lose none of the vibrations of the voice; that the disk alternately makes and breaks the connection with the battery, you might have at a distance another disk which will simultaneously execute the same vibrations."

This was certainly a remarkable prophecy of what the telephone would ultimately become, and had Boursel possessed the genius required he would doubtless have given us a telephone built on lines almost identical with the instrument in use to-day. Boursel's idea was acted upon by Philip Reis, of Frankfurt, who succeeded in constructing a telephone furnished with a receiver which actually did reproduce sounds. "And," says a biographer, "had he only understood that by adjusting his transmitter so that the contacts would remain continuously in contact, he would have had an articulating transmitter. Further than this, had he connected two of his receivers together and

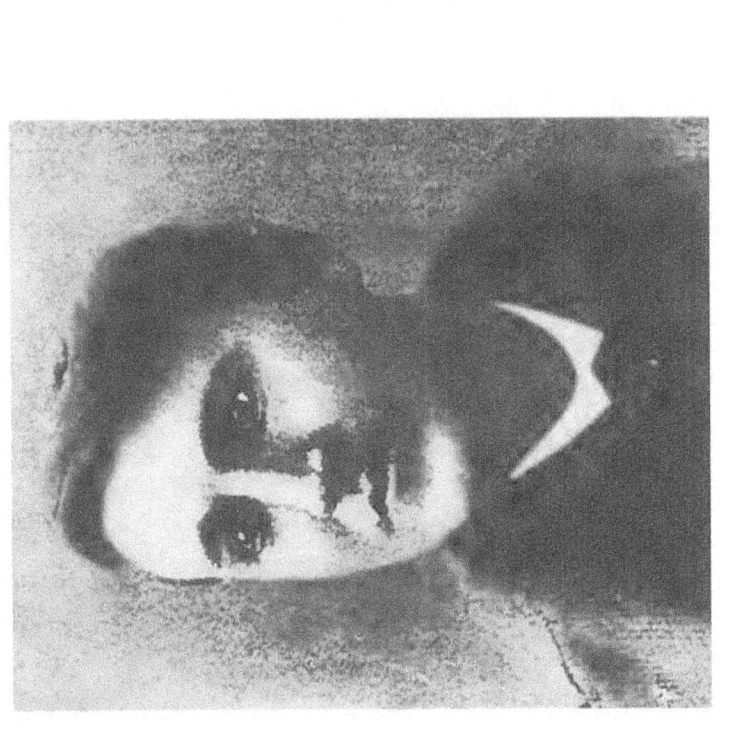

EDISON AT THE AGE OF TWENTY-FOUR

EDISON AT THE AGE OF TWENTY-EIGHT

used one as a transmitter, speech might have been transmitted. With such apparatus of such possibilities it does, indeed, seem remarkable that the mere oversight of not having turned a screw a fractional rotation on its axis, or of not having connected two particular binding posts by a wire, should have shifted the honor of having first transmitted articulate speech from the shoulders of Reis to those of men living half a generation later." Reis's telephone was designed to carry music as well as words, and probably in the whole history of invention no man ever escaped fame by so narrow a margin as Reis. Boursel did not try to turn his primitive idea to account, but became superintendent of telegraph lines at Auch, France; and the French Government, as some reward for the originality of his ideas in connection with telephony, created him Chevalier of the Legion of Honor — the only recognition he ever received.

In 1875 two men took up the question of telephony — Alexander Graham Bell, of Salem, Mass., and Elisha Gray, of Chicago, Ill. — and on February 15, 1876, two applications were filed with the Commissioner of the United States Patent Office, both covering an invention for "transmitting vocal sounds telegraphically." These came from Bell and Gray. The coincidence was a remarkable one, and, according to the Commissioner, without parallel in the annals of the Patent Office. When the applications came to be examined it was found that practically the same ground was covered by both, and therefore, in the granting of a patent, it became necessary to determine at what hour of the day each paper was filed. The chief clerk was put through a verbal examination, and his daybook examined, with the result that priority was awarded to Bell, who was granted a patent on the 7th of March, or less than three weeks after making his application. Bell lost no time. He organized a company, which he called the Bell Telephone Company, incorporated it in the State of Massachusetts, and the manufacturing of instruments commenced. But the telephone at this stage was far from perfect, the public regarding it as an interesting toy rather than an invention which had great commercial possibilities. It was not practical.

Then Edison's attention was aroused. He saw that, if perfected, the telephone would be of colossal use in business, and, abandoning telegraphy for the time being, he devoted all his energy and practical genius to overcoming those apparently insuperable difficulties which had halted Bell in his march towards success. Very soon after taking the matter in hand Edison invented the carbon telephone transmitter — a device which made telephony practical, and without which Bell's invention was useless. Bell wanted that transmitter, but Edison wouldn't sell the patent. And Edison couldn't make any practical use of his own transmitter without infringing on some of Bell's patents. Edison tried to evolve an entire system of his own, but found that there were certain Bell inventions which he must have. Bell attempted to use Edison's idea with regard to the carbon transmitter in a different way, but it was useless, he "infringed" every time. There was a contest between the two inventors and neither would give in. Their inventions were like certain elements — of very little use apart, but of immense value when brought together. Litigation followed, but the wisdom of a compromise made itself apparent to both electricians, and Edison yielded up his transmitter in exchange for certain benefits satisfactory to both.

Bell made considerable money over the telephone,

THE TELEPHONE

not by his patent rights, but by getting hold of a lot of stock and sticking to it. Before the formation of his Telephone Company, however, Bell had a strenuous time trying to get people interested in his enterprise. So hard up for money was he at one period that he offered a friend a half-interest in his invention for $2500, but in spite of his assurance that the telephone would subsequently do away with the telegraph, the friend declined. To an official in the Patent Office Bell offered a tenth interest for $100, which was also refused. In fifteen years that tenth interest was worth $1,500,000.

A short time ago Edison was asked to explain his connection with the telephone, and with his usual modesty he replied: "When I struck the telephone business the Bell people had no transmitter, but were talking into the magneto receiver. You never heard such a noise and buzzing as there was in that old machine! I went to work and monkeyed around, and finally struck the notion of the lampblack button. The Western Union Telegraph Company thought this was a first-rate scheme, and bought the thing out, but afterwards they consolidated, and I quit the telephone business."

Besides his carbon transmitter Edison has done much other work in the field of telephony, and the receivers and transmitters of various designs which he has invented are too numerous to describe in detail. Among the many systems which he evolved for the transmission of speech, however, may be mentioned the water telephone, condenser telephone, electrostatic telephone, chemical telephone, various forms of magnetic telephone, inertia telephone, mercury telephone, voltaic pile telephone, musical transmitter, and the electro-motographic receiver.

Luther Stieringer, in stating that the electro-motograph receiver and the carbon transmitter are Mr. Edison's most important and valuable contributions to telephony, adds that the inventor was the first to apply the induction coil to the transmission of speech, a factor so important that, without it, telephony on a commercial scale would be practically impossible. "The variable resistance of carbon under pressure," declared the late Mr. Stieringer, "used by Edison in other inventions, was again taken advantage of in the carbon transmitter. Its operation is briefly as follows: A carbon button, held by a light spring against the diaphragm, is placed in circuit with the primary wire of an induction coil, the battery being in the same circuit and the secondary of the induction coil connected to the line. When the diaphragm is set in vibration by the sound waves of the voice, constantly varying pressure is applied to the carbon button, altering its electrical resistance, and producing wide variations of current in the primary, and consequently similar changes in the induced current set up in the secondary. These induced currents are sent into the line and act on the receiver at the distant end.

"A curious discovery," continues Mr. Stieringer, "made by Mr. Edison, and one which he has applied in quite a number of his inventions, is what he calls the 'electro-motograph principle.' He found that by placing a sheet of rough paper, saturated with certain chemical solutions, upon a brass plate connected to one pole of a battery, on passing over the paper a piece of sheet metal (palladium) connected through a telegraph key to the other pole of the battery, when he opened and closed the key there was alternately friction and slipping of the metal strip on the paper, the passage of the current apparently producing a lubricating effect. This principle was adopted by Edison in his motograph relay, which he sold to the Western Union Telegraph Company, who, however, never put it into extensive practice, as shortly after they consolidated with a rival company controlling the patent for the electro-magnetic relay. The Edison motograph receiver, or loud-speaking telephone, is a modification of the electro-motograph, in which a cylinder of chalk revolved by a small electric motor is employed in place of the strip of chemically treated paper. The palladium-faced spring, which rests on the chalk, is attached to a mica diaphragm in a resonator. The current passes from the main line through the spring to the chalk and to the battery. The ingenious instrument produced the voice with remarkable power and distinctness, and could be heard perfectly by a very large audience. The action of the instrument depends upon the variations in adhesion of the metallic strip to the chalk cylinder caused by the current coming over the line. As the strip or spring is connected to the receiving diaphragm, these variations produce corresponding variations in the diaphragm, the voice being reproduced with startling distinctness.

It is now nearly thirty years since Edison first exhibited this telephone, and an account of the interesting event may not appear out of place. It was first shown at Saratoga on the evening of August 30, 1879, the event being reported in the New York *Tribune* as follows:

"The town hall was crowded with people, who were all interested and amused in the exhibition and description of the new chemical telephone, Mr. Edison's latest invention. On the platform were Professor Barker, Professor A. Graham Bell, Professor Borton, and Mr. Edison. President Barker, in a clear, simple, and popular way, gave a history of the telephone, and an account of the magneto receiver and transmitter, the carbon transmitter, and the improvements of the original invention. Mr. Edison amiably acted as draughtsman, illustrated the characteristics of the various machines by diagrams on the blackboard, which aided President Barker in his explanations.

"Then the comparative powers and qualities of the various forms of transmitters were tested for the enlightenment of the audience. Mr. Bachelor, Mr. Edison's assistant, who is blessed with a most powerful and resonant voice, but was afflicted last night with a cold in the head, was in a distant room in the building, to which the telephone wires were conducted. In the first place experiments were tried with the magneto transmitter and magneto receiver, and it was shown that only one person, and he only when holding the receiver to his ear, could hear Mr. Bachelor's vociferous remarks and thunderous songs, even though that worthy gentleman strained his lungs to the utmost. Then the carbon transmitter and the magneto receiver were used, and a few persons close to the instrument could hear faintly Mr. Bachelor's shouts into the transmitter. The sounds were much louder than when the magneto transmitter was used, but could not be heard at all at a little distance from the receiver.

"Finally the electro-chemical telephone was used with brilliant results. Mr. Bachelor's talk, recitations, and singing could be heard all over the hall, and the audience was delighted with such enchanting novelties as 'Mary had a little Lamb,' 'Jack and Jill went up the Hill,' 'John Brown's Body,' 'There was a little Girl,' and the like. The assembly was spared one infliction, however — no selections from 'Pinafore' were given. The telephone gave distinctly the singing of two and three persons at once, the talk of one person and the singing of another at the same time, whistling airs on the cornet, laughter loud and long, repetition of the alphabet and whistling together, and many other sounds.

"Mr. Edison described the machine which worked these wonders and drew a plan of it on the blackboard. He said, however, that he was not sure he could make it quite clear to his hearers, for he did not understand its operation entirely himself. From a diaphragm extends an arm at right angles touching the cylinder of chalk moistened with a solution of phosphate in water. The arm is pressed against the chalk cylinder by a little block of rubber, which is pressed upon the arm by a screw touched by the finger of the receiver of the message, who keeps the cylinder in rotation by a little crank. The working of the instrument depends upon the principle that the passage of a current of electricity through a moistened substance prepared in the way the chalk cylinder is prepared prevents friction. Hence, when the electric waves come from the transmitter there is no friction during the passage of a wave, and this absence of friction affects the arm projecting from the diaphragm, and the diaphragm itself vibrates with an intensity greater than all the impulse which comes over the wire from the transmitter. Hence the enfeebling of the current by the length of wire that it passes over is made up, and the voice of the speaker or singer at the transmitter is heard nearly as loudly, or sometimes even more loudly, at the receiving instrument than at the transmitter. The current, however, does not pass directly from the wire leading from the transmitter to the electro-chemical apparatus. Owing to some defects in telegraph lines, Mr. Edison said that it is necessary to have two coils a very short distance apart. The current from the transmitter reaches the first coil, and a wave is set in motion in the second coil which goes to the chalk cylinder.

"Mr. Edison said that he could, if necessary, construct instruments which would make the sound three or four times as loud as any man could shout. Three or four years ago he had a somewhat similar instrument at Saratoga, but moistened paper was used and not prepared chalk, and the instrument was imperfect. It would not transmit spoken words, but would transmit music, and a concert was given in New York and the music heard on the piazza of the Grand Union Hotel by the use of that instrument.

"The receiving apparatus in the electro-chemical telephone has no ear trumpet at the end like the magneto receiver. The apparatus is in a small box with a crank at the side and a glass front, through which the screw passes by which the receiver presses on the arm extending from the diaphragm to the chalk cylinder. There is a little round hole at the top of the box. The inventor showed that it made no difference in which direction the cylinder was turned, or whether it was turned fast or slow. But if he stopped turning the crank the sound stopped the same instant. The receiver has thus entire control over the message. No sound is heard until he begins to turn the crank, and the message only continues while the revolution of the cylinder is kept up.

"Mr. Edison's explanation pleased the people greatly. His quaint and homely manner, his unpolished but clear language, his odd but pithy expressions charmed and attracted them. Mr. Edison is certainly not graceful or eloquent. He shuffled about the platform in an ungainly way, and his stooping,

MOTOGRAPH RECEIVING AND TRANSMITTING TELEPHONE

swinging figure was lacking in dignity. But his eyes were wonderfully expressive, his face frank and cordial, and his frequent smile hearty and irresistible. If his sentences were not rounded, they went to the point, and the assembly dispersed with great satisfaction at having seen and heard the renowned inventor and having seen and heard his most recent invention. Though the distance between the transmitter and receiver was short last night for convenience and to save expense of arrangement of wires, the electro-chemical telephone can be used at long distances as well as other telephones. It is certainly a remarkable instrument."

Edison's manager at the time, Mr. Edward H. Johnson, in a statement subsequently given to the press, briefly explained how it came about that Edison became associated with the perfecting of the telephone. "The Bell patent," he said, "preceded Edison's, but soon after Edison improved the telephone by substituting the carbon button transmitter. The machine, however, was still far from what was required. It could not be used in Europe, and besides it involved law-suits brought by the Bell Telephone Company and defended by the Western Union Telegraph Company, which had bought Edison's patents. In this strait the English agent telegraphed to Edison: 'You must make a new receiver, and dispense with the magnet.' That was a difficult undertaking, for the magnet was considered indispensable in every telephone to convert sound waves into electric waves and *vice versâ*. At last it occurred to him that he might substitute moistened chalk with certain chemicals. He tried it, and it produced results which delighted him."

The first practical telephone was exhibited in America at the Centennial Exhibition in Philadelphia and the first recorded telephone message was sent over the wire by Professor Bell. It was the recital of Hamlet's "To be or not to be," and was spoken to Dom Pedro, Emperor of Brazil. The telephone was first shown in Europe at the meeting of the British Association in Glasgow, September, 1876, and pronounced by Sir William Thomson the greatest of all marvels connected with electric telegraphy.

In an old volume of Chambers's *Journal* for 1883 the following incident is recorded regarding one of the earliest forms of telephone: "The drum of the telephone," says the writer, "is a flat plate which has a fundamental note of its own, and it is more ready to vibrate in response to this note than to any other. Thus, the basic tones in the voice which harmonize with this fundamental note come out stronger in the telephone than the other tones which do not; and hence a certain twang is given to the speaker's voice which depends on the dimensions of the plate. Thus for men's low voices the plate of a telephone should be larger than for the shriller voices of women and children. This peculiarity of the instrument was amusingly illustrated at the Paris International Electric Exhibition of 1881 by Professor D. E. Hughes.

"As a member of the scientific jury who were reporting on the various exhibits in telegraphy, Professor Hughes was examining — along with his colleagues, comprising several eminent foreign electricians — a telephonic apparatus devised by Dr. Werner Siemens; but they could not make it answer to their voices. Various names of foreign savants were shouted in the mouthpiece of the telephone, but it would not respond. At length Professor Hughes, who is an accomplished musician, stepped forward and secretly ascertained the fundamental note of the telephone by tapping its plate. He then turned to his fellow-jurors with a smile, and remarked that there was a peculiarity about this telephone: it was an Anglophile and would only respond to the honored name of Faraday. The jurors naturally treated his words with amiable derision; but this, however, was soon changed to wonder when, after crying over the names of Franklin, Ohm, Volta, Ampère, and others, the telephone remained obstinately uncertain until he pronounced the magic syllables, FAR-A-DAY, to which it joyously responded. The word Faraday had simply been spoken by him in the same tone of voice as the fundamental note of the telephone plate."

It is frequently declared that there is nothing new under the sun, yet it may surprise some readers to learn, on the authority of the noted Dr. Bach, that the Catuquinary Indians in the valley of the Amazon had a system of telephony generations before the transmission of sound by electricity attracted the attention of modern scientists. "I found," wrote Dr. Bach, some years ago, in an American geographical magazine, "that each habitation or malocca occupied by the tribe was supplied with a cambarysu, or telegraph, which enabled them to communicate with each other. The machine consists of a hollow piece of hard palm wood filled with sand, hide, resin, and rubber. This is struck with a club of wood coated with rubber and hide.

"There is one of these instruments hidden in each malocca, and the maloccas are about a mile distant one from the other, and all on a direct line north and south. It appears that the instruments are *en rapport* with each other, and, when struck with a club, the neighboring ones to the north and south, if not above a mile distant, respond to or echo the blow. To this an Indian answers by striking the instrument in the malocca with which it is desired to communicate, which blow in turn is echoed by the instrument originally struck. Each malocca has its own series of signals. So enclosed is each instrument in the malocca that when standing outside and near the building it is difficult to hear, but, nevertheless, it is heard distinctly in the next malocca a mile distant in the manner indicated. The Tuchan gave me an example of signalling. With a prolonged interval, he twice struck the instrument with a club, which, as I understood, was to indicate attention or that a conference was required. This was responded to by the same instrument as a result of a single blow given by some one on the next apparatus a mile distant. Then commenced a long conversation which I could not comprehend. So, long before we had our telephone connecting house to house, these remote Indians of South America had got what served something of the same purpose."

Some time ago Edison was interviewed on the subject of telephoning across the sea. Apparently the inventor does not think this very probable, for he said: "I do not believe we shall ever be able to telephone across the Atlantic owing to the electrification of the gutta-percha covering of the cable. Every substance will electrify somewhat, so the difficulty will not be overcome by discarding what is now used. Between Valencia and Heart's Content the tons of gutta-percha on the cable play a large part in its operation. Every bit of it has to be electrified before a single signal can be sent. And when the current is cut off at Valencia after being operated it still continues to flow into Heart's Content for a comparatively long time afterwards. This all interferes with the sound waves. Even in telegraphing there is no real break between flashes, and there are only ten or twelve sound waves per second. In telephoning there would be two or three thousand in the same time. The only way to get over it would be to employ some other force that would not affect surrounding matter."

The question whether the voice causes vibration in the telephone has often been asked, and a short time ago the matter was fully discussed in the press. On the question being put to Albert H. Walker, the well-known American electrician, he replied: "In Bell's original telephone the human voice did cause the line to vibrate electrically though not mechanically; but that telephone could propagate electrical vibrations only a few hundred feet at most. The telephone in actual use to-day is the Edison variable resistance transmitter. In that system the voice supplies none of the energy that traverses the wire. The energy is supplied by a battery or a dynamo sending a constant current over the line. The voice merely vibrates the little diaphragm in the transmitter, and the vibration simply moves a little bit of carbon in the transmitter into more or less contact with another little bit of carbon. That slight movement varies the electrical resistance of the circuit and thus causes the current from the dynamo to vary in strength. The voice does not make the line wire vibrate any more than a locomotive engineer pulls a train of cars with his arm when he moves the lever that lets the steam into the cylinder of his engine."

Considerable speculation has been indulged in as to the origin of the expression "Hello!" as applied to telephonic conversation. Mr. F. P. Fish, president of the American Telephone Company, gives the credit to Edison. "Years ago," says Mr. Fish, "when the telephone first came into use people were accustomed to ring a bell and then say, ponderously: 'Are you there?' 'Are you ready to talk?' Well, Mr. Edison did away with that awkward un-American way of doing things. He caught up a receiver one day and yelled into the transmitter one word — a most satisfactory, capable, soul-satisfying word — 'Hello!' It has gone clear around the world. The Japs use it; it is heard in Turkey; Russia could not do without it, and neither could Patagonia."

It might here be remarked that Edison is also credited with coining the word "filament," a term first used in connection with his incandescent electric light system. On one occasion, during the progress of a suit brought by certain infringers of his electric light patents in England, the London *Electrician* declared that it did not know what a "filament" was. It said: "If Edison had no other claim to immortality — and most people believe he is essentially well provided in this respect — he still, we think, deserves all the credit which has ever been awarded him for his invention of the definition-defying term 'filament.' The highest available forensic, judicial, and scientific skill of this age and country have been brought to bear upon the question, and that not once only, but over and over again; and still, as Judge Cotton plaintively remarks this week, we seem to be no nearer knowing what a filament really is. His Lordship inclines to think that it must be something which 'is formed before carbonization,' but this only serves to show how far a reconciliation of legal subtilities and technical absurdities may remove the final issue from the category in which he who runs may read. For if this be indeed the definition of a 'filament,' then our admiration for the inventor of the term will be more than ever profound."

During his investigations in telephony, and about the time when he had perfected his transmitter, Edison was frequently called upon to supply telephone experts

— the requests coming from all parts of the world. Before sending out a man, however, he had a novel method of testing his capabilities — a system of examination which, if he passed, usually satisfied both Edison and his patron. "First of all," the inventor stated on one occasion to a writer in the *Electrical Review*, "we rigged up some telephones in the shop, and did all sorts of things with them. I would stick the point of a jack-knife through the insulation in spots and cut a wire, and in various ways induce 'bugs' (in electrical parlance, something difficult to find) into these instruments; then the boys were set to work to find out what was the matter with them. If a fellow could find out ten times inside of ten minutes what the various troubles were he got his passage paid to the place where his services were required, and was started. About one out of three of the boys managed to stand this test, and I believe that every one of them who went abroad made money."

As has already been stated, it was at the time of the invention and exhibition of the telephone that Edison was first referred to as the "Wizard of Menlo Park," and more was written about him, perhaps, than about any other celebrity. The public was amused as well as interested in hundreds of details published regarding the inventor — some of them true, but alas! the greater proportion false. Pick up any periodical or newspaper of the time and you will find innumerable notes about Edison which will astonish you almost as much as they astonished the inventor himself. Mr. Fox, a magazine writer of some prominence, published in *Scribner's* for 1879 several articles dealing with the work of Mr. Edison, in the course of which he states that when true facts regarding the inventor ran out the United States *litterateurs* began the work of drawing upon their imaginations. "The hero of their labors," wrote Mr. Fox, "assumed all sorts of forms. Now he was a scientific hermit shut up in a cavern in a small New Jersey village, holding little or no intercourse with the outside world, working like an alchemist of old in the dead of night, with musty books and curious chemicals, and having for his immediate companions persons as weird and mysterious as himself. Again he was a rollicking, careless person, highly gifted in matters scientific, but deplorably ignorant of everything else, a sort of scientific Blind Tom. Especially was he credited with the most revolutionary ideas concerning Nature. One Western journal represented him as predicting a complete overthrow of nearly all the established laws of Nature: water was no longer to seek its level; the earth was speedily to assume new and startling functions in the universe; everything that had been learned concerning the character of the atmosphere was based on error; the sun itself was to be drawn up in ways that are dark, and to be made subsidiary to innumerable tricks that are vain; in short, all Nature was to be upset."

A somewhat saner description of the inventor, published at the same time, came from the pen of a Mr. Bishop, who had frequent opportunities of studying the "Wizard." But neither could he resist the temptation of surrounding him with a kind of mysterious nimbus, to which Edison himself declares he never had any real right. "Of the number of persons in the laboratory," wrote Mr. Bishop, "remark one you may have least thought of selecting from the informality of his appearance. It is a figure of perhaps five feet nine inches in height, bending above some detail of work. There is a general appearance of youth about it, but the face, knit into anxious wrinkles, seems old.

THE TELEPHONE

The dark hair, beginning to be touched with gray, falls over the forehead in a mop. The hands are stained with acid, and the clothing is of an ordinary ready-made order. It is Edison. He has the air of a mechanic, or, more definitely, with his peculiar pallor, of a night printer. His features are large; the brow well shaped, without unusual developments; the eyes light gray, the nose irregular, and the mouth displaying teeth which are also not altogether regular. When he comes up his attention comes back slowly as though it had been a long way off. But it comes back fully and gradually and the expression of the face, now that it can be seen, is frank and prepossessing. A cheerful smile chases away the grave and somewhat weary look that belongs to it in moments of rest. He seems no longer old. He has almost the air of a big, careless schoolboy released from his desk."

From such a description as this one would suppose that the author were writing of a man bordering on old age, or at least nearing the seamy side of middle life. Yet at the time Edison was barely thirty and, according to those who were his associates, was just as full of fun, just as fond of a good story, just as genial and light-hearted as he was when a boy, or as he is to-day. But it was the fashion then to write of him in this strain, and the temptation to keep up the fashion was yielded to, even by those who knew him sufficiently well to describe him (had they wished to do so) as he really was. The public had taken it into its head that he was a real wizard, and the newspapers, at all events, took no steps towards dispelling the general belief.

It may not be altogether out of place here to record a few facts respecting telephony as it is to-day — facts which were related by Mr. F. P. Fish recently in an address delivered before the Beacon Society. It may, for instance, appear somewhat curious to the lay mind that the energy required for a single incandescent electric light burner is 5,000,000 times as great as that required to send a telephone message a thousand miles, and that the energy required to lift a weight of thirteen ounces is sufficient to operate a telephone for 240,000 years. The number of telephone subscribers in the States (the real home of the telephone) had, in 1905, more than doubled during three years over the total of the previous twenty-four years.

The telephone, Mr. Fish declared, would soon exceed the mail in the number of messages per day. To meet all the requirements of the service one million trees a year are necessary for poles, and the average cost of every class of message is 2.2 cents, which is not much more than the average cost of messages by mail. In 1902 twelve telephones for every hundred of the population in the United States were considered the maximum that it was possible to supply. Now the telephone people are looking ahead to a maximum of twenty for every hundred. The last report of the original Bell Company showed the existence of 4,080 exchanges and branch offices connecting 30,000 cities, towns, and villages, and requiring the constant use of 3,549,810 miles of wire. Through these wires travels a yearly total of over 3,500,000,000 telephone calls, handled by over 20,000 switchboard operators.

At Cortlandt Street, New York, may be seen the biggest telephone-wire switchboard in the world. It is 256 feet long, in the shape of a horseshoe, and cost $100,000. This remarkable apparatus was installed about a year ago, taking the place of an old one which had become inadequate, and although the substitution involved the connecting and disconnecting of more than nine thousand wires, the change from the old board to the new was completed in two hours. This switchboard was the first to be supplied with small incandescent lamps, which glow while the subscribers are talking and which become dark when the receiver is hung up. By this means the instant the line is no longer in use the fact is automatically and silently indicated. On this switchboard there are 14,000 of these electric bulbs. Two hundred and forty-six operators attend to the wants of 9300 subscribers, and the board provides for 470,000 connections, while there are 1000 incoming trunk lines and 840 outgoing.

The telephone has made its way even into the depths of the great forests, and to-day lumbermen are able to communicate with the outer world though they may be separated from it by hundreds of miles of solid timber. In the huge forest belts of the old and new worlds numerous telephones have, during the last few years, been installed, and it is now declared by those whose interests are centred in the lumber trade that the time is not far distant when telephonic communication may be had with every mile of forest where loggers are employed.

These telephones not only save an immense amount of time in the matter of communication and with the different camps, but are also of inestimable value in cases of accident. It is related that soon after the first wires were installed in the forests of Vancouver a party of three men were bringing down a "two-hundred-footer" when by some means it partly fell upon two of them, pinning the victims to the ground, but not seriously injuring them. The third man did his best to liberate his companions, but finding this impossible he communicated with the nearest camp by 'phone and was thus able to summon help, which arrived in a few hours.

In the forests of Montana many telephone boxes

have been fixed to the trees, and these are being increased so speedily that soon every logger will be able to communicate with the mills at any hour of the day, and also speak with the men who overlook the floating of the timber down the great rivers. Moreover, telephone wires are now being slung along the banks of these big waterways, and by this means of quick and easy communication it is believed that the big logjams which are so constantly occurring will be avoided.

Before the adoption of the telephone in the big Canadian and American forests, each lumber company was obliged to keep a large force of men always travelling from camp to camp, carrying instructions and messages from the mills; and, though they sometimes covered thirty miles in a day (remarkably rapid progress when one remembers the density of these forests), much time was lost. Now, with the help of a few telephone wires, the same thing may be accomplished in a few minutes and at much less cost. Most of the logging camps in Montana and other states are now "rung up" at appointed times, the foreman receives his instructions over the wire, messages are exchanged, and the loggers, being allowed the use of the 'phone at intervals, thereby feel that they are not so entirely cut off from their families as formerly.

Many of these lumbermen remain in the forests for a year at a time, and the camps are frequently one hundred and one hundred and fifty miles from civilization. During these twelve months they never see their families and, formerly, seldom had any communication with them. For six months out of the twelve they are, perhaps, snowed in, and could not make their way to the frontier if they wished. Consequently the telephone has been hailed with delight by these men. By its means they are able to receive letters from their wives very frequently, for the owners of the big mills have made arrangements whereby any logger's wife may send a letter to headquarters and have the contents telephoned to the camp where her husband is stationed.

By means of the telephone, doctors are now enabled to visit patients without leaving their consulting rooms. Deaf people need no longer make their infirmity an excuse for staying away from church, for many places of worship are providing a number of pews with receivers and transmitters in direct communication with the pulpit. The telephone is a safeguard against burglars and thieves, and almost as sure a preventer of crime as the electric light. In England, and Europe generally, the telephone is still in a somewhat primitive state, while in America it has long since been brought to a high degree of perfection.

To give some idea of the ease with which the system works in the United States, a recent "long-distance" banquet may be mentioned, where members of an Alumni Association held simultaneous telephone dinners in New York, Chicago, St. Louis, and Portland, Oregon. As it takes twenty-eight hours' continuous and rapid railroad travelling to get from New York to St. Louis, and several days to go from coast to coast, it says a good deal for the excellence of the telephone service when it is stated that no hitch occurred over any part of the line, and that the voices of those who proposed and responded to the various toasts in the four cities mentioned, were as clear and distinct as though the speakers had been all in the one room. Eighty receivers and transmitters were arranged on the tables of each banquet, and the honor of proposing the first toast was relegated to Mr. William S. Curtis, of St. Louis, Mr. Grant Beebe, of Chicago, responding. Toast followed toast alternately, the last health being drunk at midnight, at which hour good-nights were said and the receivers hung up.

CHAPTER VIII

THE ELECTRIC LIGHT

THE genesis of the electric light is thus given in Edison's own simple words: "In 1878," he says, "I went down to see Professor Barker, at Philadelphia, and he showed me an arc lamp — the first I had seen. Then a little later I saw another — I think it was one of Brush's make — and the whole outfit, engine, dynamo, and one or two lamps, was travelling around the country with a circus. At that time Wallace and Moses G. Farmer had succeeded in getting ten or fifteen lamps to burn together in a series, which was considered a very wonderful thing. It happened that at the time I was more or less at leisure, because I had just finished working on the carbon-button telephone, and this electric-light idea took possession of me. It was easy to see what the thing needed: it wanted to be subdivided. The light was too bright and too big. What we wished for was little lights, and a distribution of them to people's houses in a manner similar to gas. Grovernor P. Lowry thought that perhaps I could succeed in solving the problem, and he raised a little money and formed the Edison Electric Light Company. The way we worked was that I got a certain sum of money a week and employed a certain number of men, and we went ahead to see what we could do.

"We soon saw that the subdivision never could be accomplished unless each light was independent of every other. Now it was plain enough that they could not burn in series. Hence they must burn in multiple arc. It was with this conviction that I started. I was fired with the idea of the incandescent lamp as opposed to the arc lamp, so I went to work and got some very fine platinum wire drawn. Experiment with this, however, resulted in failure, and then we tried mixing in with the platinum about 10 per cent of iridium, but we could not force that high enough without melting it. After that came a lot of experimenting — covering the wire with oxide of cerium and a number of other things.

"Then I got a great idea. I took a cylinder of zirconia and wound about a hundred feet of the fine platinum wire on it coated with magnesia from the syrupy acetate. What I was after was getting a high-resistance lamp, and I made one that way that worked up to 40 ohms. But the oxide developed the phenomena now familiar to electricians, and the lamp short-circuited itself. After that we went fishing around and trying all sorts of shapes and things to make a filament that would stand. We tried silicon and boron, and a lot of things that I have forgotten now. The funny part of it was that I never thought in those days that a carbon filament would answer, because a fine hair of carbon was so sensitive to oxidation. Finally, I thought I would try it because we had got very high vacua and good conditions for it.

"Well, we sent out and bought some cotton thread, carbonized it, and made the first filament. We had already managed to get pretty high vacua, and we thought, maybe, the filament would be stable. We built the lamp and turned on the current. It lit up, and in the first few breathless minutes we measured its resistance quickly and found it was 275 ohms — all we wanted. Then we sat down and looked at that lamp. We wanted to see how long it would burn. The problem was solved — if the filament would last. The day was — let me see — October 21, 1879. We sat and looked, and the lamp continued to burn, and the longer it burned the more fascinated we were. None of us could go to bed, and there was no sleep for any of us for forty hours. We sat and just watched it with anxiety growing into elation. It lasted about forty-five hours, and then I said, 'If it will burn that number of hours now, I know I can make it burn a hundred.' We saw that carbon was what we wanted, and the next question was what kind of carbon. I began to try various things, and finally I carbonized a strip of bamboo from a Japanese fan, and saw that I was on the right track. But we had a rare hunt finding the real thing. I sent a schoolmaster to Sumatra and another fellow up the Amazon, while William H. Moore, one of my associates, went to Japan and got what we wanted there. We made a contract with an old Jap to supply us with the proper fibre, and that man went to work and cultivated and cross-fertilized bamboo until he got exactly the quality we required. One man went down to Havana, and the day he got there he was seized with yellow fever and died in the afternoon. When I read the cable message to the boys, about a dozen of them jumped up and asked for his job. Those fellows were a bright lot of chaps, and sometimes it was hard to select the right ones."

That is the whole history of the invention of the incandescent light according to Edison's modest statement in an old number of the *Electrical Review*. His thirteen months of unwearied experimenting with different metals in his search for a suitable filament — carbon points he had hardly considered for a moment — were forgotten, but some account of those days of anxiety, dejection, hope, and final triumph must be given lest the reader come to the erroneous conclusion that the invention of incandescent electric lighting was the thing of ease Edison would have us suppose. Had any other man encountered the difficulties — or half of them — that Edison did, we should still be reading by gas and studying by candle-light. From the moment he took the problem in hand he had no faintest doubt of being able to solve it, and to this, probably, is due the fact that however many disappointments he met with, he was never really down-hearted or despairing.

As Edison has stated, at the time that the question of electric lighting first occurred to him he was more or less a man of leisure, having just completed his carbon telephone. Moreover, he had lately returned from a vacation spent in the Rockies, feeling particularly fit and ready to solve any scientific problem which might suggest itself. After viewing the Brush light and determining that the chief and primary difficulty was one of distribution, he thought long and seriously before deciding which system he should adopt — the incandescent or the voltaic arc. Finally, he decided that the former was the more practical.

Then commenced those long months of experimenting with platinum wire — weary months spent in trying to find some means of preventing this hardest of all metals from melting when the full current of electricity was turned on. Some of these experiments and the difficulties he encountered are touched upon in the chapter devoted to a lecture delivered by Edison in 1879. Many devices were invented in order to prevent the platinum fusing, among others being an automatic lever which regulated the current when the platinum approached the melting-point. This was soon discarded, as was also a diaphragm invented for the same purpose.

At this period of his investigations Edison publicly stated that he felt no doubt of his being able to make the electric light available for all common uses, and that he would ultimately supply it at a cost below that of gas. "There is no difficulty," he said, "about dividing up the current and using small quantities at different points. The trouble is in finding a candle that will give a pleasant light, not too intense, which can be turned off and on as easily as gas. Such a candle cannot be made from carbon points, which waste away, and must be regulated constantly while they do last. Some composition must be discovered which will be luminous when charged with electricity and that will not wear away. Platinum wire gives a good light when a certain quantity of electricity is passed through it. If the current is made too strong, however, the wire will melt. I want to get something better. I have a chemist at work helping me to find the composition that will be made luminous by electricity. We shall discover it in time."

Edison had already made application for a patent in connection with what may be called his new platinum light, and the London papers were among the first to obtain a copy of the specifications. They scarcely met with approval by the British press. "This document," declared one journal, "reveals for the first time authoritatively the line on which Edison is experimenting. It reveals nothing new, however, for in one manner and another the substantial facts in regard to Edison's experiments had all been obtained previously. The Edison lamp, it appears, is a piece of metal which may be platinum, rhodium, titanium, ormium, or any other very infusible metal fashioned into a coil, helix, ribbon, plate, or any other form, and made incandescent. The current is regulated by a metal bar through which it passes. This bar expands when the current is too strong, and shunts or short-circuits the flow of electricity. Or it may be regulated by the operation of a diaphragm which is acted upon by the expansion of the air or gas enclosed in a tube. This is all that Edison's specification aims at, so far as the apparatus of the lamp is concerned, and scientific men may judge for themselves as to the probable success of the Edison light. The weak point of the lamp is this, that in order to be luminous, platinum must be heated almost to the point of melting. With a slight increase in the current, the lamp melts in the twinkling of an eye, and in practice the regulator is found to short-circuit the current too late to prevent the damage. It is this difficulty which must be overcome. Can it be done?"

An English scientific publication, commenting upon the document, also attempted a prophecy. It said: "All anxiety concerning the Edison light may be put on one side. It is certainly not going to take the place of gas, and its invention would not have been regarded with the anxiety and interest which have been displayed had it not been for the statements of newspaper reporters on the other side of the Atlantic. In the whole specification we have not one word concerning any new or extraordinary contrivance for dividing the electric light."

During the time that Edison was making his investigations towards discovering a means for dividing the electric current, and rumors were thick that he had solved the problem long before he applied for a patent, the leading scientific men of America and Europe strenuously declared it to be impossible. A committee was appointed by the British Parliament to examine into the general subject, and they called before them as witnesses nearly all the prominent scientists of the day.

With the exception of Professor Tyndall they testified that, in their opinion, the subdivision of the electric light was a problem beyond the power of man to solve. Professor Tyndall said he would scarcely go so far as that — he would not say it was absolutely impossible but he would not like to undertake its solution.

But there was one man, at least, who never doubted but that Edison would accomplish what he had set out to do. This was Grovernor P. Lowry, who had been one of the first to encourage Edison in his electric lighting investigations, and had been instrumental in getting together the necessary funds to enable him to carry on his researches. Mr. Lowry followed Edison's progress step by step with unabated interest, and spent much of his time at the Menlo Park laboratory. When newspaper men couldn't get hold of Edison they bore down on Lowry, and obtained from him just as much information as he and the inventor considered it was desirable they should know. Lowry kept a wide-open eye on the newspapers, and was constantly correcting misstatements which appeared from time to time in the American press. One of his many interesting letters, addressed to a New York paper, is before the writer at the moment, and as it bears on Edison's investigations in connection with the electric light it is here reproduced as a document of considerable contemporary interest:

"DEAR SIR, — Your columns this morning contain the following, which you will undoubtedly be glad to correct:

"'It is understood that Mr. Edison is suffering from ill-health, and has given up his experiments with the electric light.'

THE ELECTRIC LIGHT

"My relation to Mr. Edison in respect to his inventions and discoveries in electric lighting gives me opportunity to know the truth about these matters, and the public interest concerning them makes it seem a duty to correct statements which I know to be erroneous. Mr. Edison's ill-health I learn indirectly from his family physician, Dr. Leslie Ward, and directly from Dr. E. L. Keyes, who visited him professionally two weeks ago at Menlo Park, was of a temporary character and not at all serious. For two weeks past Mr. Edison has been daily and nightly, as usual, at work in his laboratory upon the electric light. I spent several hours with him a few days since. He seemed in the highest spirits and in excellent health, and very enthusiastic over the results of his work in electric lighting. Since the state of progress in this work is of interest to the public I may avail myself of this occasion to state my view of the matter as it now stands, promising that I am not an expert.

"Mr. Edison first discovered some months since his new methods of dividing the electric light, or, in other words, of taking the electric current which, by long-known methods, produces (through incandescence and slow combustion of carbon pencils) a single light equal, say, to 4000 candles, and (passing it over an extended wire) distributing it at numerous points so as to yield at each point a separate light of, say, fifteen candles — the ordinary gas-burner power. He then devised a form of lamp intended, in connection with other devices, to enable him to produce with the same current such a number of separate lights that the sum of these divided lights would equal the sum of a single light produced by the carbon.

"His first invention, as it will appear in the first patents to be issued, will but inadequately show the novel discoveries and devices which he has made even to this time, when, according to his own views, he is comparatively only upon the threshold of a new and wonderful development of electrical science. In the meantime, the proper exhibition of what has already been invented, as well as the study of the economical questions involved, require the erection of large buildings, engines, etc., which is now going on with the utmost rapidity. Pending their completion Mr. Edison, far from having given up his experiments, is pursuing the great variety of them with his customary energy and even more than his customary good fortune.

"In the meantime there is an interest somewhere to set on foot false reports affecting Mr. Edison's light, one of which, recently circulated in an up-town club, I beg space to correct. It was stated that an official paper emanating from the British Patent Office had been seen which denied a patent to Mr. Edison. The author of the report would, perhaps, have been more careful had he known that the legal period fixed for the issue or denial of such a patent has not yet been reached, and that the existence of such a paper at this time is, therefore, impossible."

Soon after the publication of Mr. Lowry's letter, Edison came to the conclusion that pure platinum was not — and never would be — suited to the purposes of successful electric lighting, and he therefore incorporated with it another material of a non-conducting nature, so that when the electric current was turned on one substance became incandescent while the other became luminous. By this means he obtained a very excellent, but not a permanent, light. Then, thinking more light-giving surface was needed, he covered many yards of platinum wire with a non-conducting material, "bunched" it together, placed it in a vacuum, and turned on the current, but the experiment was a dismal failure. More regulators were invented, more materials tried, more schemes put to the test, and — more disappointments the result. But the greater the failure the less Edison felt inclined to give up the fight. He argued that when everything had been tried and discarded, then what remained must be the right solution. And all the time he was a monument of encouragement to his associates — always good-humored, always cheerful, always certain that the next day would see the victory.

Thirteen months had passed, thirteen months of tireless investigation, and at last Edison became convinced that he was on the wrong track. Platinum and all metals must be abandoned. But what was left? He was groping about in search of a fingerpost that should point to the right path, and he couldn't find one. And then the secret was suddenly revealed to him in a way which clearly indicated that Nature, having enjoyed her year's sport, had at last made up her mind to reward the sturdy investigator for his courage by acting generously towards him. And the way she performed this gracious act is probably known to every reader, yet the story is worth retelling.

The inventor was seated in his laboratory alone one evening, a little serious over his thousand-and-one disappointments, though by no means crushed in spirit, and, as usual, thinking deeply, when his right hand, which lay idly upon the table, strayed towards a little pile of lampblack mixed with tar which his assistants had been using in connection with his telephone transmitter. Picking up a modicum of this substance he began rolling it between his finger and thumb, still wondering what one thing he had forgotten which should make the electric light possible, and little dreaming that it lay between his fingers. For perhaps half an hour he continued to ponder and at the same time to roll the mixture, until at last he had obtained a thin thread not unlike a piece of wire in appearance. He looked at it idly, and then began to speculate on its possibilities as a filament for an incandescent lamp. It was carbon, of course, and, this being so, might have strength to withstand the electric current to a greater degree than platinum itself. He determined to put it to the test, and at once began the work of rolling out fine threads of the black composition preparatory to placing them in the lamps.

At no time during his investigations had Edison been so well equipped for trying the virtues of carbon as at that moment. His experiments with platinum had all tended towards the production of a vacuum in a tube that was almost perfect — only one-millionth part of an atmosphere being left behind. Such a vacuum had never before been thought of, and therefore a better test to decide the properties of carbon as a conductor of light was hardly possible. With the assistance of his associate, Charles Bachelor, a thread of the lampblack and tar was placed in a bulb, the air exhausted, and the current turned on. A good light was the result, but it did not last — the carbon soon burnt out. But it had glowed with an intensity sufficient to prove that the inventor was at last on the right road. Edison then proceeded to look for some reason to account for the failure of the carbon to withstand the current, and he found it in the fact that it was impossible to get the air out of the lamp-black, besides which the thread had become so brittle that the slightest shock broke it even after it had been

THE ELECTRIC LIGHT

inserted in the lamp. A carbon filament, he felt sure, was the right thing, but not in the form of lampblack and tar.

Then Edison had a brilliant idea. He sent a boy out to purchase a reel of cotton, and when it was brought to him he declared his intention of seeing what a piece of carbonized thread would accomplish. It was a fibre, he explained, fairly tenacious, and did not contain any air, so that possibly it might stand a greater heat than the platinum or lampblack. His associates looked dubious — how could so frail a thing stand an electric current that would melt the hardest of metals? Nevertheless the experiment was worth trying, and preparations were at once made to carry it out. A short length of the thread bent in the form of a hairpin was laid in a nickel mould, securely clamped, and placed in a muffle furnace, where it remained for five hours, after which it was withdrawn and allowed to cool. The mould was then opened and the carbonized thread carefully taken out, when it instantly broke. Another piece of cotton was placed in the mould, carbonized, withdrawn, and again broken. Then commenced a battle for a perfect filament, which lasted two days and two nights. Let any reader try the experiment of carbonizing a bit of thread and then handling it without injury, and he will get some idea of the nerve-racking experience through which Edison and his men passed. At last they succeeded in taking from the mould one perfect and unbroken filament, but when they attempted to attach it to the conducting wire it parted again. It was not until the night of the third day after beginning their experiments with carbonized cotton — during which time no sleep or rest had been taken — that success came to them and the filament was placed in the lamp, the air exhausted, and the current turned on. A beautiful soft light met their eyes, and they knew that the secret of the incandescent electric lamp was solved.

In after years Edison thus described the wrestle he and his associate had in placing the carbonized cotton in the first electric bulb: "All night Bachelor, my assistant, worked beside me. The next day and the next night again, and at the end of that time we had produced one carbon out of an entire spool of Clarke's thread. Having made it, it was necessary to take it to the glass-blower's house. With the utmost precaution Bachelor took up the precious carbon, and I marched after him, as if guarding a mighty treasure. To our consternation, just as we reached the glass-blower's bench the wretched carbon broke. We turned back to the main laboratory and set to work again. It was late in the afternoon before we had produced another carbon, which was again broken by a jeweller's screw-driver falling against it. But we turned back again, and before night the carbon was completed and inserted in the lamp. The bulb was exhausted of air and sealed, the current turned on, and the sight we had so long desired to see met our eyes."

Edison and Bachelor watched that electric lamp for many hours. They turned on a small current at first, fearing that the frail filament would expire, but it withstood the heat so bravely that more current was called for until the tiny thread was bearing a heat under which platinum would have instantly melted. For forty-five hours the cotton thread lasted, and then with a suddenness that was startling the light vanished. But it left behind happy if weary men, who congratulated one another on the part each had played in producing a light which they knew was to be the world's future leading illuminant.

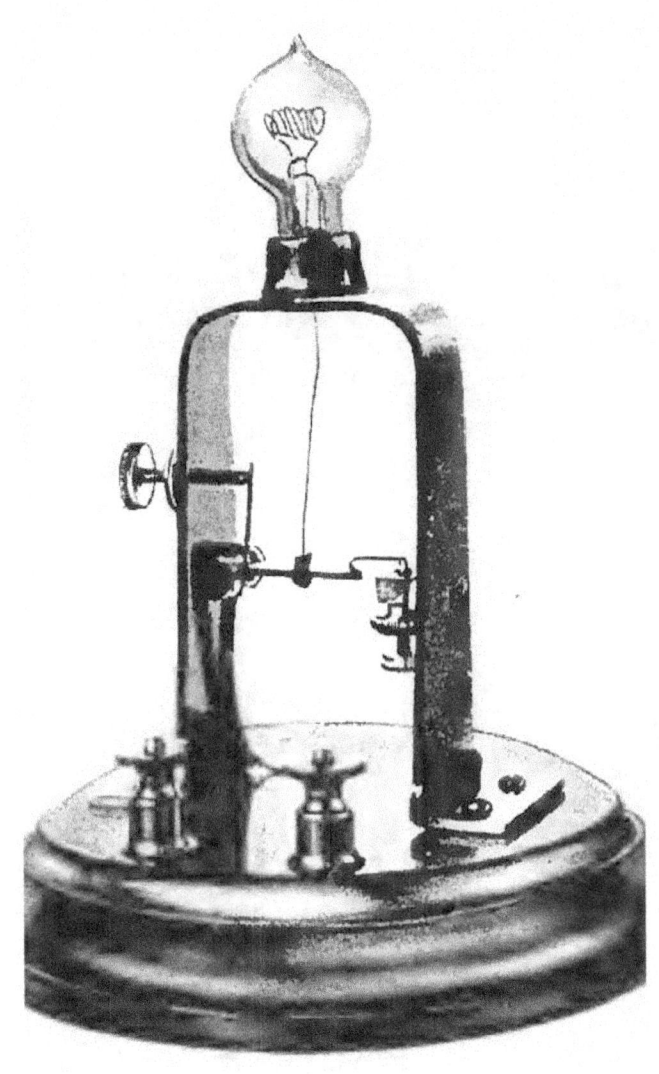

EDISON'S FIRST INCANDESCENT LAMP

THE ELECTRIC LIGHT

The man who had the distinction of putting the first filament into an incandescent lamp — Charles Bachelor — had at the time been Edison's closest associate for several years. Edison always affirmed that Bachelor was the most wonderful man with his fingers that he had ever known, and during the hours and days he spent attempting to make a perfect filament, only to break it, he never showed the slightest impatience. Just as soon as he broke one he would go ahead and make another, ever cheerful, good-tempered, untiring. And when he finally succeeded, and the filament he had spent so many days over glowed with the steady light familiar to us to-day, no one was more generous in congratulating him than Edison. He had performed a work which no other man in the laboratory could have accomplished — not excepting even the inventor himself — and ever after he was always spoken of as "Edison's hands." Later Bachelor enjoyed another distinction — he was the first man to have his portrait taken by the light of the new lamp.

But the ideal filament was not yet found, for the carbonized cotton had only lasted forty-five hours. It was necessary to find a material which would give a light for at least a couple of hundred hours or longer before there could be any hope of the new invention being a commercial success. And so, with his usual impetuousness, Edison, after a sleep lasting nearly a day, commenced carbonizing everything in sight. Under the microscope he had found that his original cotton filament was hard and polished like a piece of steel, and he believed if he could find a more homogeneous material than thread, the filament might last ten times as long. The entire staff of the laboratory was set to work carbonizing straw, paper, cardboard, wood splints, and a hundred other things. In fact, during these carbonizing days nothing was safe — umbrellas, walking-sticks, all vanished, and the probability is that if a lame man had called about that time his crutch would have gone the same way. Curiously enough, the best results were obtained with cardboard, which stood the electric current longer than the cotton thread. But after a few experiments in this line Edison concluded that cardboard was not what he was looking for either. Then the inventor got hold of a bamboo fan, tore off the rim which encircled the leaf, and from it produced a filament which gave the best results of any. As a consequence he concluded that bamboo was the material best adapted for his purpose, but though the fan had performed excellent service he believed that somewhere there was a bamboo or cane of better quality capable of being converted into a perfect filament.

Edison immediately set himself the task of learning all that there was to learn about bamboos. He obtained works on the subject, and soon made the interesting if somewhat overwhelming discovery that there were at least twelve hundred varieties of bamboo known, of which about three hundred were made use of in some way. The inventor pined to have a specimen of each one, and it only took him about half a minute to make up his mind to send men out into the world to obtain them. He wanted the most homogeneous variety of bamboo that grew, and he meant to have it if it cost him his fortune. He didn't send one man, but several, and the search for a suitable filament for the electric lamp cost in the neighborhood of $100,000. Among those who went forth on this historic bamboo hunt besides William Moore was James Ricalton, a New Jersey schoolmaster, who made his way to the Malagan Peninsula, Burmah, and southern China, covered 30,000 miles, and had many exciting encounters with wild beasts during a strenuous search for the correct kind of bamboo. Another man was sent to the Amazon and up the River de la Plata. Others to the West Indian Islands, South America, British Guiana, Mexico, Ceylon, and India. These men forwarded samples of bamboo and other fibrous plants to the Edison laboratory in bales, and all were tested by Edison. People in different parts of the world heard of his search for bamboo, and joined in the hunt on their own account, despatching samples in generous quantities. Something like six thousand specimens of bamboo were carbonized, and out of these Edison found three species of bamboo and one species of cane which gave almost perfect results. All these grew in a region of the Amazon, and were difficult to obtain owing to malaria. It is interesting to know that the only part of the bamboo used was the outer edge of the cylinder after the removal of what is known to the botanist as the "silicious epidermis," and in order to produce good filaments the sections had to be cut parallel with the fibres.

During these experiments at Menlo Park the greatest excitement was caused in Europe as well as America by rumors which stated that the electric light was a brilliant success, a dead failure, an infringement of some one else's patents, and the like, while one story was published to the effect that the inventor himself had succumbed to the strain, and was in a dangerous state of health. Menlo Park was besieged by reporters who implored admittance to the laboratory, but the gates were kept closed and watchmen put on guard to see that no unauthorized person entered. Many members of the stock company formed to introduce the new light called at the laboratory and were admitted, afterwards being eagerly buttonholed by the reporters as they made their reappearance; but they had been placed under injunctions of secrecy and would not talk. Edison, sympathizing with the "newspaper boys," as he called them, sent out a message saying that "he had encountered several difficulties which he had overcome by inventions already patented, but he had made other discoveries more important than all in the way of making the electric light available, and to disclose them to the public would endanger the success of the entire enterprise. Some delay would occur before application could be made for patents, as they related to materials which were not easily obtained in this country."

It was on October 21, 1879, that Edison discovered the carbonized cotton filament, and in January of the following year letters patent were granted him for his new and improved electric lamp. The specification in this interesting document, which is throughout in Edison's handwriting, is as follows:

"Be it known that I, Thomas Alva Edison, of Menlo Park, New Jersey, United States of America, have invented an improvement in electric lamps and in the method of manufacturing the same of which the following is a specification:

"The object of this invention is to produce electric lamps giving light by incandescence, which lamps shall have high resistance, so as to allow of the practical subdivision of the electric light. The invention consists in a light-giving body of carbon wire coiled or arranged in such a manner as to offer great resistance to the passage of the electric current and, at the same time, present but a slight surface from which radiation can take place. The invention further consists in placing such burner of great resistance in a nearly perfect vacuum to prevent oxidation and injury to the conductor by the atmosphere. The current so conducted into the vacuum bulb through platina wires sealed into the glass. The invention further consists in the method of manufacturing carbon conductors of high resistance, so as to be suitable for giving light by incandescence.

"Heretofore, light by incandescence has been obtained from rods of carbon of 1 to 4 ohms resistance and placed in closed vessels, in which the atmospheric air has been replaced by gases that do not combine chemically. The leading wires have always been large, so that their resistance shall be many times less than the burner, and, in general, the attempts of previous workers have been to reduce the resistance of the carbon rod. The disadvantages of following this practice are that a lamp having but 1 to 4 ohms resistance cannot be worked in great numbers in multiple arc without the employment of main conductors of enormous dimensions; that owing to the low resistance of the lamp, the leading wires must be of large dimensions and good conductors, and a glass globe cannot be kept tight at the place where the wires pass in and are cemented; hence the carbon is consumed, because there must be always a perfect vacuum to render the carbon stable, especially when such carbon is small in mass and high in electrical resistance.

"The use of gas in the receiver at the atmospheric pressure, although not attacking the carbon, serves to destroy it in time by air-washing or the attrition produced by the rapid passage of the gas over the slightly coherent, highly heated surface of the carbon. I have reversed this practice. I have discovered that even a cotton thread properly carbonized and placed in a sealed glass bulb exhausted to one millionth of an atmosphere, offers from one hundred to five hundred ohms resistance to the passage of the current, and that it is absolutely stable at very high temperatures; that if the thread be coiled as a spiral and carbonized, or if any fibrous vegetable substance which will have a carbon residue after heating in a closed chamber be so coiled, as much as 2000 ohms resistance can be obtained without presenting a radiating surface greater than three-sixteenths of an inch. I have carbonized and used cotton and linen thread, wood-splints, papers coiled in various ways, also lampblack, plumbago, and carbon in various forms mixed with tar and rolled out into wires of various lengths and diameters."

It is generally believed that the above was the first statement made in writing by Edison in reference to his incandescent electric light. Previous patents, however, had been granted to him covering a new generator, a modification of the Sprengel quicksilver-pump for the production of a vacuum, and other parts of the process. Since then he has taken out one hundred and sixty-nine patents on electric lights.

Having solved the difficulty of a suitable filament, he made a number of lamps which were strung along a wire and suspended from the trees in Menlo Park. They attracted world-wide attention, and the fact that they remained burning night and day for more than a week appeared marvellous to the thousands who journeyed to Menlo Park to view the wonderful lamps. "The lamps," wrote one of the visitors at the time, "are about four inches long, small and delicate, and comely enough for use in any apartment. They can be removed from a chandelier as readily as a glass stopper from a bottle and by the same motion. The current is turned on and off by the simple means of pressing a button. The lamp is simplicity itself in form and construction, and can be made for a very small sum. A few of the lamps which have been in use longest appear a little duller than the others, but this defect the inventor says will disappear as soon as he has carried out a few changes in the construction of the globe, which he contemplates doing at an early date."

During the early days of January a general illumination of Menlo Park took place for the special edification of the New York Board of Aldermen, who went out to the laboratory at Edison's invitation on a special train. The inventor so arranged matters that the visitors arrived after dark, and the effect of the hundreds of brilliant incandescent lamps glowing among the leafless trees was very remarkable. The lamps were strung along two big wires, and the way in which one could be extinguished or lit without interfering with the others appeared to strike the aldermen as being particularly wonderful. Among the visitors on this memorable occasion was Hiram Maxim.

And during all this time that Edison had been perfecting the incandescent lamp his mind had been busy with another great idea — that of a central station from which consumers might obtain their electric light in the same way that they drew their gas. The initial difficulties of such an undertaking were gigantic. It must be remembered that electric lighting was an absolutely new art, and outside the Edison laboratory there was no one who knew what it was all about. There were no factories to manufacture the apparatus, no skilled artisans to carry out the installing of an electric light system; no one, in fact, with the exception of Edison's immediate associates, who could be trusted even to put a carbon filament in an exhausted globe. But Edison's mind had long been made up. His ambition was to see a central station built somewhere in New York, and he never rested until his ambition was realized. The story of how this first central station was built is one of the most interesting in the whole history of electric lighting. Many years ago Edison related some of his experiences in connection with this work in the *Electrical Review* — the first and, I believe, last occasion on which he referred to the subject at any length — and to the editor of this magazine I tender my thanks for permission to reproduce here some of the inventor's remarks:

"I had the central station idea in my mind all the time that I was pursuing my investigations in electric lighting. I got an insurance map of New York, in which every elevator shaft and boiler and house-top and fire-wall was set down and studied it carefully. Then I laid out a district and figured out an idea of the central station to feed that part of the town from just south of Wall Street up to Canal and over from Broadway to the East River. I worked on a system, and soon knew where every hatchway and bulkhead door in the district I had marked was and what every man paid for his gas. How did I know? Simplest thing in the world. I hired a man to start in every day about two o'clock and walk around through the district noting the number of gas lights burning in the various premises; then at three o'clock he went around again and made more notes, and at four o'clock and up to every other hour to two or three o'clock in the morning. In that way it was easy enough to figure out the gas consumption of every tenant and of the whole district; other men took other sections.

"After various other preliminaries we were fairly committed to the lighting project and started in to

THE ELECTRIC LIGHT

build the central station. You cannot imagine how hard it was. There was nothing that we could buy or that anybody else could make for us. We built the thing with our hands, as it were. At Menlo Park we started a lamp factory. Krusei was set to work making the tubes over in Washington Street, and we hired a kind of a second-class machine shop in Goerck Street and there started out making the dynamos, while Bergmann had a little place on the East Side where he made gas fixtures, and he went into making sockets and fixtures for us and did well with them. We started with our own money and credit — mostly credit. But we soon got the money put up for the station by starting the New York Edison Illuminating Company.

"I planned out the station and found where it ought to go, but we could not get real estate where it was wanted. It cost us $150,000 for two old buildings down in Pearl Street where we finally settled. We had very little room and we wanted a big output. There was nothing else for it but to get high-speed engines, and — there were no high-speed engines in those days. I had conceived the idea of a direct-coupled machine, and wanted to hitch the dynamo direct to the engine without belting. I could not see why, if a locomotive could run on that speed, a 150 horse-power engine could not be made to run 350 turns a minute. The engine builders, when I asked them about it, held up their hands and said, 'Impossible!' I didn't think so. I found C. H. Porter, and I said to him, 'Mr. Porter, I want a 150 horse-power engine to run 700 revolutions per minute.' He hummed and hawed a little while, and then agreed to build it — if I could pay for it! I believe he charged me $4200 for it. He got it finished and sent it out to the Park.

"We set the machine up in the old shop, and we had some idea of what might happen. So we tied a chain around the throttle valve and ran it out through a window into the wood shed, where we stood to work it. Now the old shop stood on one of those New Jersey shale hills, and every time we opened up the engine and she got to about 300 revolutions the whole hill shook under her. We shut her off and rebalanced and tried again, and after a good deal of trouble we finally did run up to 700, but you should have seen her run! Why, every time the connecting rod went up she tried to lift that whole hill with her! After we got through with this business we tamed her down to 350 revolutions (which was all I wanted), and then everybody said, 'Why, how beautifully it runs, and how practicable such an engine is!' We closed a bill for six engines, and I went to work in Goerck Street to build the dynamos on to them. Of course, we built them by guesswork. I guessed at 110 volts — and I didn't guess enough. So we put extra pole-pieces on them, and in that way managed to raise the voltage to what I wanted.

"While all this was going on in the shop we had dug ditches and laid mains all around the district. I used to sleep nights on piles of pipes in the station, and I saw every box poured and every connection made on the whole job. There was nobody else who could superintend it. Finally we got our feeders all down and started to put on an engine and turn over one of the machines to see how things were. My heart was in my mouth at first, but everything worked all right, and we had more than 500 ohms insulation resistance. Then we started another engine and threw them in parallel. Of all the circuses since Adam was born we had the worst then. One engine

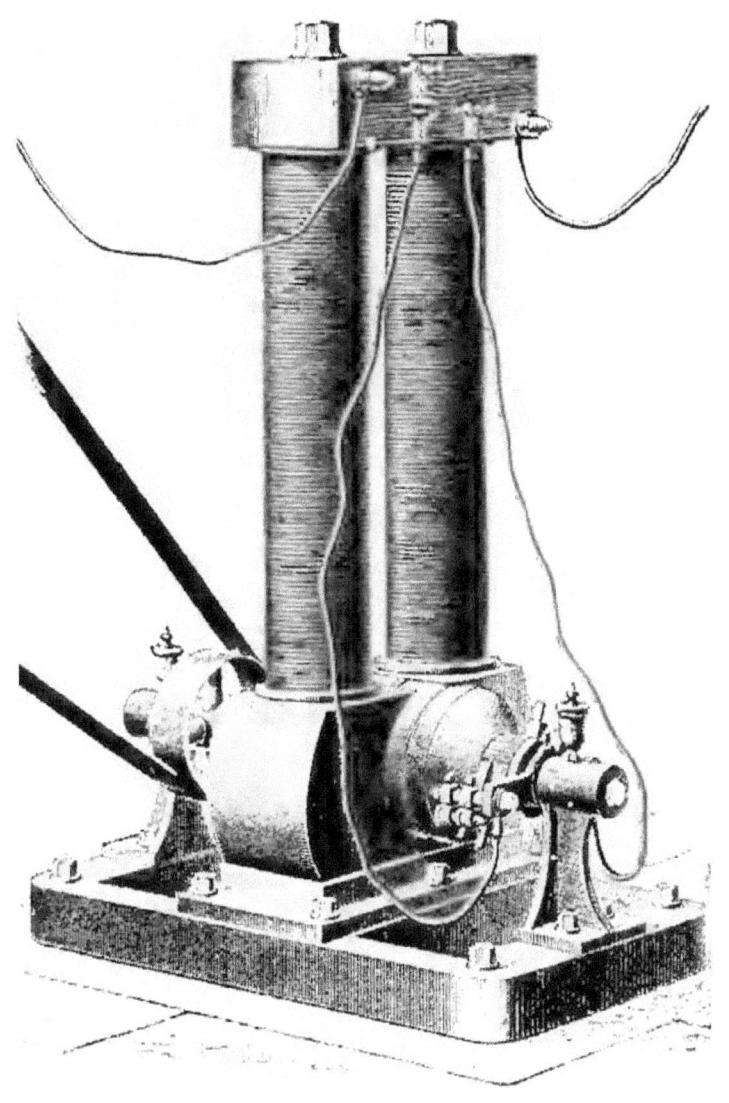
EDISON DYNAMO OF 1880

would stop and the other would run up to about a thousand revolutions, and then they would see-saw.

"What was the matter? Why, it was these Porter governors! When the circus commenced the men who were standing around ran out precipitately, and some of them kept running for a block or two. I grabbed the throttle of one engine and E. H. Johnson, who was the only one present to keep his wits, caught hold of the other and we shut them off. Of course I discovered then that what had happened was that one set was running the other one as a motor. I then put up a long shaft connecting all the governors together, and thought this would certainly cure the trouble, but it didn't. The torsion of the shaft was so great that one governor still managed to get ahead of the others. Then I went to Goerck Street and got a piece of shafting and a tube in which it fitted. I twisted the shaft one way and the tube the other as far as I could and pinned them together. In this way, by straining the whole outfit up to its elastic limit in opposite directions, the torsion was practically eliminated, and after that the governors ran together all right.

"About that time I got hold of Gardiner C. Sims, and he undertook to build an engine to run at 350 revolutions and give 175 horse-power. He went back to Providence and set to work and brought the engine back with him. It worked, but only a few minutes, when it busted. That man sat around that shop and slept in it for three weeks until he got his engine right and made it work the way we wanted it to. When he reached this period I gave orders for the works to run night and day until we got enough engines, and when all was ready we started the engine. The date was September 4, 1882 — a Saturday night. That was when we first turned the current on to the mains for regular light distribution, and it stayed on for eight years with only one insignificant stoppage. One of these engines that Sims built ran twenty-four hours a day for 365 days before it was stopped.

"In those days we used the old chemical meters, and these gave us a lot of trouble, for, as they contained two jars of a liquid solution, there was always a danger of freezing in the cold weather. So I set to work to negative this difficulty and succeeded, as I thought, by putting an incandescent lamp in each meter with a thermostat strip, which would make a contact through the lamp when the temperature fell to 40 degrees. That idea, simple as it was, caused us a whole lot of trouble. The weather became cold, and then the telephone in our office began to ring every five minutes and people would say —

"'Our meter's red hot. Is that all right?'

"Then some one else would call up and say —

"'Our meter's on fire inside, and we poured water on it. Did that hurt it?'

"As to voltmeters, we didn't have any. We used lamps. And I hadn't much use for mathematicians either, for I soon found that I could guess a good deal closer than they could figure, so I went on guessing. We used to hang up a shingle nail, tie it on a string alongside one of the feeders, and used that for a heavy current ammeter. It worked all right. When the nail came close to the feeder we screwed up the rheostat a little, and in this way kept the lamps looking about right.

"I invented the fuse wire about the time of the aldermen's visit to Menlo Park. It had occurred to me that an interruption would be serious, and I had thought out the scheme of putting some fine copper wire in as fuses in various places. And when the aldermen came one fellow in the party who had a little piece of heavy wire in his hand managed to short-circuit the mains with his wire. He was very much surprised because only three lamps went out. The real reason that led me to think of the fuse wire was that we were not very flush of dynamos in those days. I had burned out two or three, and I saw that something was needed to prevent that happening again. After my experience with my short-circuiting friend, I had fuses put in all over."

To the late Luther Stieringer I am indebted for the following brief description of the various methods adopted by Edison for registering the quantity of current supplied to consumers in those days:

"Many experiments were made with all sorts of mechanism, motors, clockwork, electro-magnets, springs, heat, electrolysis, and electro-deposition. Finally the Edison meter was evolved, and was found to answer perfectly. It consists of a small glass cell, containing a solution in which two zinc plates are immersed. A certain proportion of the current entering the building is diverted through this combination, and an electro-plating action is set up in the cell, zinc being deposited on one plate from the other. According to a well-known scientific law, a current of certain strength will deposit just so much zinc in a given time, no more and no less. Therefore, it is easy to see that if the plates are periodically weighed, the amount of current supplied between the times of weighing can be calculated to a nicety.

"Mr. Edison has also invented various other instruments for measuring electric-light currents, such as a weighing voltmeter, in which the current acts on coils of wire at one end of the beam, the other end being balanced by a cup filled with shot. The deflection of the pointer indicates the pressure of the current traversing the coil. In another instrument he causes the pressure, or electro-motive force, of the current to be registered on a sheet of paper, revolved by clockwork; and in a third, which he has styled the 'sonorous voltameter,' the action of the current makes itself known by a series of small explosions in a glass cell. Two platinum wires are immersed in water in the cell, and the current passing between them decomposes the water, causing small bubbles to rise to the surface and explode; the cell is closed over, with the exception of an aperture provided with a funnel to magnify the sound."

It is interesting at this date, when the thirtieth anniversary of the invention of the incandescent lamp is in sight, to look back and note the buildings which were first illuminated by electric light. It is claimed that the first office building to adopt the incandescent lamp was that of the New York *Herald*, where a complete plant was installed, and when that enterprising paper sent out the sailing vessel *Jeanette* to find the North Pole, one of her chief novelties was a complete installation of the Edison electric-light system. She was lost in Arctic seas, and so it is more than possible that some of Edison's first lamps are still reposing beneath the waters of those icy regions.

The first church lighted by electricity is generally supposed to have been the City Temple, London, while the first theatre was the Bijou, Boston, which was lighted by an Edison isolated plant, December 12, 1882. There were 650 lamps used, and the first attraction given with the new illumination was, very appropriately, Gilbert and Sullivan's fairy opera "Iolanthe." The proscenium arch was surrounded by 192 lamps; 140 were placed in the borders, and 60 in the chandelier of the auditorium, making a total of 392 lamps — the balance being placed in different parts of the building. No other method of lighting was provided, and there were no footlights.

The first hotel to be lighted by electricity was the Blue Mountain House, in the Adirondacks, where an Edison plant was started in 1881. There were 125 lamps, each with an average life of 800 hours. It was also at this hotel that the first electric lamp was placed in an elevator car — July 12, 1882. The Blue Mountain House is situated at an elevation of 3500 feet above the sea, and was, at the time of the electric-light installation, forty miles from the railroad. The machinery was taken in pieces on the backs of mules from the foot of the mountain. The boilers were fired with wood, as the commercial transportation of coal was a physical impossibility. For a six hours' run of the electric plant, one-quarter of a cord of wood was required at a cost of 25 cents per cord. Regulation of the dynamo was effected by a rheostat in the office, about 100 feet from the centre of distribution.

The first electrolier was wired and placed in service some time during 1880, at the residence of Mr. Francis R. Upton, at Menlo Park, near Edison's laboratory. Great care was taken to distinguish the polarity of each conductor, the positive wires being of red and the negative wires of blue flexible cord. The lamps were from the first placed in an inverted position, which is now so familiar but was then so novel. This electrolier was shown at the St. Louis Exposition in 1904. The first private residence to be lighted by Edison lamps was that of J. Hood Wright, New York, while the first steam vessel to employ the same illuminant was the *Columbia*, running between San Francisco and Portland, Oregon.

The country which probably lagged longest behind in a general adoption of the electric light was England, due, no doubt, to the fact that in 1880 Parliament passed a law whereby it was enacted that at the expiration of twenty years electric-light plants were to be bought by the Government. The result can be imagined. Private enterprise was strangled, and gas as an illuminant remained triumphant. Eight years later, however, the law was repealed, and soon the electric light began to glow in every village and hamlet throughout the country.

Over the electric light there has been more litigation than over any other of Edison's inventions. As he himself says: "I fought for the lamp for fourteen years, and when I finally won my rights there were but three years of the allotted seventeen left for my patent to live. Now it has become the property of anybody and everybody." One writer, in a letter addressed to the press, endeavored to show that the incandescent light was used in the thirteenth century, and to prove his point quoted the following from a work entitled "Sorcery and Magic," published in 1852:

"During the thirteenth century, for profit of the common people, Virgilius, on a great mighty marble pillar, did make a bridge that came to the palace. The palace and bridge stood in the middle of Rome, and upon this pillar made he a lamp of glass that always burned without going out, and nobody might put it out; and this lamp lightened over all the city of Rome from the one corner to the other; and there was not so little a street but it gave such a light that it seemed two torches there did stand; and upon the walls of the palace made he a metal man that held in his hand a metal bow that pointed over and upon the lamp to shoot it out; but always burned the lamp and gave light over all Rome.

"And upon a time went the burgesses' daughters to play in the palace, and they beheld the metal man, and one of them asked in sport why he shot not; and then she came to the man and with her hand touched the bow, and then the bolt flew out and break the lamp that Virgilius made. And it was wonderful that the maid went not out of her mind for the great fear she had, and also the other burgesses' daughters that were in her company, of the great stroke that it gave when it hit the lamp. And this forsaid lamp was abyding after the death of Virgilius by the space of three hundred years or more."

According to this original correspondent, the lamp of Virgilius was, without doubt, an electric lamp, and the newspaper that published his curious letter plaintively inquired, "What will the Patent Office do about it?" The Patent Office, however, took no action in the matter, but confined its attention to those living claimants who labored under the delusion that they had invented the incandescent electric-light system, and who cropped up as suddenly as mushrooms in June.

While Edison was still experimenting at Menlo Park, and soon after he had given the exhibition of his first electric lamps, considerable excitement was caused by some humorous newspaper man spreading the report that what every one thought was the evening star was really an electric lamp which Edison had sent up attached to an invisible balloon. It seems almost incredible, but by thousands of people the story was believed, and for many nights within a radius of a hundred miles faces were turned upward to gaze on the mysterious light. After a time people in other states declared that they also could see the wonderful sight. The newspapers were inundated with letters asking for information as to how the light was really suspended, and what Edison's object was in sending it up such a height. When the papers assured the public that the wonderful light was nothing but the evening star, at least half the people didn't believe it, and for years afterwards the subject would be revived from time to time by the publication of letters in the local press. As late as 1895 the light was referred to as the "Edison Star," and the inventor often had a quiet chuckle over the idea that he should have attempted the illumination of the firmament. Edison himself received many letters on the subject, but he never replied to them, hoping that the absurd story would die a natural death — which it did after reaching years of discretion.

No other industry has grown to such mighty proportions as that of the incandescent electric light. Twenty years after its invention the investment in electric-lighting plants in the United States alone amounted to the enormous sum of $750,000,000. "This extraordinary achievement," said the statistician who made the estimate, "represents a struggle with powerful and well-organized competition of a long-established industry — that of gas illumination. It made its way against bitter opposition, against corrupt councils, and the difficulties and failures consequent upon over-capitalization, to where it is now — one of the solid, certain industries of the world. Beyond any question the most marvellous development of this or any other century in the field of applied science may be seen in the electric-lighting industry. There is nothing comparable to it in the whole history of civilization. The average layman who sees the streets of the

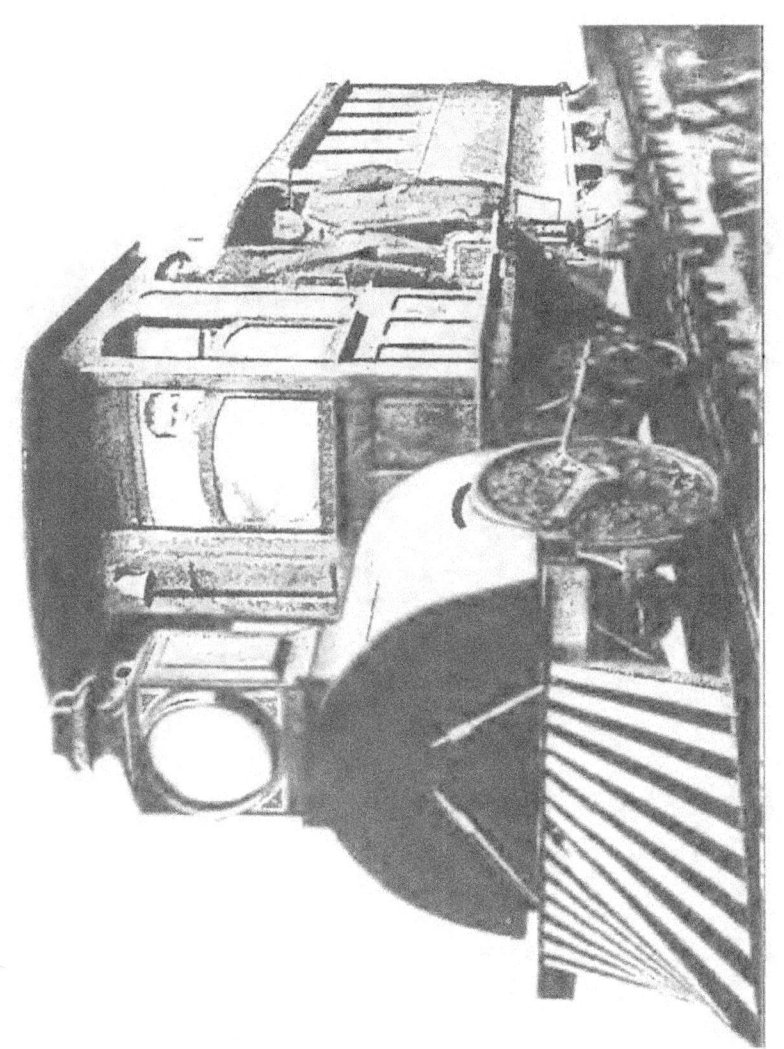

EDISON DRIVING HIS FIRST ELECTRIC LOCOMOTIVE

modern city and its stores made light as day has little conception of the amazing growth of the industry that has reached the highways of human progress with millions upon millions of incandescent bulbs."

CHAPTER IX

EXPERIMENTS WITH PLATINUM WIRE

Edison has not often lectured in public, and the majority of those lectures which he has delivered have not, unfortunately, been preserved. One of his most valuable addresses, however, he still possesses, and as it shows some of the inexhaustible energy he displayed in his search for a suitable filament in connection with his invention of the incandescent light, besides describing many curious phenomena arising from the heating of metal *in vacuo* by means of the electric current, we reproduce it here with the inventor's permission. It was delivered before a New York audience on September 2, 1879, a short time prior to his discovery of the bamboo filament.

"In the course of my experiments on electric lighting," read Mr. F. R. Upton from the writer's exquisite manuscript — for Edison himself was too busy to deliver the lecture —"I have developed some striking phenomena arising from the heating of metal by flames and by electric current, especially wires of platinum and platinum alloyed with iridium. These experiments are still in progress. The first fact observed was that platinum lost weight when heated in a flame of hydrogen, that the metal colored the flame green, and that these two results continued until the whole of the platinum in contact with the flame had disappeared. Platinum wire $\frac{4}{1000}$ of an inch in diameter, and weighing 306

EXPERIMENTS WITH PLATINUM WIRE

milligrammes, was bunched together and suspended in a hydrogen flame. It lost weight at the rate of a fraction less than 1 milligramme per hour as long as it was suspended in the flame. When a platinum wire is stretched between two clamping-posts, and arranged to pass through a hydrogen flame, it is colored a light green, but when the temperature of the wire is raised above that of the flame, by passing a current through it, the flame is colored a deep green.

"To ascertain the diminution in the weight of a platinum wire when heated by the electric current, I placed between two clamping-posts a wire $\frac{5}{1000}$ of an inch in diameter, and weighing 266 milligrammes. This wire, after it was brought to incandescence for about twenty minutes by the current, lost 1 milligramme. The same wire was then raised to incandescence; for about twenty minutes it gave a loss of 3 milligrammes. Afterward it was kept incandescent for one hour and ten minutes, at which time it weighed 258 milligrammes, a total loss of 8 milligrammes. Another wire weighing 243 milligrammes was kept moderately incandescent for nine hours, after which it weighed 201 milligrammes, showing a total loss of 42 milligrammes.

"A platinum wire $\frac{20}{1000}$ of an inch in diameter was wound in the form of a spiral $\frac{1}{8}$ of an inch in diameter and $\frac{1}{2}$ an inch in length. The two ends of the spiral were secured to clamping-posts, and the whole apparatus was covered with a glass shade $2\frac{1}{2}$ inches in diameter and 3 inches high. Upon bringing the spiral to incandescence for twenty minutes that part of the globe in line with the sides of the spiral became slightly darkened; in five hours the deposit became so thick that the incandescent spiral could not be seen through the deposit. This film, which was most perfect, consisted of platinum, and I have no doubt but that large plates of glass might be coated economically by placing them on each side of a large sheet of platinum kept incandescent by the electric current.

"This loss in weight, together with the deposit upon the glass, presented a very serious obstacle to the use of metallic wires for giving light by incandescence, but this was easily surmounted after the cause was ascertained. I coated the wire forming the spiral with oxide of magnesium by dusting upon it finely powdered acetate of magnesium; while incandescent the salt was decomposed by the heat, and there remained a strongly adherent coating of the oxide. This spiral so coated was covered with a glass shade and brought to incandescence for several minutes, but instead of a deposit of platinum upon the glass there was a deposit of the oxide of magnesia.

"From this and other experiments I became convinced that this effect was due to the washing action of the air upon the spiral; that the loss of weight in, and the coloration of, the hydrogen flame was also due to the wearing away of the surface of the platina by the attrition produced by the impact of the stream of gases upon the highly incandescent surface, and not to volatilization, as commonly understood. And I venture to say, though I have not tried the experiment, that metallic sodium cannot be volatilized in high vacua by the heat derived from incandescent platinum; in effect, what may be produced will be due to the washing action of the residual air.

"After the experiments last described I placed a spiral of platinum in the receiver of a common air pump, and arranged it in such a manner that the current could pass through it while the receiver was exhausted. At a pressure of two millimetres the spiral was kept at incandescence for two hours before the deposit was sufficient to become visible. In another experiment at a higher exhaustion it required five hours before a deposit became visible.

"In a sealed glass bulb, exhausted by a Sprengel pump to a point where a quarter of an inch spark from an induction coil would not pass between points one millimetre apart, was placed a spiral, the connecting wires passing through the glass. The spiral was kept at the most dazzling incandescence for hours without the slightest deposit becoming visible.

"I will now describe other and far more important phenomena observed in my experiments. If a short length of platinum wire, $\frac{1}{1000}$ of an inch in diameter, be held in the flame of a Bunsen burner, at some part it will fuse and a piece of the wire will be bent at an angle by the action of the globule of melted platinum; in some cases there are several globules formed simultaneously, and the wire assumes a zigzag shape. With a wire $\frac{4}{1000}$ of an inch in diameter this effect does not take place, as the temperature cannot be raised to equal that of a smaller wire owing to the increased radiating surface and mass. After heating, if the wire be examined under the microscope, that part of the surface which has been incandescent will be found covered with innumerable cracks. If the wire be placed between clamping-posts and heated to incandescence for twenty minutes by the passage of an electric current, cracks will be so enlarged as to be seen with the naked eye, the wire under the microscope presents a shrunken appearance and is full of deep cracks. If the current is continued for several hours, these effects will so increase that the wire will fall to pieces.

"This disintegration has been noticed in platina long subject to the action of a flame by Professor John

W. Draper. The failure of the process of lighting invented by the French chemist Tessic du Motay, who raised sheets of platinum to incandescence by introducing them into a hydrogen flame, was due to the rapid disintegration of the metal. I have ascertained the cause of this phenomenon, and have succeeded in eliminating that which produces it, and in doing so have produced a metal in a state hitherto unknown, and which is absolutely stable at a temperature where nearly all substances melt or are consumed; a metal which, although originally soft and pliable, becomes as homogeneous as glass and rigid as steel. When wound in the form of a spiral it is as springy and elastic when at the most dazzling incandescence as when cold, and cannot be annealed by any process now commonly known.

"For the cause of this shrinking and cracking of the wire is due entirely to the expansion of the air in the mechanical and physical pores of the platinum and the contraction upon the escape of the air. Platinum, as sold in commerce, may be compared to sandstone in which the whole is made up of a great number of particles, with many air spaces. The sandstone upon melting becomes homogeneous, and no air spaces exist. With platinum or any metal the air spaces may be eliminated and the metal made homogeneous by a very simple process. This process I will now describe.

"I have made a large number of platinum spirals all of the same size and from the same quality of wire; each spiral presented to the air a radiating surface of three-sixteenths of an inch; five of these were brought by the electric current up to the melting-point, the light was measured by a photometer, and the average light was equal to four standard candles for each spiral just at the melting-point. One of the same kind of spirals was placed in the receiver of an air-pump and the air exhausted to two millimetres; a weak current was then passed through the wire slightly warming it for the purpose of assisting the passage of the air from the pores of the metal into the vacuum. The temperature of the wire was gradually augmented at intervals of ten minutes until it became red. The object of slowly increasing the temperature was to allow the air to pass out gradually and not explosively.

"Afterward the current was increased at intervals of fifteen minutes. Before each increase in the current the wire was allowed to cool, and the contraction and expansion at these high temperatures caused the wire to weld together at the point previously containing the air. In one hour and forty minutes this spiral had reached such a temperature without melting that it was giving a light of twenty-five standard candles, whereas it would undoubtedly have melted before it gave a light of five candles had it not been put through the above process. Several more spirals were afterward tried with the same result. One spiral, which had been brought to these high temperatures more slowly, gave a light equal to thirty standard candles. In the open air this spiral gave nearly the same light, although it required some current to keep it at the same temperature.

"Upon examination of these spirals, which had passed through the vacuum process, by the aid of a microscope, no cracks were visible; the wire had become as white as silver, and had a polish which could not be given it by any other means. The wire had a less diameter than before treatment, and it was exceedingly difficult to melt in the oxyhydrogen flame. As compared with untreated platinum it was found that it was as hard as the steel wire used in pianos, and that it could not be annealed at any temperature.

"My experiments with many metals treated by this process have proved to my satisfaction, and I have no hesitation in stating, that what is known as annealing of metals to make them soft and pliable is nothing more than the cracking of the metal. In every case where a hard drawn wire had been annealed a powerful microscope revealed myriads of cracks in the metal.

"Since these experiments of which I have just spoken, I have, by the aid of Sprengel mercury pumps, produced higher exhaustions, and have by consuming five hours in excluding the air from the wire and intermitting the current a great number of times, succeeded in obtaining a light of eight standard candles from a spiral of wire with a total radiating surface of $\frac{1}{32}$ of an inch, or a surface about equal to a grain of buckwheat. With spirals of this small size, each having passed through the process, the average amount of light given out before melting is less than one standard candle. Thus I am enabled, by the increased capacity of platinum, to withstand the high temperatures, to employ small radiating surfaces, and thus reduce the energy required for candle-light.

"I can now obtain eight separate jets, each giving out absolutely steady light, and each equal to sixteen standard candles or a total of 128 candles by the expenditure of 30,000 foot-pounds of energy, or less than one horse-power.

"As a matter of curiosity I have made spirals of other metals and excluded the air from them in the manner stated. Common iron wire may be made to give a light greater than platinum not heated. The iron becomes as hard as steel and just as elastic. Nickel is far more refractory than iron. Steel wire used in

EXPERIMENTS WITH PLATINUM WIRE

pianos becomes decarbonized, but remains hard and assumes the color of silver. Aluminium melts only at a white heat.

"In conclusion it may be interesting to state that the melting-point of many oxides is dependent upon the manner of applying the heat. For instance, pure oxide of zerconium does not fuse in the flame of the oxyhydrogen blow-pipe, while it melts like wax and conducts electricity when on an incandescent platinum spiral which is at a far lower temperature; on the other hand, oxide of aluminium easily melts in the oxyhydrogen flame, while it only vitrifies on the platinum spiral."

CHAPTER X

THE PHONOGRAPH

The phonograph was the result of pure reason based upon a very happy inspiration. In his early work with automatic telegraphs operating at high speeds, Edison had occasion to experiment with embossed strips impressed with dashes and dots thereon which were moved rapidly beneath a stylus to vibrate it. It was observed that this stylus in vibrating produced audible sounds. A small thing such as this would pass unnoticed by the ordinary observer as of no interest, but to a mind that is not only intensely alert but highly analytical it was regarded as a curious phenomenon. At this time Edison was actively working on his telephone experiments, so that his attention was largely absorbed by matters connected with acoustics. Simply as a matter of inspiration the idea of a talking machine occurred to him, and, remembering his experiments with the automatic telegraph transmitter, he concluded that, if the undulations on the strip could be given the proper form and arrangement, the diaphragm could be vibrated so as to reproduce any desired sounds.

The next step was to form the proper undulations in the strip, and the idea was then suggested to Edison's mind that these undulations could be produced by sounds themselves, which could then be reproduced. When this complete conception was reached the phonograph was produced. Obviously, the change from a

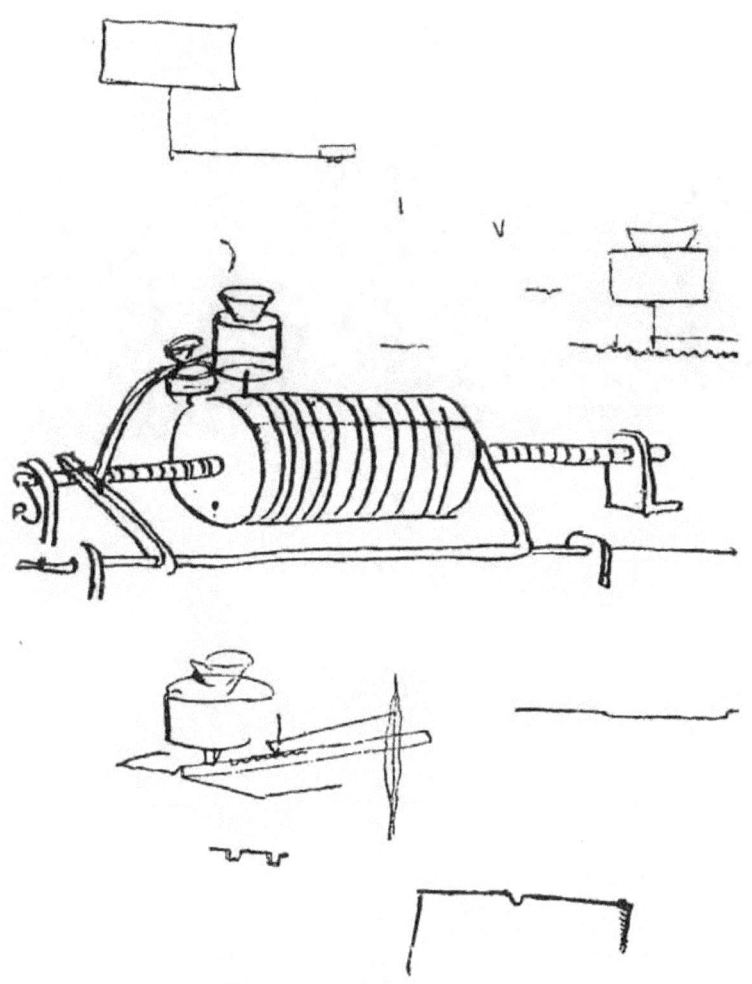

EDISON'S FIRST SKETCH OF THE PHONOGRAPH

strip of material capable of being impressed by sound-waves to a cylinder of such material on which the sound-waves could be impressed in a spiral line was a refinement of the original conception which simply involved mechanical considerations. It is, therefore, rather an interesting fact that in the development of the phonograph the reproduction of the sounds *preceded* the original production of the record.

Ten years after inventing the phonograph Edison wrote an article on the subject for the pages of the *North American Review*. From this interesting paper we quote the following paragraphs:

"In the phonograph," he writes, "we find an illustration of the truth that human speech is governed by the laws of number, harmony, and rhythm. And by these laws we are now able to register all sorts of sounds and all articulating utterances — even to the lightest shades and variations of the voice — in lines or dots which are an absolute equivalent for the emission of sound by the lips; so that, through this contrivance, we can cause these lines and dots to give forth again the sound of the voice, of music, and all other sounds recorded by them, whether audible or inaudible. For it is a very extraordinary fact that, while the deepest tone that our ears are capable of recognizing is one containing sixteen vibrations a second, the phonograph will record ten or less, and can then raise the pitch until we hear a reproduction of them. Similarly, vibrations above the highest rate audible to the ear can be recorded by the phonograph and then reproduced by lowering the pitch until we actually hear the record of these inaudible pulsations.

"To make the idea of the recording of sound more clear, let me remark one or two points. We have all been struck by the precision with which even the faintest sea-waves impress upon the surface of a beach the fine, sinuous line which is formed by the rippling edge of their advance. Almost as familiar is the fact that grains of sand sprinkled on a smooth surface of glass or wood on or near a piano sift themselves into various lines and curves according to the vibrations of the melody played on the piano keys. These things indicate how easily the particles of solid matter may receive an imparted motion, or take an impression, from delicate liquid waves, air-waves, or waves of sound. Yet, well known though these phenomena were, they apparently never suggested until within a few years that the sound-waves set going by a human voice might be so directed as to trace an impression upon some solid substance with a nicety equal to that of the tide recording its flow upon a sand beach.

"My own discovery that this could be done came to me almost accidentally while I was busy with experiments having a different object in view. I was engaged upon a machine intended to repeat Morse characters which were recorded on paper by indentations that transferred their message to another circuit automatically when passed under a tracing-point connected with a circuit-closing apparatus. In manipulating this machine I found that when the cylinder carrying the indented paper was turned with great swiftness, it gave off a humming noise from the indentations — a musical, rhythmic sound resembling that of human talk heard indistinctly. This led me to try fitting a diaphragm to the machine, which would receive the vibrations or sound-waves made by my voice when I talked to it, and register these vibrations upon an impressible material placed on the cylinder. The material selected for immediate use was paraffined paper, and the results obtained were excellent. The indentations on the cylinder, when rapidly revolved, caused a repetition of the original vibrations to reach the ear through a recorder, just as if the machine itself were speaking. I saw at once that the problem of registering human speech so that it could be repeated by mechanical means as often as might be desired was solved."

John Krusei, the man who made the first phonograph, died in 1899, but his voice is still preserved among hundreds of other records in the store closets of the Orange laboratory. Edison has often affirmed that Krusei was the cleverest mechanic who ever worked for him, and it was in no small way due to him that the invention of the phonograph was brought to so speedy and successful an issue. He was wonderfully quick at grasping the principles of any new discovery, and was an adept at making models which would perform all the duties expected of them.

When Edison had conceived the phonograph he called Krusei to him, showed him a rough sketch of the proposed machine, and asked him to build a model as quickly as he could. In those days Edison's model makers worked by piece, and it was customary to mark the price on each model. In this instance the cost agreed upon was eight dollars. Krusei was asked how long it would take him to complete the model, and he replied that he couldn't tell, but he promised that he wouldn't rest until it was finished. This was in the Menlo Park days, when Edison was looked upon as the sleepless wonder. He was accustomed to his chief assistants' working with him for two and three days at a stretch without rest, and no man showed more tireless energy than Krusei. He could do with as little repose as the inventor himself, and would become so absorbed in his work that fatigue was unfelt and time forgotten. The principles of the phonograph he absorbed with lightning rapidity, but it took him thirty hours to make the model — thirty hours without rest and very little food. At the end of that time he brought to Edison the historic machine which is now preserved in the South Kensington Museum. It was a large, clumsy affair; tinfoil was used as the material on which the indentations were to be made, and the cylinder was revolved by hand.

If Edison was in any way excited on receiving the first model of his invention for recording human speech he did not show it, and those who were with him on that memorable occasion affirm that he regarded it at the time more in the light of a queer toy than that of a machine which would create any great sensation. Among those who were present when Krusei brought in his model was Carman, the foreman of the machine-shop; and this man, unable to believe what he had been told, bet Edison a box of cigars that the thing wouldn't work. The inventor, with much good-humor, accepted the wager, and then with a smile, born of absolute faith in his deductions, slowly turned the handle of the machine and spoke into the receiver the first verse of "Mary had a little Lamb." Then the cylinder was returned to the starting-point, and faint, but distinct, came back the words of that juvenile classic faithfully repeated in Edison's familiar tones. Those present were awed rather than astonished, and the tension was not broken until Carman, in accents of pretended disappointment, and with a look of assumed disgust, exclaimed, "Well, I guess I've lost."

The first patent on the phonograph was filed in the United States, December 24, 1877, and was granted February 19, 1878, No. 200,521. Prior to this, however, in an application filed in Great Britain on July 30, 1877, No. 2909, Edison disclosed not only a cylinder

EDISON'S ORIGINAL TIN-FOIL PHONOGRAPH

phonograph, but also an apparatus embodying his original conception of an embossed strip. Under these circumstances, perhaps, it is not unreasonable that Great Britain should now possess Krusei's original model, though its loss is one which America will doubtless deplore in years to come.

The phonograph has been described as the simplest machine ever invented — there is absolutely no complicated mechanism of any kind in its make-up — yet it is difficult to believe this when confronted by a description subsequently given in a court of law when "infringements" began to come in with that customary regularity attendant upon every new and successful invention. A document was filed describing the "talking machine" in a way which made the inventor smile. "The phonograph," it declared, "is a machine for recording and reproducing sound, and from a commercial standpoint consists of two articles, one of which is commonly known to the public as the 'phonograph' and the other as the 'record.' The 'phonograph,' as designated by the public aforesaid, consists practically of a lathe mechanism, having a revolving shaft to which is attached a tapering mandrel, connected by intermediate gearing, with which is a frame arrangement to move longitudinally with the shaft as the shaft revolves; in this frame may be placed either of two apparatuses which are called respectively a 'recorder' and a 'reproducer.' Each of these consists of a glass diaphragm to which by intermediate mechanism is attached either a cutting-point or a reproducing-point; the mechanism having attached to it a cutting-point is called a 'recorder,' and the one having attached to it a reproducing-point is called the 'reproducer.'

"The record referred to consists of a tubular tablet

or record blank of metallic soap, cylindrical on its exterior, and having a tapering bore suitable to be placed in the tapering mandrel. When this tablet or blank is placed on the mandrel, and the recorder is put in operative relation with it, and sound-waves are directed against the diaphragm of the recorder, and the mandrel is revolving, the sound-waves are on the tablet in the shape of a helical groove with indentations and elevations in the bottom of the groove corresponding to the sound-waves. The tablet with this record of sound upon it becomes a record as the word is used by the public. When the sounds so recorded are to be reproduced the same operation is repeated, except that a reproducer is substituted for a recorder."

On reading this lucid and interesting description, Edison said it made his head swim, and that he never before realized what a wonderful and remarkable invention the phonograph really was. The document deserved to be placed in the archives of phonographic curiosities.

On the model of the first phonograph about fifty other machines were built, but these were almost all destroyed in subsequent experiments. Early in his work of perfecting his invention Edison discovered that tinfoil was practically worthless as a recorder — it did not retain the impression accurately, and after being used once or twice was useless. So he turned his attention to discovering a new and better composition on which to record sound-waves. Wax immediately suggested itself, but after experimenting with many kinds he was convinced that a pure product was not what he was looking for. He studied works on the subject of animal and vegetable oils, and obtained samples of almost every known fat in the Old and New Worlds. Then he set half-a-dozen men to work melting, blending, and mixing a hundred different varieties, and finally obtained a combination of waxes which seemed to answer his purpose. But the stuff was costly, and in order to economize it he made the cylinders of paper and covered them with the wax to a depth of about an eighth of an inch. The result was good records, but the cylinders were very fragile, and considerable care had to be taken in handling them.

Edison was not satisfied. He saw with the eye of a practical man that the phonograph to be popular must be furnished with records capable of withstanding a certain amount of free usage, and this convinced him that a composition cylinder was the thing he wanted, so he discarded wax and tried stearate of soda. The result was all that he had looked for, and the Edison record as we know it to-day is made of a combination of ingredients which much resembles soap. Stearin, it may be mentioned, is, according to Webster, "one of the proximate principles of animal fat, as lard, tallow, and the like. The various kinds of animal fat commonly consist of two substances, principally stearin and elain, of which the former is solid and the latter liquid. In particular instances several other different and distinct proximate principles are found in animal fats." Readers may be glad to remember this when next listening to an Edison record!

A few months after the invention of the phonograph Edison was asked to forecast its usefulness, and it may not be without interest to recall here what he said thirty years ago. He believed that the greatest use for the phonograph would be found in the office, where it could take all the correspondence and repeat it for the benefit of the letter writer. Authors, he thought, would use the phonograph instead of the pen, and printers would set up the type direct from records.

In the law courts witnesses would be compelled to speak their evidence into a "talking machine," which would also record the sayings of judge and counsel. For public speakers the phonograph would be valuable in enabling them to be heard simultaneously in a hundred different towns. It would take the place of readers in blind asylums and hospitals, and as an elocutionary teacher, or as a primary teacher for children, it would, he declared, be invaluable.

Continuing his prophecies, Edison said: "The phonograph will undoubtedly be largely devoted to music — either vocal or instrumental — and may possibly take the place of the teacher. It will sing the child to sleep, tell us what o'clock it is, summon us to dinner, and warn the lover when it is time to vacate the front porch. As a family record it will be precious, for it will preserve the sayings of those dear to us, and even receive the last messages of the dying. It will enable the children to have dolls that really speak, laugh, cry, and sing, and imitation dogs that bark, cats that meow, lions that roar, and roosters that crow. It will preserve the voices of our great men, and enable future generations to listen to speeches by a Lincoln or a Gladstone. Lastly, the phonograph will perfect the telephone and revolutionize present systems of telegraphy."

How much of this forecast has been realized is well known to the reader — certainly sufficient to stamp Edison as a very good prophet. Up to the present, however, the combination of phonograph and telephone has not proved a success; but there is time yet, and the inventor still hopes to realize this prophecy made by him in 1878. A few years ago the combination was tried in San Francisco, and a New York man on his return from a Western trip volunteered some

EDISON LISTENING TO A PHONOGRAPHIC RECORD

information regarding the experiment of applying an automatic phonograph to a telephone switchboard to do the work of an operator. "The result," he said, "was satisfactory to the telephone company, but it must have been heart-breaking to some of their subscribers. This phonograph was so arranged that when a subscriber called up a number that was busy the phonograph answered, 'Busy now. Call up later.' This was the invariable reply whenever a busy number was called over, and it was given in a monotonous tone of voice.

"I admired the cleverness of the application until the manager said to me, 'You know some of our subscribers are very profane, and perhaps you would like to hear their opinions. Here is Captain Blank, who has been calling a busy number now for five minutes. Listen to him.' Captain B.'s wire was swung on to a receiver, which I put to my ear. I never heard anything like it. 'You blankety blank, blank idiot,' he was saying, 'can't you say anything else but "Busy now. Call up later"? There you go again, you blamed idiotic chump. I am going up to the Central Office and kill you right away.' 'That,' said the manager, 'is one of the drawbacks to this invention. It excites profane men unduly, and it might lead to violence.' I heard the opinion of several other San Franciscans who called busy numbers and received over and over again this monotonous reply, and I think the invention is open to serious objection."

Two writers at least have predicted the phonograph. In 1839 an unidentified author — generally believed to have been the poet Hood — wrote: "In this country of inventions, when a self-acting drawing-paper has been discovered for copying invisible objects, who knows but that a future Niepce, or Daguerre, or Herschel or Fox Talbot might find out some sort of Boswellish writing-paper to repeat whatever it hears?"

The second writer to predict the phonograph was a woman — Miss Jean Ingelow — and she came out with her prediction only five years before it was realized. In a fairy story written by her in 1872, and entitled "Nineteen Hundred and Seventy-two," wherein she sought to forecast events a hundred years hence, there is such explicit reference to the phonograph that it appears to be something more than a coincidence. Miss Ingelow certainly possessed the idea of such a machine, and had she been born with the inventive genius of Edison she might, perhaps, have forestalled him. The particular paragraph which has reference to the modern "talking machine" is here quoted:

"He began to describe what was evidently some great invention in acoustics, which, he said (confusing his century with mine), you are going to find out very shortly. 'You know something of the beginnings of photography?' I replied that I did. 'Photography,' he remarked, 'presents a visible image; cannot you imagine something analogous to it which might present an audible image? The difference is really that the whole of a photograph is always present to the eye, but the acoustigraph only in successive portions. The song was sung and the symphony played at first and it recorded them, and gave them out in one simultaneous, horrible crash; then when we had once got them fixed science soon managed, as it were, to sketch the image — and now we can elongate it as much as we please.' 'That is very queer!' I exclaimed. 'Do you mean to tell me these notes and those voices are only the ghosts of sounds?' 'Not in any other sense,' he answered, 'than you might call a photograph a ghost of sight.'"

"The phonograph," relates a writer in an old number of the New York *Herald*, "came to the Edison laboratory and the first baby to the Edison home about the same time, and when the baby was old enough to say 'Goo-goo' and pull the great inventor's hair in a most disrespectful manner, the phonograph was near enough perfection to capture the baby talk for preservation among the family archives. So Mr. Edison filled up several rolls with these pretty articulations and laid them carefully away.

"But this was not sufficient. The most picturesque thing about the baby's utterances was its crying, and the record of this its fond father determined to secure. How it would entertain him in his old age, he thought, to start the phonograph a-going and hear again the baby wails of his firstborn! So one afternoon Mr. Edison tore himself away from his work, and climbed the big hill leading to his house. He went in a great hurry, for he is a man who grudges every working moment from his labors. A workman followed at his heels, carrying the only phonograph that at that time had been sufficiently completed to accomplish really good results.

"Reaching home and the nursery, Mr. Edison started the phonograph and brought the baby in front of it. But the baby didn't cry. Mr. Edison tumbled the youngster about, and rumpled its hair and did all sorts of things, but still the baby didn't cry. Then the inventor made dreadful faces, but the baby thought they were very funny, and crowed lustily. So back to the laboratory went Mr. Edison in a very unpleasant frame of mind, for the baby's untimely good-humor had cost him an hour of work. The phonograph was also taken back.

"But he didn't give it up. The next afternoon he

went home again, and the phonograph with him. But if the baby was good-natured the day before, this time it was absolutely cherubic. There was nothing at all that its father could do that didn't make the baby laugh. Even the phonograph with its tiny whirring wheels the baby thought was meant for its special entertainment, and gurgled joyously. So back to work the inventor went again with a temper positively ruffled. The next day and the next he tried it, but all to no purpose. The baby would not cry even when waked suddenly from sleep.

"But to baffle Edison is only to inflame his determination, which, as has been remarked before, is one of the secrets of his success. So at length, after much thought, he made a mighty resolve. It took a vast amount of determination on his part to screw his courage to the point of committing the awful deed, but he succeeded at last, and one morning, when he knew his wife was down town, he went quietly home with the phonograph and stole into the nursery, where the baby greeted him with its customary glee.

"Starting the machine, Mr. Edison ordered the nurse to leave the room. Then he took the baby on his knee and bared its chubby little leg. He took the tender flesh between his thumb and finger, clenched his teeth, shut his eyes tight, and made ready to — yes, actually to pinch the baby's leg. But just at the fateful moment the nurse peeped through the door, and, perceiving the horrid plot, flounced in and rescued the baby in the nick of time. Mr. Edison breathed a mighty sigh of relief as he gathered up the phonograph and went back to the laboratory. He then gave up the project of phonographing the baby's crying.

"But not long afterwards he accomplished his purpose in spite of everything, and quite unexpectedly, too. As soon as the baby was old enough to 'take notice' its mother took it down to the laboratory one sunny day, and when the big machinery was started a-roaring, the baby screwed up its face, opened its mouth, and emitted a series of woful screams that made Mr. Edison leap to his feet. 'Stop the machinery and start the phonograph,' he shouted, and the record of his baby's crying was there and then accomplished."

Of all Edison's inventions the phonograph probably caused the greatest sensation. There was something so inexpressibly weird in the idea of capturing speech and preserving it for centuries to come, that the inventor was regarded more than ever as a "Wizard." Every one wanted to hear the phonograph, and as soon as it was possible to make the machines a number were despatched to all parts of the world. In England and on the Continent it was the talk of the hour, and monopolized the attention of crowned heads and commoners alike, to the exclusion of everything else. Edison's name was in everybody's mouth, and if he had visited France at that time he would probably have been hailed more rapturously than even Napoleon when he escaped from Elba. But though he would not at that time risk visiting the Old World himself (he hates to be lionized), he sent several of his best machines, one of which he despatched by his faithful co-worker, A. T. E. Wangemann, the manager of the Phonograph Experimental Department, to Berlin. This was in 1888, and the young Emperor of Germany had expressed the liveliest interest in the invention. As soon as it became known that Mr. Edison's representative was in Berlin, together with one of the "talking machines," there was intense excitement.

The newspapers were full of more or less exaggerated accounts of what the wonderful instrument would do, though few in that city had yet heard it. It was to be shown first of all to Emperor William.

At his Majesty's special request, Mr. Wangemann took the phonograph one morning to the Palace, where, in the Emperor's private apartments, he explained how the machine was worked. He took it apart, put it together again, explained the principles, and made records, until the young monarch knew almost as much about the phonograph as did the inventor. But his Majesty was not satisfied until he, too, had taken the thing to bits, put it together again, made records, and was able to explain things as readily as Mr. Wangemann. Then he desired the latter to bring the machine to the Palace again that evening in order that the Court might listen to it. He would not be required to lecture on the subject as his Majesty himself would attend to that part of the entertainment.

Mr. Wangemann, of course, was quite agreeable and that night a brilliant assembly gathered at the Palace to hear the latest Edison wonder. The astonishment of those present, however, was increased a hundredfold when the Emperor himself appeared as lecturer, exhibiting the machine and explaining its mechanism as though he had spent his life in the Edison laboratory. With admiration they listened to the young monarch discourse on acoustics, soundwaves, and vibrations, and when he inserted a record, adjusted the machinery, set the electric motor going, and spoke to his audience through the medium of the phonograph, the excitement was intense, if suppressed. The royal lecturer remained for a couple of hours, alternately explaining details and reproducing records, after which he withdrew, leaving behind him the impression among his courtiers that if the phonograph were wonderful the Emperor was more so.

While Mr. Wangemann was still in Berlin, the Emperor again sent for him and requested that he would make some records of the playing of the Court orchestra. For this purpose the band assembled in the concert chamber, the performers being arranged according to their usual positions. Mr. Wangemann explained to the conductor that he would like to place the band a little differently, putting certain instruments a little further back and bringing others more to the front. But the conductor, a hot-tempered German, flatly declined to change the position of his men,—they had always been placed so, and even for the phonograph, or the great inventor himself, he was not going to alter them. In vain Dr. Wangemann argued with him that for the making of a successful record the instruments had to be arranged according to their power and quality, the less obtrusive tones being nearer and the loud or shrill tones more distant. But it was no good, the conductor was unconvinced, and the band would play according to his views or not at all.

Then Dr. Wangemann appealed to the Emperor, and to convince his Majesty he took a cylinder of the playing of the orchestra in the positions the conductor insisted they should be. His Majesty listened critically to the result. Nothing but a confusion of sounds assailed his ears. Was that his own matchless orchestra? Impossible. He ordered the conductor to place his men in any position Dr. Wangemann desired, and the musician sadly obeyed. Then the phonograph was adjusted and a record made. The difference was extraordinary, all the beauties of tone and orchestration being clearly brought out.

The Emperor was delighted. The conductor apologized, and in compliment to Dr. Wangemann his Majesty ordered the orchestra to play that evening in the position it would be if performing for the phonograph. At all future Imperial functions, however, the bandsmen returned to their ordinary places, greatly to the relief of the conductor and the comfort of the audience.

Since then the German Emperor has taken the greatest interest in the progress made by the phonograph, and when a few years ago he was asked to give a record of his voice to be deposited in the Phonographic Archives at Harvard University, he graciously consented. The application was made by Dr. Edward Scripture, a psychologist, of Yale University, through the United States Ambassador in Berlin, and in a memorandum sent to the Court Marshal, Dr. Scripture wrote: "The Phonographic Archives are to include records from such persons as will presumably have permanent historical interest for America. The importance of the undertaking can be estimated by considering what would have been the present value of voice records by Demosthenes, Shakespeare, or Frederick the Great. I wish to record his Majesty's voice as the first European record deposited in the Archives." The Emperor received Dr. Scripture one Sunday after morning church, and referred to the occasion when Dr. Wangemann paid his first visit to Berlin so many years previously. During the making of the record the Emperor was alone with the phonograph. He spoke into it twice. The first cylinder, made specially for Harvard University, contained observations on Frederick the Great, while the other, intended for the Congressional Library and the National Museum, Washington, was a short disquisition on

TESTING A PHONOGRAPHIC RECORD IN THE EXPERIMENTAL ROOM

THE PHONOGRAPH

"Fortitude in Pain." His Majesty afterwards listened to some special records which Dr. Scripture had brought for the amusement of the Imperial family.

During the early days of the phonograph it formed the basis of many amusing jokes in the Edison laboratory. The "boys" were not slow to find out that the matrix, after having been used to record one conversation or poem, as the case might be, would also admit of another being superinduced, the two being reported in a very jumbling manner. In this way a lot of fun was obtained. On one occasion the affecting words of the first verse of "Bingen on the Rhine" came out as follows:

"A soldier of the legion lay dying in Algiers,
  'Oh, shut up! Oh, bag your head!'
There was lack of woman's nursing, there was
  'Oh, give us a rest!'
    lack of woman's tears.
  'Dry up!'
But a comrade stood beside him while his life
  'Oh, what are you giving us? Oh,'
    blood ebbed away,
  'cheese it!'
And bent with pitying glances to hear what he
  'Oh, you can't read poetry! Let'
    might say.
  'up!'
The dying soldier faltered, and he took that com-
  'Police! Police! Po-'
    rade's hand,
  'lice!'
And he said, 'I shall never see my own, my,
  'Oh, put him out! Oh, cork'
    'native land.'
  'yourself!'"

Edison enjoyed these phonographic liberties and laughed like a schoolboy. The inventor himself was not slow to have his joke with the phonograph, and once hid a machine in a guest's room. Just as his friend was about to get into bed a sepulchral voice exclaimed, "Eleven o'clock, one hour more!" The visitor sat up for some time in anything but a peaceful frame of mind, but as nothing further happened he composed his nerves and lay down again. But sleep refused to visit his eyelids. He lay awake wondering what the end of the hour was to bring when the midnight chime sounded, and a second voice, deeper and more sepulchral than the first, groaned out, "Twelve o'clock, prepare to die!" This was a little too much for the astonished guest, who leaped out of bed, opened the door, and dashed into the landing, where he was confronted by the inventor, who was holding his sides with suppressed laughter. The mystery was explained and the guest returned to his bed, much relieved, if somewhat abashed, that all his fright had been caused by a phonograph.

Many interesting experiments were made with the phonograph, and it was soon found that by reversing the machinery while working the most remarkable sound effects could be produced. One writer on the subject says: "It is impossible for the human voice to be so manipulated as to produce sounds exactly backwards. Even with the letter 'A,' which is one of the simplest sounds made by the voice, the articulation cannot be reversed. At the first thought it would appear that 'A' is 'A' no matter how it is said, backwards, or forwards, or sideways, but the phonograph shows this to be a mistake. The little intonation that follows the first sharp sound of the letter is scarcely noticeable when spoken, but when the phonograph is reversed it seems that it is a most important part of the sound. It is as though the phonograph were

THE PHONOGRAPH

trying to say 'ear,' but could not quite make it. The simplest sounds, such as the alphabet or counting from 1 to 10, are as confusing as Greek, and a complete sentence is worse than unintelligible. Musical sounds are reversed in the same way, and the intonation of a banjo makes that instrument sound like a church organ, while piano music would be thought to come from a harmonium by nine out of ten musicians. Such familiar pieces as 'Home, Sweet Home,' lose their identity completely. In some cases music that is entirely new and very sweet is produced by the reversing process. This opens a new field for composers, as they can take ideas from a reversed phonograph without being accused of plagiarism."

The first public exhibition of the phonograph in England took place at the Crystal Palace in 1888, but prior to that a "private view" was given at Norwood in the presence of a distinguished gathering, including Mr. Gladstone, Sir Morell Mackenzie, the Earl of Aberdeen, Lord Rowton, Sir John Fowler, Sir William Hunter, and others equally noted. The entertainment consisted of various musical items specially chosen to display the phonograph's remarkable capabilities, a message from Edison, an "Address" to the London press from the phonograph itself, and a "Salutation," also supposed to have originated with the "talking machine." Mr. Edison's message was in the form of a private phonographic letter addressed to his agent, but nevertheless it was listened to by those present with greater interest than the songs or instrumental pieces which had preceded it. As this was the first letter in the form of a phonogram ever made by Edison, we cannot refrain from quoting it. The following is an exact transcript:

"AHEM! IN MY LABORATORY IN ORANGE,
NEW JERSEY.

"June 16, 1888, 3 o'clock A.M.

"FRIEND GOURAUD, — Ahem! This is my first mailing phonogram. It will go to you in the regular United States mail from New York *via* Southampton, North German Lloyd Steamer *Eider*. I send you by Mr. Hamilton a new phonograph, the first one of the new model which has just left my hands.

"It has been put together very hurriedly, and is not finished, as you will see. I have sent you a quantity of experimental phonogram blanks, so that you can talk back to me. I will send you phonograms of talk and music by every mail leaving here until we get the best thing for the purpose of mailing.

"Mrs. Edison and the baby are doing well. The baby's articulation is quite loud enough, but a trifle indistinct; it can be improved, but is not bad for a first experiment.

"With kind regards,
"Yours,
"EDISON."

The greetings of the phonograph itself were in poetry as well as prose. The "Address" to the London press was given out in a clear, distinct voice as follows:

"GENTLEMEN, — In the name of Edison, to whose rare genius, incomparable patience, and indefatigable industry I owe my being, I greet you. I thank you for the honor you do me by your presence here to-day. My only regret is that my master is not here to meet you in the flesh as he is in the voice. But in his absence I should be failing in my duty, as well as in my pleasure, did I not take this, my first opportunity, to thank you and all the press of the great city of London, both present and absent, for the generous and flattering reception with which my coming to the Mother Country has been heralded by you to the world."

The "Phonograph's Salutation" was composed and spoken into the machine by the Rev. Horatius Nelson Powers, D.D., of Piermont on the Hudson. The poem is said to have received the commendations of Mr. Gladstone himself:

"THE PHONOGRAPH'S SALUTATION

"I seize the palpitating air, I hoard
 Music and speech. All lips that breathe are mine;
I speak, the inviolable word
 Authenticates its origin and sign.

I am a tomb, a Paradise, a shrine,
 An angel, prophet, slave, immortal friend;
My living records, in their native tone,
 Convict the knave, and disputations end.

In me are souls embalmed. I am an ear,
 Flawless as truth, and truth's own tongue am I.
I am a resurrection; men may hear
 The quick and dead converse, as I reply.

Hail! English shores, and homes, and marts of peace,
 New trophies, Gouraud, yet are to be won.
May sweetness, light, and brotherhood increase;
 I am the latest born of Edison."

Edison was particularly anxious to obtain a record of Gladstone's voice, and had given his agent strict injunctions, before leaving America, to ask the statesman to send him a phonographic message. At this "private view" the request was made, and Gladstone at once consented. The phonograph was adjusted, and into the receiver the late Premier spoke these words, addressed to the inventor: "I am profoundly indebted to you for, not the entertainment only, but the instruction and the marvels of one of the most remarkable evenings which it has been my privilege to enjoy. Your great country is leading the way in the important work of invention. Heartily do we wish it well; and to you, as one of its greatest celebrities, allow me to offer my hearty good wishes and earnest prayers that you may long live to witness its triumphs in all that appertains to the well-being of mankind. — GLADSTONE."

The phonogram made by Gladstone was but the first of many which subsequently helped to form a wonderful collection of "voices of the great" now in the "Wizard's" possession at Llewellyn Park. The collection includes records made by Bismarck, Tennyson, Beecher, Browning, and many other famous men living at the time of the perfecting of the phonograph. Years after Gladstone had "talked back," as Edison termed it, the explorer Stanley and his wife visited the inventor's laboratory at Orange, and while listening to the phonograph Mrs. Stanley said to Edison, "Whose voice, of all the great men of the past, would you like best to recall and register?" The question had never been put to Edison before, and he pondered it for some time. Then, in tones which showed clearly that he had fully made up his mind, he replied, "Napoleon's." The visitors, somewhat surprised, suggested that in past centuries there were voices of other men greater than Napoleon. The argument waxed warm, but Edison never wavered in his choice. Napoleon's was the voice he wanted to hear most, and for it he was willing to barter the entire collection of records then in his possession.

The phonograph has made its way into strange lands, and there are now probably few places on the globe where its voice has not been heard. "In 1897," says a writer, "it appeared, for the first time, in Lhassa, Thibet, the religious capital of the Buddhist faith. To this ancient town no European or other man than a Buddhist is supposed to be allowed to penetrate, though, as a matter of fact, some Europeans have been there and returned safe and sound. Travellers of the Buddhist faith may visit Lhassa if they are under no suspicion of being emissaries of the Christians. Among such travellers was a certain Burmese merchant, who, familiar with the resources of civilization, took with him, to show the Grand Lama, or sacred and miraculously appointed Head of the Buddhist Church, an Edison phonograph. This was a good idea on the part of the Burmese trader, for in the Buddhist cult great account is made of mechanically repeated prayers. Praying wheels to reel off written or printed prayers are employed, and it struck the merchant that if he could introduce a machine which would actually repeat the prayers aloud he might make a fortune in supplying the apparatus.

"He succeeded in getting the Grand or Dalai Lama and the dignitaries that surround him to inspect the phonograph, and as he had read into it a chapter of the sacred writings of the Buddhists, he was able to make it repeat this chapter aloud, to the great astonishment of the Grand Lama, who thought he was witnessing a miracle. The merchant asked the Dalai Lama to speak into the machine, and he did so, declaiming the beautiful prayer called 'Om mani padme cum,' or 'Jewel in the Lotus.' Then the cylinder being put in place the phonograph repeated the prayer in the Dalai Lama's voice, to the stupefaction and great edification of all the auditors. For many days thereafter the phonograph was kept busy with this and other utterances holy to the Buddhists, and now the phonograph has taken its place as the favorite 'praying machine' of Lhassa."

In Russia the phonograph did not receive quite so hearty a welcome, and it was some time before it was looked upon with anything like favor by the Russian Government. Even to-day all records have first to be submitted to the "Press Censor" before they can be enjoyed by the public, and it is a serious offence to have in one's possession a cylinder which has not been inspected by the censor. Ten years ago in the pavilion of the public gardens in Tagonrog the machine was exhibited for the first time and attracted large crowds. It played and sang and laughed for some time undisturbed, until a police officer heard the machine reciting one of Kirloff's famous fables, but with some variations of the original text. The officer got suspicious, and, not trusting to his memory, he ran at once and got Kirloff's book, and came again to listen to the phonograph's version of the fable. To his horror he found the fable reproduced not at all as it was passed by the censorship more than half a century ago. An alarm was raised at once, the higher local authorities communicated with, and the manager of the pavilion was called upon to explain the conduct of that "speaking mechanical beast." All the poor manager could do was to open the mysterious inside of the criminal machine, and hand over to the authorities the indiscreet cylinder which threatened to tell the peaceful inhabitants so many undesirable things. But the arrest of the chief criminal was considered insufficient, as it could not have acted without a human accomplice, and so the poor manager was haled to court, sentenced to three months' imprisonment, a heavy fine, and the forfeiture of his phonograph, which was forthwith smashed to pieces by the sensitive officials.

The phonograph has been employed for many queer purposes, perhaps the queerest being to assist a certain American professor in his study of the language of cats. This gentleman interested himself many years ago — together with one or two others — in the Simian language, but ultimately abandoned the problem of interpreting "monkey talk" in order to find out what a cat means when it stands on the back fence at night and emits those blood-curdling cries which make householders so reckless regarding their personal property.

"It is not easy," said this gentleman to the writer, "to secure good records of cat language, and, in fact, I have waited night after night in my backyard for the purpose only to be disappointed. It is, of course, necessary to place the phonograph pretty near the cats' rendezvous in order to bottle up their voices, and it is seldom that felines are so absorbed with their musical efforts as to become oblivious to their surroundings. One record took me several nights to secure, and the reason that I did finally succeed was almost due to an accident. These particular cats were known for a mile around, and I do not suppose there was any one occupying a room looking on the back who had not voluntarily lost property in a vain endeavor to break up their musical evenings. But the cats seemed to lead charmed lives, and the manner in which they dodged missiles and at the same time continued singing was marvellous. But having made up my mind to secure a record of their voices, I crept into a dark corner of my yard one night and awaited their coming. For four evenings in succession they had been tuning up just below my window, and whether they had got wind that I was there with the phonograph and felt shy in consequence I don't know, but they never showed up that night, though I could hear them halfway down the block giving No. 19 a serenade.

"After waiting about three hours I was so cold that I packed up my machine and went to bed, but I had scarcely got between the sheets when I heard them below singing away as though their hardened hearts would burst. I slipped on a pair of trousers, grabbed the phonograph, opened the back door and crept out. They were on the top of the water-butt, and I was quietly making my way towards them when I fell over the india-rubber plant and with an ear-splitting yell they disappeared. The next night and the next I had no better luck, and I was almost giving up in despair when a friend suggested that I should place the phonograph in the yard, run an electric wire from the motor into my room and await the cats' arrival comfortably in bed. That very night I tried the experiment. Placing the phonograph in a spot which appeared to be a favorite one with the cats (to judge by the queer things I used to pick up near it) I adjusted the horn, arranged the wire so that by pressing a button I could start the motor, and then returned to bed. I was just beginning to feel sleepy when they arrived. They must have taken their stand quite close to the phonograph, and it wasn't long before they began their choir practice. When they were fairly started I pressed the button and set the machinery in motion. The yowling became awful after a bit, and I was very much afraid that the missiles which began to fly would strike my machine, but fortunately they didn't, and when I thought I had secured a sufficient quantity of the cats' vocal powers I put on some clothes and brought in the phonograph. When I tested the record I found it an excellent one. I was exceptionally lucky in this instance, for a few nights later the cats completely and mysteriously disappeared. I am afraid that they finally fell victims to their art, and we shall never hear their voices again, save in the phonograph.

"I have, by the aid of Mr. Edison's invention, secured records of cats purring, cats in pain (a wounded or sick cat emits a peculiarly mournful sound quite different from its ordinary voice), cats spitting, and so forth. It is not difficult to secure the record of an angry cat's voice, for all you have to do is to hold the animal near the mouth of the phonograph and give its tail a twist. It will make plenty of noise then, but I never follow this method myself as I only wish to obtain records of the natural voice. All together I have secured twenty-five cat records, which repeat twenty-five different cries. I believe that when a cat yowls at night she has some object in view other than that of annoying the neighbors, though I know the majority of people wouldn't believe you if you said so. I am convinced there is a cat language just as there is a Simian language, and if I live long enough I am going to find out what it means. I feel I have a difficult task before me, but with the aid of the 'talking machine' I think I shall succeed.

"Sometimes I place the phonograph near my own cat (a quiet respectable parlor animal that doesn't go out at night) and turn on a few nocturnal yowls for her especial benefit. When she hears the sounds of the other cats having a good time she races round the room in a remarkable manner and does her best to perform a feline harlequin act through the window. It is perfectly evident that she knows what is being said, and if she'd only respond in some intelligible way I should begin to understand. However, I am not without hope.

"I have succeeded in determining by the aid of the phonograph the different emotions of cats, and can tell fairly accurately which is the cry of fear, of delight, of contempt, of amusement, and of affection. I can also tell the peculiar cry a cat makes when he or she wishes to attract a friend's attention, and also the sound of warning on the approach of an enemy. In a short time I intend to give a serious lecture on the Feline Language illustrated with cat cries on the phonograph. People will laugh, of course, but I hope in the end that they will come to believe with me that even cats have a language of their own, and one which, if we study sufficiently, we shall some day understand."

As a matter of fact, the phonograph has been put to queerer uses than Edison ever anticipated. Here is one case which greatly amused the inventor when he heard of it. About two years ago in one of the busiest parts of London, where almost the entire road is taken up with costers' barrows, Edison's invention played an important part in helping the proprietor of a big stand to dispose of his entire stock of "greens."

Around the well-filled barrow a crowd of hilarious buyers and idlers congregated, while one could distinctly hear above the general clamor a voice in coster accents declaring that "termarters" were "tuppence a pahnd" and "green peas fippence the 'alf peck." Under ordinary circumstances, of course, this information would not have attracted more than the usual number of Saturday night buyers, but the reason of the jostling crowd became clear when it was observed that the voice proceeded apparently from the very midst of the vegetables, while the owner of the cart, a delicate, weak-looking man, stood quietly by attending to his customers' wants without saying a word.

When asked to explain the meaning of this strange affair the coster replied in husky tones that some months ago he had almost entirely lost his voice through an attack of fever, and was subsequently in great danger of also losing his trade through being unable to announce the quality and price of his goods in tones equal to those of his competitors, when a friend suggested that he should engage the services of a phonograph to discharge that duty for him.

The idea was a good one, and the coster promptly adopted it with the most satisfactory results, the "talking machine" generally enabling him to sell out his entire stock while his rivals were still making the night-air hideous with their vocal efforts to attract customers. The records were made for him by a friendly coster whose voice was the pride and admiration of the entire "push-cart" community.

Frank D. Millet, and other artists, often make use of the phonograph while painting a portrait, as they declare that it helps to banish the bored look which a subject usually assumes when sitting for any length of time. In the case of children especially they find that the little one is able to sit much longer without becoming restless or fatigued if the phonograph is turning out melodies or funny speeches. The smile becomes natural and the expression interested — a state of things which, under ordinary circumstances, is sometimes impossible to obtain.

Many other amusing, interesting, or remarkable incidents in connection with the phonograph might be related were it not that their recital would possibly prove tedious, for so accustomed have we become to the "talking machine," and so true is it that familiarity breeds contempt that it is now difficult to understand the tremendous sensation it created twenty years and more ago. The rising generation who have always had the phonograph with them cannot be expected to regard it as so great a wonder as do those who have followed its development from its inception, but, nevertheless, even in the dim future, it will probably still remain one of the most marvellous inventions of the nineteenth century.

CHAPTER XI

THE KINETOSCOPE, MAGNETIC ORE SEPARATOR, AND OTHER INVENTIONS

IT was during the year 1887 that Edison invented the "Kinetoscope," or moving picture machine. The idea was not an original one, nor does he claim it to have been, but frankly states that it was suggested to him by that interesting little instrument called the Zoëtrope. Edison had known this toy for many years, and after he had invented the phonograph he argued that it should be possible to make a machine "which would do for the eye what the phonograph does for the ear." Later, when the kinetoscope was perfected, he declared that it would be comparatively easy to combine the two inventions, and with their aid give an entire opera on the stage of a theatre — the acting and singing being supplied entirely by the kinetoscope and phonograph. During the spring of 1907 the writer questioned Edison on the subject, and he replied:

"The time is coming when the moving picture and the phonograph will be combined so naturally that we shall be able to show a trumpeter or any other musician so life-like in appearance that when he puts his instrument to his lips it will be impossible for any one to say positively that it is not the living man himself who is playing. I look forward to the day when we shall give grand opera in so realistic a manner that the critics themselves will be deceived. We are working on these lines now, and though the difficulties are great we shall overcome them by and by."

The invention of the kinetoscope took Edison into a realm of science into which he had not previously penetrated — that of photography. Up to the time when the idea of the kinetoscope first occurred to him he had never taken a snapshot, developed a plate, or, in fact, touched a camera. But he soon saw that if he was to have any success with his new enterprise he must study the subject of photography from A to Z, and with his customary enthusiasm he threw himself at once into the work of mastering the art. He realized that the pictures, to indicate natural movements successfully when thrown on a screen, would have to be taken with extraordinary celerity — from forty to sixty a second, in fact. By this means only would the eye be unable to detect the change from one position to the other.

Edison endeavored to find plates (films) which would be quick enough to do this, and discovered that there were none in existence. Thereupon he opened a photographic laboratory and by innumerable experiments succeeded in making films sufficiently quick for his purpose. He learned all there was to learn regarding the taking, developing, printing, and toning of negatives, and soon began to make discoveries which were of inestimable benefit to him in the perfecting of the kinetoscope. In this work Edison had the assistance of W. K. L. Dickson, who labored unceasingly with his chief in the development of the machine. The two men worked together early and late, and thousands of experiments were made before the results satisfied them.

From the very first, of course, it was necessary that the photographs should be taken on strips of film,

THE KINETOSCOPE 167

and literally miles of this sensitive material were exposed for the purpose of obtaining interesting subjects for the kinetoscope. Every sort of incident was photographed, and the assistants in the laboratory were called upon to go through all kinds of "turns" (or "stunts," as they called them) for the benefit of the kinetoscope. Fred Ott, who was known to occasionally indulge in the luxury of an ear-splitting sneeze, was requested to give an illustration of his famous performance before the moving picture camera. He protested at first but was compelled to yield, and by some means or other known only to himself was able to go through all the grimaces of a real, *bonâ-fide* sneeze while the camera clicked away at the rate of fifty pictures to the second. Boys in the laboratory were told to turn somersaults, stand on their heads, play leap-frog, and perform other manœuvres supposed to be dear to youth, while various members of Edison's staff were "taken" busily engaged experimenting. When these pictures were thrown on to the screen they caused the liveliest interest and amusement. Edison himself was asked to give "sittings," but declined. Then when the machine came nearer to being the perfected thing it is to-day a stage was put up in the Orange laboratory and various celebrated dancers came down from New York — Miss Loie Fuller among the number — and rehearsed their dances before the kinetoscope. All this, of course, cost a good deal of money, and it is more than probable that this invention gobbled up at least a hundred thousand dollars before it could be considered a commercial success.

Later on Mr. Dickson obtained special permission to make some moving pictures of Pope Leo XIII., on which occasion he took no fewer than 17,000 photographs. "It was only by great diplomacy," said Mr.

Dickson afterwards, "that I obtained the necessary permission, and it was a good deal due to the kindness of Count Pecci, the Pope's nephew, that I succeeded. And after I had entered the Vatican and commenced 'operations' I was much afraid that the Pope would send out word that he was too fatigued to appear. True, he had given me an appointment, but I imagined that indisposition, or the weather, or a dozen unlooked-for events would cause a postponement. But I was mistaken. His Holiness had set a date in April, and — kept it. I made 17,000 photographs during that and subsequent days, and all the time the Pope was kindness itself. I and my assistant had to dress in black, and before we commenced the work of photographing his Holiness we were drilled in various formalities which had to be observed. The Pope himself was extremely interested in everything, and I had to explain the whole process to him.

"The first series of pictures were made while the Pontiff was on his way to the Sistine Chapel, being driven thither in his carriage. I explained to him that in order to obtain good results it would be necessary to have the hood down, and he cheerfully consented to its being lowered. He held an umbrella over his head, for the sun was hot, but this he closed as soon as I began to make the pictures. Another series of photographs showed the Pope, with uplifted finger, bestowing the Apostolic benediction on an imaginary crowd, while a third depicted him walking in the Vatican grounds. The Pope afterwards witnessed many of these moving pictures, and showed unbounded delight and wonder at the faithfulness of the reproductions. 'Now,' he said on this occasion, turning to Cardinal Rampolla, 'I know how I look when I am blessing my people.'"

KINETOSCOPE RECORD OF CARMENCITA'S DANCE

During these days when rumor was busy with the "sensations" to be depicted by means of the kinetoscope, an announcement appeared in a great number of American papers to the effect that Edison had permitted a *bonâ-fide* prize fight to take place in his laboratory for a series of moving pictures, the pugilists being the noted Jim Corbett and a Jerseyman. One-ounce gloves were used, and the prize was a purse of five thousand dollars, it was stated. This, however, was an exaggeration, as no purse was offered.

Since those days the kinetoscope has been accused of reproducing greater sensations than a prize fight — among other things the agonized contortions of a negro being burned at the stake — but these are merely "newspaper stories" which have originated in the brains of imaginative space writers. Of the many thousand series of moving pictures which have issued from the Edison laboratory there has not been a single instance of one calculated to produce a "sensation" in the generally accepted sense of the word. And the same thing may be said of Edison's phonographic records.

Another invention on which Edison worked soon after he had conceived the idea of the kinetoscope was the magnetic ore separator — a means whereby the magnetic substances may be separated from the non-magnetic. The origin of this invention is interesting. It is stated that Edison was one day walking along the sea-coast when he came across a patch of black sand. Curious to know what it contained, he filled his pockets with it, and when he returned to the laboratory he poured it out on to the bench. As he did so, a workman stumbled against the table and dropped the big magnet he was carrying across the sand. When he picked it up again it was covered with tiny black grains, proving the sand to consist chiefly of metallic particles. Edison took the magnet in his own hands, and sitting there became lost in thought. His mind was busy with fresh ideas which the accidental dropping of the magnet had generated. He saw no reason why magnetic attraction should not be employed to separate the metal from low-grade ores, and there and then he commenced his experiments which ultimately gave birth to what is now known as the magnetic ore separator.

For many years Edison struggled with the problem and finally brought it to such a state of perfection that, by his system, a piece of ore weighing a couple of tons may be crushed to powder, and the metal extracted by means of an electro-magnet. The method is an extremely simple one, the crushed ore being allowed to fall in a steady stream from a hopper past the electromagnet, which attracts the iron particles and causes them to curve away and fall into a bin under it. The non-magnetic substances, being uninfluenced by the magnet, fall straight and are collected in another bin placed directly beneath the hopper.

In connection with this separation of ores by magnetic attraction, Edison had to invent a tremendous amount of machinery, which included crushers, pulverizers, conveyers, and presses, before the scheme was workable. Then he bought a big tract of land in Sussex County and commenced operations. A little town soon sprang up, which was called "Edison" after the founder, and about two hundred neat houses were erected. The work of quarrying and crushing the ore continued for several years, and Edison is said to have put several hundred thousands of dollars into the venture; but the shipping facilities were bad, and ten years ago the works were shut down and the inhabitants began gradually to creep away, until to-day "Edison" is deserted. The magnetic ore separator is still regarded as the best and simplest method of separating iron from low-grade ores, and the system is carried on in many parts of the world. In Edison's case, however, it was one of those things which, while successful as an invention, was not so financially, and he therefore closed down the mine and turned his attention to other things more remunerative. No one lives at Edison now, and it is as lonely and silent as the "Deserted Village." Many of the buildings still stand, but they are falling quickly to decay, and the little houses where the miners and operators used to dwell, and which were lighted by electricity and contained all "modern conveniences," seem to regard one in mute protest against their abandonment. At one time Edison was the most up-to-date mining town in America, and people came for miles to see the magnetic ore separator, but when the works were closed down there was nothing there which would support a community, and so the inhabitants drifted away. A few hopeful ones remained behind and endeavored to eke out a living, but it was too strenuous an existence, and after a few months they too fled. The inventor never once revisited the little town named in his honor, after finally turning his back upon it now nearly ten years ago.

A far more prosperous undertaking is Edison's method of turning rock and limestone into cement. His works for this purpose are situated at Stewartsville, N.J., and cover close upon eight hundred acres of ground. A short description of his methods in this line may not be without interest. The rock after blasting is picked up by ninety-ton vulcan steam shovels, which are the most powerful things of the kind in the world. One of these mighty "scoops" can pick up a six-ton piece of rock as though it were a walnut and handle it as freely as a child would a rubber ball. These giant pieces of stone are loaded on "skips" and drawn by locomotives about a mile distant to the "crushers." In the crushing house are terrible-looking rollers capable of breaking up a five-ton piece of rock as easily as a pair of nut crackers would smash a filbert. These rolls are five feet long and fifteen feet in circumference, each roller alone, without any of its appurtenances, weighing twenty-five tons. They are made of chilled iron plates and rotate in opposite directions. The motors which work these rollers are enclosed in dust-proof chambers, for otherwise they would soon become clogged with the powdery particles which rise from the crushers like gigantic clouds. The rock is dumped into these crushers direct from the "skips," and some idea of the former's appetite may be gathered from the fact that they eat up no less than fifteen tons of material every four minutes.

After passing through these giant rollers the rock is dropped into hoppers feeding a set of thirty-six-inch rolls — so called because they are thirty-six inches long and thirty-six inches in diameter. These rolls break up the rock in pieces about the size of one's fist, after which it passes through a second and third set of crushers, finally emerging broken up in pieces of the size of lump sugar. The rock is now ready for the drying room. Here it is dropped upon grates heated by gases and shaken until thoroughly dried. Then it goes to the stockhouse — an immense building 500 feet long containing ten bins, each one capable of holding 1500 tons. Six of these bins are used for the cement rock, three for carbonate of lime, and one

EDISON MAGNETIC ORE SEPARATOR

for mixing. Mixing is absolutely necessary, for the rock never contains the same amount of lime, and in order to give satisfactory results the proportions must be "just so."

The cement rock and the limestone are next taken to the storehouse, which contains two bins each with a capacity of sixty tons. Here the chemist's formula is kept and carefully followed by the mixers. So much limestone must go with so much rock. The quantities are weighed automatically by a process highly interesting to the visitor. Each bin (one containing limestone and the other rock) deposits so much of its contents into the scale, which is worked electrically so that when the right quantity has been dropped into the weighing pan further supply is instantly cut off by the scale beam closing an electrical circuit. The cement rock and limestone then pass through chutes into a feed roll which thoroughly mixes the two materials. After passing under chalk grinding rolls the mixture arrives at the summit of the "blower-house," from which it falls through grids. As it falls a current of air is passed through it, the fine dust being carried to a large settling chamber where it accumulates in miniature mountains at the bottom. The coarser material which has defied the "blowers" is returned to the chalk crushers for further reduction. The pressure of these rollers varies from 14,000 to 18,000 pounds per square inch. The cement is finally passed through a 200-mesh screen, "bagged" and "barrelled" by machinery, and conveyed to the forwarding-houses.

The roasters are 150 feet long, made of cast iron lined with fire-brick, and built in the form of huge cylindrical shells. On the outside they are nine feet in diameter and on the inside six feet. Each roaster can turn out 900 barrels of cement every twenty-four hours. As a rule the works are in action during the night as well as the day, and the great crushers revolve ceaselessly from year's end to year's end. Most of the machinery used in these cement works is the result of Edison's inventive mind, and there are a hundred other interesting facts connected with the making of Portland cement by his remarkable system which it is impossible to touch upon here. Mention, however, may be made of a wonderful electrical signalling apparatus recently erected whereby the manager in his office may communicate with the heads of the different departments without leaving his desk, while by means of an "annunciator" system a foreman can call a messenger at any time during the night or day. There is also a remarkable system of oiling whereby every part of the machinery is automatically lubricated. The oil passes continuously through the machinery, is collected (by gravity) in tanks, filtered, and again used. After filtration and re-filtration the oil is pumped into tanks situated at the top of each building, from which it again drops to the different parts of the machinery. The supply is regulated by means of needle valves.

Edison is also the originator of a novel method of building houses of solid concrete. He was some years working out the details of this scheme to his own satisfaction, but twelve months ago he completed his experiments and now it is possible to "build" a ten-room house in about four days. The simple method is as follows: a steel mould is made into which the concrete is pumped, allowed to harden, and the mould then removed. At present an entire house has not been made in one piece. The foundations, walls, floors, and ceilings are made by pouring concrete into separate moulds and afterwards piecing them together.

Even the window frames are temporary shells into which concrete is pumped. When these shells are removed they leave behind solid window frames which it will take centuries to weaken. The origin of Edison's idea is said to have been the increasing cost of brick and lumber.

The time will most certainly come when whole houses will be turned out in one piece, though each part is now separately moulded. These metallic moulds may be ornate or plain as the fancy of the householder dictates, and it will be no dearer to have the latter than the former. It only requires some smart architects to draw up designs for a few houses of different patterns and of about the size to suit the family of the average mechanic. The moulds made for each part of the house may even be joined together *before* the concrete has been pumped in. If more convenient, then the parts may be made separately and joined together with cement afterwards. The concrete will dry in a few hours, though it is considered better to leave the liquid material in the moulds for four days, when the latter may be removed with perfect confidence that a solid and almost bomb-proof house will remain behind.

Moulds for a house of ten rooms would cost about $25,000, but they could be used five hundred times if necessary, so that the charge of $500 for a dwelling of the size mentioned would pay the builder very handsomely. This idea of erecting houses in moulds is a very simple and feasible one, and it seems strange that it should have occurred to no one until Edison suggested it. In America to-day many houses are being erected according to Edison's plans, and are fulfilling all that was expected of them.

CHAPTER XII

SOME LESSER INVENTIONS

EDISON'S work as an inventor extends over a most varied field. In addition to his better-known patents, granted in connection with the development of the electric lamp, the phonograph, the telephone, ore-milling machinery, and storage-batteries, the inventions include typewriters, electric pens, vocal engines, addressing machines, methods of preserving fruit, cast-iron manufacture, wire-drawing, electric locomotives, moving-picture machines, the making of plate glass, compressed-air apparatus, and many other things.

To describe these numerous inventions in detail would take up too great a part of this book, but a brief description of some of them is necessary in order to convey to the reader a faint idea of the tremendous scope of Edison's researches. He has been by far the most prolific inventor and patentee of any time, having filed more than twelve hundred applications in America alone, for which over eight hundred patents have so far been granted. For foreign patents in most of the countries of the world his applications number more than two thousand. Such a record as this is unique, yet because the public has come to regard Edison as a kind of favored mortal to whom Nature generously whispers her secrets, the inventor scarcely receives that amount of credit for the work entailed to which he is entitled.

The commonly accepted idea of him is that by brilliant flashes of intellect inventions spring fully developed from his brain, or that he has the singular good fortune to be the instrument whereby Nature communicates her discoveries. Neither of these views is correct. Edison draws a very broad line between "discovery" and "invention." In his parlance a discovery is a "scratch" — something that might be disclosed to any one, and for which he thinks little or no credit is due. Invention, on the other hand, is the result of that peculiar faculty which perceives the application of some phenomenon or action to a new use. As an inventor, therefore, Edison possesses two qualifications preëminently. First, the inventive faculty, or the special intuition by which the adaptability of some observed result to a useful end is presented; and secondly, the physical energy and patience necessary for the investigation by which that result may be ascertained.

Although capable of flashes of great genius, his mind is necessarily analytical, and when a problem is presented to his attention it may be safely presumed that most of its solutions will be considered by him and the most successful selected. Notwithstanding this mental equipment, his success has depended very largely on his physical make-up, as well as upon a certain solidity of his nervous system that takes no account of fatigue or ennui. In other words, day after day, with only a few hours' sleep, he can devote himself enthusiastically to the investigation of a single problem the very monotony of which would drive most men into nervous prostration.

In a recent argument in a suit on one of Edison's patents opposing counsel sought to show that Edison was more an inventor than a discoverer, and the remark made was entirely complimentary. Said the learned gentleman: "If your honor wished him to, Mr. Edison could go into a field of grass a mile square *and select therefrom the most perfect blade!*" The popular conception of Edison is that of a man who accomplishes startling results by instantaneous flashes of intellect. The real Edison is a man of indefatigable industry, who attains his ends by patient effort intelligently applied.

On the subject of "scratches" but very few real discoveries have been made by him. In one of them experiments were being made in the early days with automatic telegraphs, where the effect of the current was to produce chemical changes in moving paper strips with various substances. In making these experiments Edison held in his hand a pen, through which the current passed, and which pressed upon the strip. It was found that, with some chemicals, the passage of the current increased the friction between the pen and the strip, so as to subject the pen to slight pulls. Later, when experimenting with the telephone, these earlier observances occurred to him, and as a result the "motograph," or "chalk telephone receiver," was invented, wherein the same phenomena take place. Although this work Edison regards as a "scratch," probably very few men would have had the inventive faculty to foresee that the original discovery could have been used for making a new telephone.

At the Paris Exposition of 1889 the chief attraction was the exhibition of Edison's leading inventions, which created an immense sensation. The following year they were shown in the United States, and visited by hundreds of thousands of individuals interested in the progress of invention. Each exhibit was accompanied by a card giving a short description of the invention, and there was also published a small descriptive catalogue or pamphlet, prepared by the late Luther Stieringer, friend and co-worker of Edison, and to this little work — copies of which are now very difficult to obtain — I am indebted for the succinct descriptions of some of these lesser-known inventions.

Stieringer was with Edison in the early Menlo Park days, and worked almost as untiringly and energetically as the inventor himself. He ultimately became famous in the electrical world through his development of the wiring system, and the illuminating effects which he obtained when the electric light was yet in its infancy will always be remembered in the history of the incandescent lamp. The lighting of the Omaha Exposition was carried out by Stieringer with such consummate skill, and the electrical effects were so striking, that a special medal was designed in his honor and presented to him as a small recognition of the success of his work. The illuminations of the Grand Court at the World's Fair, Chicago, were also placed in his hands, and again he proved in a remarkable way the possibilities of electric lighting. Stieringer owned the first electrolier ever made, and this was shown, among other interesting Edison exhibits, at the St. Louis Exposition of 1904.

Stieringer was one of Edison's stanchest admirers, and the inventor's capacity for work was a source of constant wonderment to him. He it was who on one occasion declared his belief that if Edison could have chosen his birthplace he would have located it in the planet Mars, so as to have secured the advantages of a day forty minutes longer than ours. It was with Edison's sanction that Stieringer prepared the pamphlet, already referred to, descriptive of those inventions which he knew so well, and the majority of which he had seen grow from crude beginnings to perfected entities. Stieringer was generally credited with having a "roving commission" from Edison, empowering him to investigate anything and everything which he considered might prove of use or interest to the inventor. Any scientific door which was double-locked or which bore the legend "No Admittance" immediately attracted Stieringer's attention, and he never rested night or day until he had opened it. Of the many men who gathered around Edison in the days when the brilliancy of his inventive genius began to be recognized Stieringer takes a high place, and his death was a very real loss to the scientific and electrical world.

Mention has already been made of the fact that the motograph was invented at a time when Edison was experimenting with automatic telegraphs. Another invention which came to him about the same period was the electric pen. This was one of his most useful clerical devices, and its great success was soon proved by the number of imitations which immediately afterwards began to flood the market. The instrument, as originally conceived, was very simple in construction, consisting, as it did, of a hollow wooden tube, the size and shape of an ordinary penholder, fitted with a steel shaft. Attached to the head of the pen was a tiny motor communicating with the shaft, while a needle projected from the writing end of the instrument and performed the duties of a pen-point. To work the pen the miniature motor was attached to a battery by flexible wires, and when in operation the steel shaft vibrated at so great a speed that the needle, on being guided over the surface of a sheet of paper, perforated it. By means of this electric pen the stencil of a plan or letter was made, and then, with the help of a duplicating press and an inked roller, as many copies could be run off as were required.

Soon after this novel pen made its appearance many so-called inventors attempted to better and cheapen it. Among these was a New Orleans man, who got up a pneumatic pen on the same principle, except that it was worked by air. Instead of the steel shaft a small tube was employed. The air set a little drumhead quivering in the top of the pen, and that moved the needle. The motor was in the form of a tiny bellows operated by clockwork. "It was all beautifully simple," said the luckless inventor some years later, "and I figured out that it could be sold for half the price of the electric machine. I believed I was on the eve of reaping a big harvest when Edison thought again, and calmly knocked me out by merely fastening a diminutive toothed wheel to the point of a pencil. When the pencil was moved over the paper the wheel naturally revolved, and the teeth cut the stencil. It cost about a dollar to make, and shelved both the electric and pneumatic pens in just one fell swoop. When I heard of Edison's improvement I couldn't understand why I hadn't thought of it myself, but inventions are mighty queer things, anyway."

The mimeograph, with which every city clerk is familiar, followed close on the heels of the electric pen. It was more economical, did not need any electric power, and yet was equally useful for manifolding manuscript. The apparatus consisted of a steel plate, a sheet of sensitive paper, and a stylus. The paper was laid on the smooth plate, over which the stylus glided with the greatest ease, perforating the sensitive sheet. In this way a stencil was made from which any number of copies could be rolled off. By placing the stencil paper, backed with a piece of silk, in the typewriter, and removing the ribbon, the same result may be obtained for manifolding typewritten matter. The mimeograph was immediately recognized as an indispensable piece of office furniture, and to-day it is to be found in thousands of business houses.

As far back as 1885 Edison applied for a patent covering wireless telegraphy, and was allowed one in 1891, but he did not pursue his investigations in this direction with his customary zeal. He was content to give way to Marconi, for whom he has a very sincere admiration. Edison's "grasshopper telegraph" was an invention whereby communication could be made between telegraphic stations and moving trains. The feature of this system was the absence of any special wire between or along the tracks. Electrical induction served to transfer the currents from the apparatus in the train to the ordinary Morse wires alongside the track, no other medium than the air being required to facilitate the transfer. The currents which were thus induced in the wires did not in any way interfere with the ordinary business which was being carried on over them. The apparatus on the train and at the stations along the line consisted of an ordinary battery, an induction coil with vibrator, a Morse key, and a pair of telephone receivers. By means of the induction coil the current from the battery was transformed into a rapidly alternating, highly penetrative current, capable of producing a similar current in neighboring wires or apparatus. The effect was a continuous humming sound heard in the phonetic receivers, this being broken into the dots and dashes of the Morse system by means of the key. The roofs of the cars were all connected together and to the instruments, and these were connected to the earth through the car-wheels and track. By means of this simple and inexpensive system messages have been transmitted across an air space of 560 feet intervening between the wires and the cars. The "grasshopper telegraph" was, at one time, used on many of the long-distance trains of America, but it never became a very great commercial success, probably for the reason that few people find it necessary to send messages while travelling by rail — even in the United States. In the perfecting of this invention Edison worked in coöperation with W. Wiley Smith, who therefore shares with the inventor the distinction of originating this unique form of telegraphy.

While engaged in his acoustic researches, carried on in connection with the telephone, the idea occurred to Edison that it would not be difficult to construct an instrument whereby two persons at considerable distance from each other might carry on a conversation without unduly straining their lungs. So he set to work and evolved the megaphone. To-day that instrument is still largely employed as a means of conveying sound to distant points, though its construction is somewhat different to what it was at the time of its invention. In those days "twin" funnels were employed, made either of metal or wood, each funnel being from 6 to 8 feet in length, with a width from 30 to 36 inches at the mouths. These huge funnels ended in tiny apertures, which were provided with tubes, and which the operator placed in his ears. Between the funnels was a large speaking trumpet, and the whole apparatus was mounted on a substantial steel tripod. Remarkable results were obtained by using these megaphones, and two people provided with instruments were able to keep up a conversation at a distance of two miles without in any way raising their voices above the normal. The telephone has rendered the megaphone less useful than it might otherwise have proved, but it remains, nevertheless, one of Edison's most valuable inventions connected with acoustics.

Another invention — more interesting, perhaps, than useful — also owes its being to experimental work connected with the telephone. This Edison called the "phonomotor," or "vocal engine." It consists of a mouthpiece and a diaphragm, to the centre of which is attached a brass rod carrying a steel pawl; the pawl acts on a ratchet wheel with very fine teeth, mounted on a shaft carrying a flywheel, and driving a colored disk by means of a belt or cord. The vibrations of the voice — which he had discovered were capable of developing considerable energy — in speaking or singing into the instrument, caused the pawl to impinge upon the teeth of the ratchet-wheel, producing a rapid rotation of the flywheel and colored plate; a continuous sound gives the flywheel such momentum that considerable force is needed to stop it. By means of this queer toy it is quite possible to bore a hole through a board or even saw wood.

Two startling inventions in connection with astronomy and hydrography are the work of Edison. These are, respectively, the tasimeter and the odoroscope. The former is an ingenious instrument in which the electrical resistance of carbon has been taken advantage of, as in many other of Edison's inventions. The name "tasimeter" is derived from the words meaning "extension" and "measure," because the effect is primarily to measure extension of any kind. The apparatus consists of a strip of hard rubber with pointed ends resting perpendicularly on a platinum plate beneath which is a carbon button, and below this

EDISON EXPERIMENTING IN HIS PRIVATE LABORATORY

SOME LESSER INVENTIONS

another platinum plate. The two plates and the carbon button form part of an electric circuit containing a battery and a galvanometer. The hard rubber is exceedingly sensitive to heat; the slightest degree of warmth imparted to it causes it to expand, thus increasing the pressure on the carbon button and producing a variation in the resistance of the circuit, which is, of course, immediately registered by the galvanometer. The instrument is so sensitive that with a delicate galvanometer the warmth of a person's hand at a distance of thirty feet affects it very considerably. In astronomical observations it has been used most successfully. On one occasion the heat of the rays of light from the star Arcturus was measured in a very satisfactory manner.

The principle of the odoroscope is similar to that of the tasimeter, but a strip of gelatine takes the place of the hard rubber. Besides being affected by heat, it is exceedingly sensitive to moisture, a few drops of water thrown on the floor of the room being sufficient to give a very decided indication on the galvanometer in circuit with the instrument. Barometers, hygrometers, and similar instruments of great delicacy can be constructed on the principle of the odoroscope, and it may be employed in determining the character or pressure of gases and vapor in which it is placed.

Other inventions of Edison's — too technical for description in a work such as this — are the carbon rheostat, an instrument for altering the resistance of an electrical circuit; the pressure or carbon relay, for the translation of signals of variable strengths from one circuit to another; acoustic telegraph system, chemical telegraph, private line printers, printing telegraphs, electro-magnets, rheotomes or circuit directors, telegraph calls and signalling apparatus.

Edison was the first to see how important it was that dynamos should be made with massive field-magnets. His first large steam dynamo was built at Menlo Park, and was used to supply the current for 700 lamps. In 1881 he built a dynamo of a size which staggered the electrical world. It weighed twenty-seven tons, the armature being built of bars of copper instead of wire, which alone weighed six tons. It was exhibited at Paris, London, Milan, and New York, and created the greatest sensation.

The pyro-magnetic motor, the pyro-magnetic generator, the microphone (called after him), the magnetic bridge (for testing the magnetic properties of iron), the electro-motograph, the motograph receiver, the etheroscope, the chalk battery, methods for preserving fruit *in vacuo* without cooking, vacuum pumps, the telephonograph, and the "dead beat" galvanometer (peculiar from the fact that it has no coils or magnetic needle) are a few more inventions for which Edison has been granted patents. It might here be mentioned that a single invention often carries with it scores of patents, and this is the case with several of Edison's conceptions. In the line of phonographs, for instance, he has secured a hundred and one patents, on storage batteries twenty patents, on electric meters twenty patents, on telegraphs a hundred and forty-seven patents, on telephones thirty-two patents, on electric lights a hundred and sixty-nine patents, and on ore-milling machinery fifty-three patents. When it is remembered that an incandescent lamp consists simply of a carbon filament in an exhausted glass globe, the ingenuity in devising one hundred and sixty-nine different patentable modifications and improvements on such device appears really marvellous.

Queer inventions have been ascribed to Edison

from time to time, and the great electrician is of immense service to the imaginative American reporter who finds himself hard up for a "good story." The conscienceless newspaper man will get hold of what he believes is a brilliant, if impracticable, idea, and which he knows would look well (with a few nightmare illustrations) in a Sunday newspaper, so he sets to work and proceeds to turn out something really startling. It is necessary, however, to father the "story" on some scientist, and who better known than Edison? So the unblushing space-writer couples with his imaginings the name of the great inventor, feeling pretty safe in the thought that his victim, like royalty, is far too busy to contradict all the wonderful statements which are published about him.

Some time ago, for example, an American paper came out with a startling story of how Edison had conceived a plan whereby torpedo-boats would henceforth be rendered useless in times of war. "The apparatus," said this sensation-loving journal, "is in the form of canisters of calcium carbide with a small quantity of calcium phosphide mixed in, to be placed in the scouting boats or fired into the water at a distance from a mortar. These canisters, being provided with buoyant chambers and water vents, would give off acetylene gas, and also spontaneously inflammable phosphoretted hydrogen, which would serve to ignite continuously the acetylene gas. The result would be powerful lights, very cheaply produced, in great numbers over an area of several square miles. Any torpedo-boat coming nearer than one mile of those lights would be thrown into silhouette, which, to the eye, would be at least fifty times more powerful than the small reflection from the light-absorbing surface of a torpedo-boat illuminated by the most powerful electric light. This is Edison's plan.

It simply cuts the torpedo-boat out of naval warfare as an important factor."

Many other queer inventions have been ascribed to Edison. At one time an enterprising newspaper, whose policy might be described as saffron-hued, for several months published an "interview" with the inventor weekly, ascribing to him such weird and wonderful things that he at last became really alarmed lest a lunacy commission should be appointed to inquire into his sanity. Something had to be done, and the editor of the paper in question received an intimation that unless the series of "stories" came to an end legal proceedings would be taken. Being a wise man, the editor reflected that it was scarcely dignified to go to law over the matter, and the series of "interviews" came to an abrupt conclusion. Among other strange inventions which this newspaper ascribed to Edison was one to be used for melting snow as rapidly as it fell. The work was to be accomplished by the use of electric and sunlight reflectors. "This," said the newspaper in question, "will make many a city boy, who has to shovel snow from the sidewalk, very happy, but it will at the same time rob many a poor man of a meal that he would otherwise get for doing that work. The invention will have its greatest utility in clearing transcontinental railway tracks."

These "interviews" called forth an angry letter from the inventor in 1898, addressed to a leading New York daily, of which the following is a copy:

"SIR, — I wish to protest through the *Sun* against the many articles appearing in the sensational papers of New York from time to time purporting to be interviews with me about wonderful inventions and discoveries made or to be made by myself. Scarcely a single one is authentic, and the statements purporting to be made by me are the inventions of the reporter. The public are led from these articles to draw conclusions just the opposite of the facts. I have never made it a practice to work on any line not purely practical and useful, and I especially desire it to be known, if you will permit me, that I have nothing to do with an article advertised to appear in one of the papers about Mars.

"T. A. EDISON."

But the story which, perhaps, caused Edison the greatest amount of annoyance was one published half a dozen years ago. "I laugh at it now," said the inventor, "but at the time I did not think it quite so amusing. One of the 'boys' (newspaper men) came down here one day, and not being able to see me or get any startling information from any of my associates, he went home, probably feeling somewhat aggrieved, and wrote up a story of his own invention. He declared, in a very lucid and descriptive way, that I was shortly bringing out a new and very ingenious shirt which would last the ordinary man twelve months or longer if he were economical. The front of the shirt, he declared, was made up of 365 very thin layers of a certain fibrous material — the composition of which was known only to the inventor — and each morning that the wearer put the garment on, all he had to do to restore the front to its usual pristine spotlessness, was to tear off one of the 'layers,' when he would have practically a new shirt. The writer declared that I myself wore these shirts, and that I considered the invention the biggest thing I had yet accomplished. Well, the story was published in about five hundred papers in the States, and the queer part was that so many of the readers believed the statements to be true. Every one seemed to hanker after possessing one of these shirts, and I soon began to receive requests for supplies varying from one to a hundred dozens from all parts of the country. At first I gave orders that a letter should be sent to these would-be buyers of the 'Edison shirt' informing them that the story was untrue and that I hadn't tried my hand at patent clothing yet, but the letters continued to come in in such numbers that this soon became impossible. Many of the writers enclosed drafts and checks, and these, of course, had to be returned. Then the story got into the papers of other countries, and every race of people from Chinamen to South Africans, all seemed desirous of getting some of these shirts. Many writers begged that if I didn't sell the shirts myself would I inform them where they could be obtained. The idea, they were pleased to add, was a grand one, and they'd be happy if they could only get hold of a few. Did I want any agents to push the goods? For more than a year orders for the 'Edison Patent Shirts' poured in, until at last the public began to realize that it had been hoaxed and turned its attention to something else. But it was a foolish story, and if I could have got hold of the young man who wrote it up, I guess he wouldn't have wanted a shirt or anything else on his back for a few weeks."

Edison was once asked if he could not invent something to prevent people growing old. He laughed at the question, and declared that though he didn't think he could some one else might in the dim future. He referred to the sacrifice of animal life and the injection of serums to replace worn tissues. The interviewer published his remarks at length, with some additions, and even stated that it was the belief of Edison and others that old age was simply due to molecular physiological changes made in a certain direction. In other words, when we are enabled to reverse the motion of these molecules we can make each birthday reduce our age one year, or go backward or forward alternately as we wish. This novel idea, which in all probability had its origin more or less in the brain of the interviewer, called forth a good deal of interesting and amusing correspondence, and many poets waxed eloquent on the possibilities of "reversing molecules."

It is said that the medical pharmacopœia owes to Edison the discovery of one of the drugs now used in the treatment of gout, viz., hydrate of tetra-ethyl ammonium. The story of its discovery is thus related:

"Edison met a friend one day, and on hearing that he was a great sufferer, and noting the swellings of his finger-joints, asked, with his usual curiosity:

"'What is the matter?'

"'Gout,' replied the sufferer.

"'Well, but what is gout?' persisted Edison.

"'Deposits of uric acid in the joints,' came the reply.

"'Why don't the doctors cure you?' asked Edison.

"'Because uric acid is insoluble,' he was told.

"'I don't believe it,' said Edison, and he straightway journeyed to his laboratory, put forth innumerable glass tumblers, and into them emptied some of every chemical which he possessed. Into each he let fall a few drops of uric acid and then awaited results. Investigation forty-eight hours later disclosed that the uric acid had dissolved in two of the chemicals. One of these is used to-day in the treatment of gout diseases."

CHAPTER XIII

WAR MACHINES

TEN or twelve years ago, when the Venezuelan matters came to a crisis, a discussion arose in America as to the capabilities of the country to defend herself in case of war. The press was full of suggestions for self-defence from all kinds of people — from men expert in warfare and from others who, apparently, had never seen a gun. Many scientists and electricians whose opinions were considered valuable were consulted, and among these was Edison. An interviewer called at the Orange laboratory one morning and plied the inventor with so many questions that Edison proceeded to fill him up with an astounding number of electrical devices whereby America might protect herself from the invader. He had hundreds of original and startling ideas, and he handed them out as freely as a home missionary distributes tracts.

Edison had some years before invented, in conjunction with W. Scot Sims, a submarine torpedo-boat to be operated by electricity, and he first of all suggested that this deadly instrument of war would prove a machine of excellent use in case of trouble. In this invention — Edison's solitary contribution to those devices whose primary object is the destruction of life — the torpedo proper is suspended from a long float so as to be submerged a few feet under water, and contains the electric motor for propulsion and steering, and the explosive charge. The torpedo is controlled from the shore or ship through an electric cable, which it pays out as it goes along, and all operations of varying the speed, reversing and steering, are effected by means of currents sent through the cable. Edison pointed out that this torpedo-boat could be sent a couple of miles ahead of a man-of-war, and could be kept at that distance under absolute control ready to blow up anything within reach.

Having referred to his torpedo-boat, Edison next proceeded to discuss other ideas for the defence of the country which were then simmering through his brain. He declared that electricity would play a leading part in any war between America and another country, and it would be possible to keep an enemy very much at bay by merely using streams of water charged with electricity. From small forts occupied by a dozen men or less it would be easy to control the advance of the enemy, no matter in what numbers they might come. Each fort would be furnished with an alternating machine of 20,000 volts capacity, and it would require but one man to operate a stream of water connected with the deadly current and play on the enemy. Just as soon as the water struck an invader, or a group of invaders, the circuit would be complete, and the men would go down so quickly that they'd never know what had hit them.

When once started on a description of this novel means of defence Edison himself became deeply interested, and, being a humane man, assured his interviewer, whose eyes were beginning to bulge, that the wholesale destruction might be modified and the current so reduced that those who felt its force would merely be stunned. It would all depend on the temper of the operator. If he felt in a stunning mood the enemy would be shocked only, but, on the other hand, if he saw that death was necessary he might turn on the full current. Supposing he decided that to stun was sufficient, then, after those who had escaped the deadly stream had retired, the occupants of the forts could go out and pick up the enemy and make them prisoners. Should the prisoners become so numerous that it was impossible to control them, however, they might be treated to another and a stronger dose of electrically charged water, and thus be permanently put out of the way of doing further damage. This was an alternative, however, which Edison, being tender-hearted, did not advocate.

But the inventor had other ideas equally novel and effective. He had visions of an aërial torpedo-boat which would fly over the ship of an enemy and drop a hundred pounds of dynamite down her hold. These birds of destruction would be furnished with a self-steering gear and a fuse timed to act so many minutes or hours after being cut loose from the ship. The cost of these aërial torpedo-boats would not be great, and those who used them might well afford to send up a flight of a hundred or so if the result was the destruction of a five-million-dollar war vessel.

The inventor then discussed other powers of destruction such as dynamite guns, after which the interviewer went home and wrote an article which not only brought great joy to his countrymen, but attracted the attention of European powers. England took the statements somewhat seriously, and a leading provincial daily newspaper — it would be unkind to mention its name — published the following remarks in a "leader":

"For the moment we are tempted to think that Mr. Edison must be mad, if there is any truth in the report which has appeared of an interview with that very

EDISON REPLYING TO SOME PUZZLING QUESTIONS

wonderful man, in the course of which he spoke of the murderous inventions he has ready for the service of his country in the event of war with any other nation. We protest against Mr. Edison directing his extraordinary inventive genius which God has given him into such channels. We would even give our hearty adhesion to the old sentiment, that all things are fair enough in love and war. But to attack an enemy with such 'resources of civilization' as those of which Mr. Edison speaks is not war, it is simply wholesale slaughter of a kind which would be intolerably wicked and cruel, and which no nation with any self-respect would permit to be exercised. Let Mr. Edison continue to direct his enormous talents into more peaceful channels for the benefit of a world which is heavily indebted to him already for his marvellous inventions. We do not say this because we fear for our soldiers. They have faced danger so bravely and in so many ways, and have held their lives as nought where the honour of old England has been concerned, that we do not doubt they would meet Edison's engines of destruction if they knew it was their duty. But the sentiment of the matter does not excuse the wickedness of the ideas attributed — we hope unjustly — to the greatest inventor of his time."

Then the London papers took up the matter and discussed Edison's propositions in all seriousness. Lord Armstrong was appealed to by an excited correspondent, and received from the British inventor the following letter:

"CRAGSIDE, ROTHBURY, *December* 27, 1895.

"DEAR SIR, — If the words attributed to Mr. Edison are correctly reported, which I greatly doubt, I must say that this great inventor is both hard to understand and extravagantly sanguine. Designs which exist only in idea are seldom of much account, and Mr. Edison would be more than human if his brain were capable of evolving matured inventions of astounding potency in war requiring no protracted trials to fit them for practical application. In such matters models and laboratory experiments go for very little on this side of the Atlantic. Nothing short of trials on a scale of actual practice can be relied upon, and these, if made, would, from their nature, be incapable of concealment, so that the advantage of sole possession would speedily vanish. Transcendent inventions, even when coming from an Edison, should always be received with incredulity in the absence of tangible proof, and Lord Salisbury is himself too much of an electrician to be moved from his serenity by any threats of wholesale electrical destruction which Mr. Edison in the fervour of his patriotism may have uttered."

France also took an interest in Edison's war inventions, and while England was discussing the proposed dynamite guns and aërial torpedoes, a Parisian paper made its appearance with the following skit, which imagines Edison in his laboratory hearing the news of a declaration of war between Great Britain and the United States. A young man, his assistant, rushes in, pale and out of breath, and exclaims to the great electrician:

"Oh, master, war is declared! It is terrible!"

"Ah!" says the master. "War declared, eh? And where is the British army at this moment?"

"Embarking, sir."

"Embarking where?"

"At Liverpool."

"At Liverpool — yes. Now, my friend, would you

WAR MACHINES

please join the ends of those two wires hanging there against the wall? That is right. Now bring them to me. Good. Now be kind enough to press the button."

The assistant, wondering and half-amused, presses the button.

"Very well," says the inventor. "Now do you know what is taking place at Liverpool?"

"The British army is embarking, sir."

The inventor pulls out his watch and glances at the time. "There is no British army," he says curtly.

"What?" screams the assistant.

"When you touched that button you destroyed it."

"Oh, this is frightful!"

"It is not frightful at all. It is science. Now, every time a British expedition embarks at any port please come and tell me at once. Ten seconds afterwards it will simply be out of existence. That is all."

"There does not seem to be any reason why America should be afraid of its enemies after this, sir."

"I am inclined to believe you," says the master, smiling slightly. "But in order to avoid further trouble, I think it would be best to destroy England altogether."

"To — to destroy England, sir——"

"Kindly touch button No. 4 there."

The assistant touches it. The inventor counts ten.

"... eight, nine, ten — it is all over. There is no more England."

"Oh! oh!" screams the young man.

"Now we can go on quietly with our work," says the master. "And if we should be at war with any other nation you have only to notify me. I have an electric button connected with every foreign country which will destroy it when pressed. In ten minutes I could destroy every country in the world, the United

States included. Be careful, now, that you don't touch any of those buttons accidentally — you might do a lot of damage!"

All these stories and skits were highly diverting to Edison, who was vastly astonished that his innocent, if imaginative, remarks on what might be accomplished in the way of electrically devised war engines should have been taken so seriously and created such a sensation. What he did regret, however, was the statement that he was especially inventing destructive machines for use in case of war with England. There would never be such a war, he declared, and so the suggestion that he was devising engines to assist in the annihilation of the old country was absurd. At the time of the discussion Edison gave his opinion on England and her wars, in the course of which he said that usually Great Britain took from two to three years to get down to business, during which time most things went wrong. But she hung on and finally "got there" when the other fellow was tired out. In substance he agreed with the man who declared that what had made England was not its head but its body. This opinion was curiously verified some years later when war broke out between that country and South Africa.

But though Edison has not given much attention to the creation of war machines he has experimented quite a little with explosives, and their peculiarities have always had a fascination for him. In his early days — when he was a boy selling newspapers — he liked experimenting with things that might possibly explode, and while a "cub" operator he compounded a kind of gun-cotton sufficiently strong to blow the front of the stove out. Edison does not consider dynamite, even when roughly handled, in any way dangerous, but regards it as the safest explosive we possess. In the magnetic separation of ores Edison used a great deal of dynamite, and as an object-lesson to the men he on several occasions took them into the woods surrounding the mines to prove to them how safe an explosive dynamite really was. He would burn it before them, throw rocks at it, and all together treat it with considerable contempt. He did this in order to prove to them that with ordinary care dynamite might be relied upon to behave itself. The men learned their lesson well, for ever since then, though they have handled tons of the explosive, not a single accident has occurred.

Nitro-glycerine, on the other hand, is dangerous at all times. Put a drop of it on a table and touch it with a hammer and you and the table and the hammer will in all probability leave the house together. But even this explosive is comparatively safe compared with iodide of nitrogen, whose explosive power is equal to 4000 feet a second, which is nearly four times the velocity of sound. In his experiments with explosives Edison has made some so sensitive that they would "go off" if shouted at. A drop placed on the table and yelled at would explode. "You see," he said in explaining this curious phenomenon, "the thing is in a state of very delicate equilibrium. It is a question depending on surrounding conditions as to which it will do — remain a liquid or turn into gas. When this balance is about equal it takes very little to incline it toward a gaseous form, so that even the sound of the voice will cause a change. A violent fit of coughing will produce the effect, and so would a heavy weight dropped on the floor."

Edison regards these highly sensitive explosives with a good deal of affection, for by means of one he was, years ago, enabled to find a way out of what appeared at the time to be something of a difficulty. While conducting his experiments in explosives he was one morning visited by some ministers who insisted on boring him very considerably in his laboratory. The inventor treated them, as he treats every one, courteously and kindly, but as the day wore on and there was no sign of their retiring, he began to think that it would be necessary to hint to them that they were monopolizing rather more of his time than he could very well afford to spare. So he casually informed them that he was experimenting with very delicate explosives and he would be sorry if any of them got hurt.

But this only had the effect of increasing their interest, and they got in his way, distracted him by foolish questions, and made him generally nervous and — almost — irritable. The inventor heaved a scarcely concealed sigh and set himself the task of evolving a plan whereby he could get rid of them without appearing to be rude. After a few minutes an excellent idea suggested itself, and taking some of the material that he had been experimenting with he put a drop or two about the room — in places where there was no danger of a minister being blown through the window. The visitors watched him with growing interest, apparently felt no uneasiness at his actions, but rather crowded round him the more. Then the inventor took a seat at the bench and continued his investigations. Presently he jumped up with a dramatic "I have it!" and knocked a heavy board off the table, which fell with a crash to the floor. What followed was rather worse than even Edison had intended. No windows were broken, but through the deafening explosion which occurred, a number of glass bottles were smashed, an electrical apparatus put out of business, a table overturned, and the ministers frightened almost out of their wits. They put their hands to their heads in evident fear of something worse, and then asked what had happened. Edison took the matter very coolly, and explained that such explosions were constantly happening, though he was glad to say they hadn't killed any one since the fall. He hoped there would not be another bust-up that day, but you never could tell. The ministers declared it was all very interesting, but they guessed they'd better be going, and grabbing their hats they hastily bade the inventor good-by and departed.

The above story recalls the fact that Edison's faculties are frequently put to severe tests in devising methods for getting rid of unwelcome visitors. "On one occasion a reporter called to see the inventor, and as the paper he represented was not one which had Edison's sympathy — it had several times been guilty of ascribing to him various ridiculous statements which had no foundation — he was desirous of getting rid of him speedily but without offence. So he asked the reporter if he objected to his talking while continuing his experiments in the inner chemical laboratory, and the visitor expressed himself as being delighted. It would give an added interest to the interview. So they adjourned to Edison's own private room in the laboratory, and the inventor again asked to be excused talking until he had his apparatus in order.

"He got out a machine peculiar for its power of charging the surrounding atmosphere with a certain form of oxygen highly objectionable to any one but the most enthusiastic scientist, and soon had the engine going full blast. Of course, Edison didn't mind the fumes in the least, and he smilingly turned to his caller with his usual cheery 'Well, what can I do for you?'

But the reporter was speechless, the fumes had got down into his throat and into his eyes, and, it appeared to him, were making their way through his ears into his brain. He attempted to put the questions with which he had come fully charged, but it was impossible by reason of his choking and coughing. He was obliged himself to bring the interview to a sudden close, and begged leave to retire, greatly to the well-feigned surprise of the inventor, who, by his manner, appeared somewhat offended at the reporter's hasty retreat. Whether the man ever suspected the trick that had been played upon him is a question, but there is no doubt about his failing to return to the laboratory to continue his interrupted interview with the joke-loving inventor."

CHAPTER XIV

ELECTROCUTION

THE question is sometimes raised as to whether Edison invented the machine by which condemned criminals in certain states are electrocuted. He did not, though when the apparatus was being installed at Auburn, he visited the prison and inspected the interesting instrument whereby murderers who commit their crimes in the state of New York are sometimes shocked out of existence. Moreover, when experiments were being conducted to decide whether or not electrocution should be adopted as the capital sentence in lieu of hanging, Edison placed his Menlo Park laboratory at the disposal of the investigators and allowed some of his electricians to assist in the work of investigation.

When the idea of adopting electrocution as a means of punishing murderers was first suggested it was laughed at, and the majority of the newspapers made merry over what they regarded as a jest. They declared that such a form of execution would never be adopted in America. But, to the surprise of many, the idea found favor with the Governor of New York State, and a commission consisting of Dr. Carlos F. MacDonald, Medical Superintendent of the Auburn Asylum for Insane Criminals; Dr. A. D. Rockwell, a celebrated investigator of electrical phenomena; Dr. Edward Tatum, Harold P. Brown, an electrical engineer, and others, was appointed to inquire into the matter, and the members at once set about making certain experiments to determine whether electrocution was not, after all, a more humane form of execution than hanging.

Edison was appealed to, and though the subject was not one with which he had much sympathy — he declared that he would be sorry to see electricity put to so bad a use — he acceded to the request that certain experimental work might be conducted at Menlo Park, and cheerfully put at the disposal of the investigators a large building at the rear of the laboratory, where numerous experiments were conducted. Harold P. Brown was appointed by the state to carry out these experiments, the primary object of which was to decide the place and method of applying the electrodes in order to produce death with the minimum amount of pain. It had previously been decided that the only current producing a satisfactory result was that known as the "alternating," and in all experiments conducted at Menlo Park this current was employed. It may be mentioned that this alternating current is one which, instead of giving the victim a continuous shock, strikes a series of blows at the rate of three or four hundred a second. In all electrocutions carried out at Sing Sing and Auburn prisons the alternating current is employed.

The experiments to decide the merits of electrocution over hanging took place on March 2, 1889, in the large wooden building which Edison had had fitted up with every electrical appliance necessary for the purpose. The victims chosen were several dogs, four calves, and a horse. The dogs claimed the attention of the experimenters first, and a big black Newfoundland quietly submitted to being weighed — he turned the scale at close on ninety pounds — and then with the same docility allowed a small plate of brass, covered with felt and soaked in a solution of salt, to be tied to his head, while a bandage moistened with the same lotion was fixed to his right leg with a piece of copper wire. Lest he might show a desire to run away, the animal was made to stand in a box, but flight seemed far from his intention. He seemed as interested in the experiments as any one present.

The dog's "resistance" was next computed by means of two fine wires connected with the electrodes, to which was attached a registering instrument. A slight shock was then sent through the animal — so slight that he scarcely winced — but of sufficient strength to correctly record his power to withstand the electric current. Heavy wires then took the place of the fine ones, the current was turned on, and the animal immediately stiffened. There was a slight tendency to leap forward, but it was momentary, and the animal remained perfectly still. The current was kept up for ten seconds, and when turned off the dog dropped in a heap perfectly dead.

The calves died just as easily. They weighed about 100 pounds and were given 800 volts each, and the current kept up for fifteen seconds. In the case of the horse 1000 volts of electricity were used and continued for twenty-five seconds. Death in each case appeared to be instantaneous. All those who took part in the experiment declared that they proved that death by electricity was more rapid and less painful than any other form of execution. The commission recommended that for the greater comfort of human victims a well-fitting helmet should take the place of the brass plate, while the bandage on the leg might with advantage be discarded in favor of a shoe furnished with a metallic sole. They added that the prisoner should be bound in an arm-chair, and inasmuch as human resistance was always greater than animal resistance — though it varied in every individual — 2000 volts might be counted upon to satisfactorily perform the happy despatch. It was at that time stated on the authority of the commission that a 1000-volt continuous current might be taken by any person in ordinary health without permanent inconvenience.

During the time that these experiments were in progress the state held prisoner a certain murderer named Kemmler, on whom they were very anxious to try the new form of execution. He was ultimately sentenced "to suffer death by electricity at Auburn Prison within the week beginning Monday, June 24, 1889."

But after many experiments had satisfied the commission that electrocution was the most humane of capital punishments, W. Bourke Cockran, an ex-Congressman, "in the interests of love of humanity and a desire to prevent an inhuman execution" (to quote his own words), took up the case, and for months fought the state's agent, Harold P. Brown, in an effort to save Kemmler from the chair. The case created the greatest sensation, and twice the prisoner was reprieved while evidence was collected to prove the unlawfulness of the new method of execution. Edison figured prominently in this evidence, and Mr. Cockran, knowing his views to be opposed to capital punishment, called him early as a witness. But he proved a disappointment in furthering the cause of the humane lawyer, for the question was not one of sentiment but whether or not electrocution meant instantaneous death. Edison had had the "resistance" of several hundred men in his employ taken, and was therefore well primed on the subject. The day on which he gave his evidence the court room was crowded to the doors by people attracted, not so much by the peculiarly morbid nature of the case as by a burning desire to see and hear the great electrician. It was one of the few occasions on which the inventor appeared in a court of justice, and he proved an excellent witness. Deputy Attorney-General Poste conducted the case, and the distinguished witness was put through a stiff cross-examination. At this late date it is interesting to recall Edison's remarks in court on this occasion. He was evidently quite at his ease, and answered the questions promptly.

"What is your calling or profession?" Mr. Poste asked.

"Inventor," briefly replied the witness.

"Have you devoted a great deal of attention to the subject of electricity?"

"Yes."

"How long have you been engaged in the work of an inventor or electrician?"

"Twenty-six years."

In reply to questions he said he was familiar with the various dynamos and their construction, and that they all generated either a continuous or an alternating current.

"A continuous current," Edison said, "is one that flows like water through a pipe. An alternating current is the same as if a body of water were allowed to flow through the pipe in one direction for a given time and then its direction reversed for a given time."

The witness said he had been present when the measurements were made in his laboratory to determine the resistance of human beings. Two hundred and fifty persons were measured, and their average resistance was 1000 ohms, the highest being 1800 ohms, and the lowest 600.

"Will you describe the method of the application of your tests?" Mr. Poste asked.

"We took two battery jars about seven inches in diameter and ten inches high, and put in each jar a plate of copper. In the jar we put water with a 10 per cent solution of caustic potash. The men we measured plunged their hands into the liquid so that the ends of their fingers touched the bottom of the jars. After waiting thirty seconds the measurement was taken.

"Where, in your opinion, is the major part of the resistance located?" Mr. Poste asked.

"I should say 15 per cent at the point of contact. The balance in the body."

"What is the law that governs the passage of an electric current, when several paths of varying resistance are offered to it?"

"It divides in proportion to the resistance encountered."

"Please explain the burning effects sometimes produced in the case of contact with an electric wire."

"It is due to bad contact, and the difference in resistance between the wire and the flesh."

"In your judgment can an artificial electric current be generated and applied in such a manner as to produce death in human beings in every case?"

"Yes."

"Instantly?"

"Yes." He advised placing the culprit's hands in a jar of water diluted with caustic potash and connecting the electrodes therewith, and, he said, 1000 volts of alternating current would surely produce death instantaneously. He did not think so small a continuous current would, although by mechanically intermitting the continuous current it could be made very deadly.

Mr. Cockran, in his cross-examination, laid much stress upon Edison's views as to the resistance of human beings.

"Did you make the experiments on the men which you have mentioned with a view to ascertaining just how to measure the resistance of Kemmler and find out how men may differ in the matter of resistance?" asked Mr. Cockran.

"I did. I made experiments the day before yesterday," Edison replied.

"And you found out there were different degrees of resistance in different men?"

"Yes, but that does not mean that the same current would not kill all men."

"What would be the effect of the current on Kemmler in case the current was applied for five or six minutes? Would he not be carbonized?"

"No," replied Edison, with a ghost of a smile. "He would be mummified. All the water in his body would evaporate in five or six minutes."

With what he had found to be the average resistance of the human body, Edison said that 1000 volts would give a man an ampère of current, which is ten times as much as any man needs to kill him. In reply to a question, he replied that there was an alternating dynamo in London that generated a 10,000-volt current, and he considered it safe to double up dynamos to increase the current for use in executions.

"That is your belief, not from knowledge?" Mr. Cockran asked.

"From belief. I never killed anybody," the witness quietly replied.

Many other witnesses were called to speak for and against electrocution, hundreds of scientists, electricians, and doctors were consulted; opinions of well-known men and women were cabled over from England and the Continent, thousands of editorials were written on the subject in the daily press, and letters from private individuals addressed to newspapers of all countries poured into their offices in one continuous stream. Meanwhile Kemmler remained in jail mildly wondering whether it was to be hanging or electrocution. Apparently the question was not one which greatly disturbed him, for he spent the greater part of his time composing doggerel verses and singing them at the top of his voice to tunes which he had learned when he was free. He had been reprieved twice, but this was principally owing to a desire on the part of the authorities to preserve him until the question of electrocution had been satisfactorily settled, and in no way indicated any sentiment in his favor. In July, 1890, it was finally decided that punishment by electricity should come into force in the state of New York, and Kemmler was the prisoner chosen to prove the wisdom or otherwise of the decision. His death was fixed for August 6, in Auburn Prison, and when informed of this he merely smiled without making any remark. In face of the fact that he was going to an uncertain and perhaps torturing death his courage was remarkable. To witness his death — perhaps the most dramatic that has ever taken place in connection with American criminal law — the warden of Auburn Prison was empowered to send out "twenty-one invitations." With two exceptions he invited men from the ranks of science. Each man accepted and each was present at Kemmler's death, with the exception of Edison.

The room in which the dynamo stood was in the northeast wing of the prison, from 800 to 1000 feet from the execution room. The dynamo used was the ordinary commercial Westinghouse machine capable of producing a current of 1500 volts. The current employed on Kemmler varied from 800 to 1300 volts. The dynamo was run by an engine in the basement of the prison. The wires which carried the current were run out of a window of the dynamo room to the roof of the jail and along the roof to a point directly over the room first chosen for the death-chamber in the southern wing of the prison. From this room two small wires ran to the engine and dynamo room. These wires were the means of communication between the room in which the switchboard was fastened and the men in charge of both the dynamo and engines, and a code of signals had been arranged by them. The wires were attached to electric bells. Two rings of the bell was the signal to start the engine, and a succeeding double ring was a command to increase the power. One ring meant to stop the machinery.

The switchboard was 5 feet long by $3\frac{1}{2}$ feet broad, and upon this were a voltmeter, resistance-box, lamp-board, a regulating switch which governed the lamps, an ammeter to measure the quantity of electricity in the current, and the switch which when turned sent the current through Kemmler's body. The wires used were of the largest size electric-light wires. One of these ran directly from the chair, while the other passed through the ammeter to the switch. The voltmeter was governed by a wire leading directly to the death-chair, by two branches running from it. One branch ran into the resistance-box, and the other into the voltmeter. The electrodes in which the wires ended were in rubber cups, in each of which was a sponge saturated with a solution of caustic soda.

Since that first electrocution in Auburn Prison there

have been close upon a hundred similar executions in the state of New York. The methods adopted seventeen years ago are very similar to those in use to-day, and death in the chair is a good deal easier than hanging, guillotining, or garrotting; but still Edison, who unwillingly assisted in electrocution becoming law, continues to affirm he deeply regrets that electricity ever came to be put to so bad a use. But apart from that, he is averse to capital punishment, and one of his wise sayings which will be remembered is the following: "There are wonderful possibilities in each human soul, and I cannot endorse a method of punishment which destroys the last chance of usefulness."

CHAPTER XV

THE STORAGE BATTERY

EDISON has secured twenty patents on his storage battery, and in working out the details of what may be regarded as one of his favorite inventions he has spent many years of unceasing labor. Literally thousands of experiments have been made, but the final results have been so satisfactory that the battery has at last passed out of his hands and is now in charge of the manufacturers. During 1906 he devoted almost his entire time to the perfecting of his storage battery, for though he had brought it to such a state of perfection that out of five thousand less than 4 per cent were imperfect, this did not satisfy him. Throughout his life Edison has always adhered to one inflexible rule — a rule which he made in the early days when he first began to be known as an inventor — never to send anything out of his laboratory that was not absolutely perfect. He has therefore refrained from placing his storage battery on the market, in spite of the temptation to thereby refute the many statements that have appeared in the press declaring that his experiments in this direction have ended in failure. Now the huge factories which are going up in Orange for the sole purpose of making the Edison storage battery bear silent witness to the final success of this important invention.

Said one of his men who has worked with him on

the storage battery for many years: "Ninety-nine out of every hundred — perhaps nine hundred and ninety-nine out of every thousand — inventors would have been satisfied with the improvements made four or five years ago, and put the battery on the market and reaped a rich reward, but Edison is made differently. He aims at perfection, and as a rule hits the mark. He doesn't 'blow' about a thing until it is completed, and when it is he lets the thing blow for itself. These batteries, which the public will soon be able to sample for themselves, have been subjected to tests which can only be described as 'heroic.' A year or so ago we had half a dozen machines, all of different designs and weights, fitted with Edison storage batteries, and then sent, in charge of skilful mechanics, over the roughest roads in New Jersey. The trips were scheduled by Mr. Edison himself, who was determined to subject the batteries to tests which would reduce the machines themselves to scrap-iron. Daily each machine had to accomplish a hundred miles until five thousand miles had been covered. The worst possible roads were chosen, and when a machine struck a track which was particularly heavy and bad, that track was covered several times during the day until the hundred miles had been accomplished. For sixty days these trials continued, and at the end of that time the machines were little less than wrecks. Many sets of tires were worn out, axles split, and screws wrenched out in the terrible jolts, but when we came to examine the batteries we found that in no single instance had the slightest injury been received. The automobiles were fit only for the scrap-heap, but the batteries were in perfect condition for another five-thousand-mile trip.

"Besides these tests which the batteries underwent

CHARGING AN EDISON STORAGE BATTERY IN THE GARAGE ATTACHED TO THE LABORATORY

THE STORAGE BATTERY

in covering the rough New Jersey roads, they were subjected to another trial of their strength in the laboratory — a final test which, one might think, would have smashed them to bits. This test was carried out as follows: A cell was fastened to the loose end of a four-foot board, to which a small electric motor was geared. Every five minutes or so the motor would raise that end of the board to which the cell was attached three feet in the air, and let it drop with a crash which would have 'busted' any ordinary piece of machinery. But the cell evidently felt little of the jar, for after every hour or so when damage was looked for the battery appeared as strong and healthy as before."

In his storage battery Edison made the interesting discovery that cobalt was the material best suited to the making of the condenser. He had a long search for this remarkable metal, which is generally found in small quantities only, and he was lucky enough to strike a rich vein running from a point just east of Nashville, Tenn., across the line into North Carolina. This discovery of a bed of cobalt was to Edison a find as rich as a gold mine would be to the ordinary mortal, in spite of the fact that up to that time it was not regarded in any way as a precious metal or even a useful one. Indeed, its uselessness is signified by its name, which is derived from the German "Kobold," meaning "evil-minded spirit."

It will be readily understood that in the manufacture of a perfect storage battery one of the hardest nuts to crack was the invention of an ideal accumulator or condenser — that portion of the battery capable of containing large quantities of electricity. Early in his experiments Mr. Edison discarded lead as being heavy and cumbersome, and with his usual remarkable powers of deduction concluded that the metal he was looking for was cobalt. But he was confronted by an almost insuperable difficulty. Cobalt had never been found save in small quantities, and it was necessary to discover a mine of it if the metal was to be of any real use. He set experts to work hunting for cobalt, and they carried on the search with the same persistency which had characterized those men in bygone days who had set out to find a bamboo suitable for an incandescent filament. And the result, as before stated, was the discovery of cobalt in Tennessee, and in quantities which even satisfied the inventor himself. Cobalt, as readers are probably well aware, is invariably associated with nickel compounds or united with arsenic and sulphur, never being found native save in some meteorites. It is a reddish white metal, lustrous, tenacious, difficult of fusing, may be magnetized, and will retain its magnetism even when raised to a red heat. Cobalt was the material, therefore, for an ideal accumulator, and went far towards assisting in the perfecting of the Edison storage battery.

Two years ago Edison made the following statement in the press: "I believe that the problem of vehicular traffic in cities has at last been solved. The new electric storage cell weighs 40 pounds per horsepower hour. The present lead battery of the same efficiency weighs from 85 to 100 pounds. I believe that the solution of vehicular traffic in cities is to be found in the electric wagon. Leaving off the horse reduces the length of the vehicle one-half. Electric power will double the speed. With the new electric wagon, the vehicular traffic of cities can be increased four times without producing any more congestion than at present. That will be a great gain in every way.

The new storage cell will last from six to eight years. That is proved by actual experiments. I have one cell which has been in constant use for more than five years. The new cell will not cost more than the painting and the tires of the wagon. I do not think the cost of operation will be quite as great as the cost of horses. There again we shall have an advantage."

The Edison storage battery may be run fifty, seventy-five, and a hundred miles without recharging, and the construction is simplicity itself. It contains no acid and no organic matter in any form, so that corroding is impossible. The only attention it needs is to be kept full of water in order that "a liquid pathway may be provided along which oxygen may travel between the nickel and the iron." The weight of the cell is 40 pounds per horse-power hour, and it is as good at the end of a year as at the beginning. The weight of a storage battery, as every one who has run an automobile knows, is a serious consideration, for the greater the weight in the carriage the more speedily will the tires wear out. It therefore stands to reason that with a battery less than one-half the weight of that now in use the life of a tire will be doubled and perhaps trebled. And so the cost of automobiling will again be reduced. An Edison cell has been charged and discharged four hundred times without showing defects. In size it is $11\frac{1}{2} \times 5 \times 2$ inches, very compact and easy of handling. It contains a solution of potash in which are immersed steel plates containing oxide of iron and oxide of nickel. As soon as the battery is charged the oxide of iron is reduced to metallic iron, the oxide of nickel absorbs the freed oxygen and is thus raised to a higher oxide. When the battery is discharged, the oxygen absorbed by the nickel goes through the liquid over to the metallic iron and so oxidizes the iron back to the original state. That is to say, the oxygen burns the iron; but instead of getting heat we get electricity as a substitute. It is a species of internal combustion in which the oxygen is stored up in the nickel to burn the iron. There is no other reaction. The simple metallic elements are iron, nickel, and steel.

To recount all the details of the development of this perfected Edison storage battery would require an entire book — a book of much human nature, of intense interest, of hopes and fears, of many disappointments, and of final successful realization. In the first place, the defects of the old forms of storage batteries had to be analyzed, from which it was found that the objections were inseparable from these types. Consequently a definite ideal was fixed — a battery that should be cheap, light, compact, mechanically strong, absolutely permanent, and generally "fool" proof — and for the accomplishment of this ideal the energies of Edison and his assistants were directed.

It was immediately perceived that the use of an acid solution was out of the question, since that meant the employment of lead — the objections to which were fully appreciated. At the outset, therefore, it was determined to use an alkaline electrolyte, and the question then presented was as to the character of active materials to be used. In this search for suitable active materials practically the gamut of chemical elements was run; nothing was left untried, and in this investigation many remarkable and heretofore unknown discoveries were made.

After months of patient experimenting it was finally decided that the metals which possessed all the desirable properties *theoretically* were iron and nickel. When this was settled, the real inventive work began. That work involved the solution of the question how to obtain iron and nickel so as to get those elements in the proper condition of activity for practical use in a storage battery. Literally thousands of experiments were made in this particular direction, and processes were gradually developed by which the materials were finally secured in the desirable condition. The development of the two metals was carried on simultaneously, the effort, of course, being to obtain practically the energy which the metals should give theoretically. In this work the development of the iron would sometimes be far ahead that of the nickel, and then some new discovery would be made or some new process suggested by which the nickel would exceed the iron. Finally, the work had so far developed that practically the entire theoretical efficiency was secured for both materials.

At this point the mechanical make-up of the battery required consideration in order that a cell might be obtained capable of cheap manufacture, mechanically strong, durable, and compact. Unforeseen difficulties were met with in these investigations, as, for example, it was found that, in charging or discharging, one or other of the active masses in absorbing oxygen tended to swell; no solder was known that would resist the effects of electrolysis in a caustic solution; and it was also found that during charging the generated gases tended to carry off a fine spray of the alkali, so as thereby to deplete the electrolyte. All these difficulties and many others had to be overcome.

Even when the battery had been experimentally developed both mechanically and chemically, machines and processes had to be designed and invented by which the active materials could be made, the mechanical parts produced, and the battery assembled on a commercial scale. In all this work Edison was in the forefront, directing the experiments, suggesting modifications, preparing new processes, and designing new mechanical appliances, until to-day the Edison storage battery is a perfected entity, realizing all the ideal conditions that were laid down at the start, and crowning with success many years of the most patient, persistent, and indefatigable investigations that can be imagined.

CHAPTER XVI

THE LABORATORY AT ORANGE

The Edison laboratory at Orange consists of a group of buildings of impressive proportions, erected in the midst of green meadows and shady trees, and is probably more picturesquely situated than any other place of the kind in the world. The town of Orange is but forty minutes by rail from the metropolis, and is noted for its unrivalled scenery of hill and dale. Within a stone's throw of the laboratory is Llewellyn Park, the private residential quarter of the town, and one of the most beautiful localities in New Jersey. On the Orange Mountain were fought most of the "battles" which took place during the South African war — for the kinetoscope; and the writer well remembers seeing the eastern slope of Orange Mountain alive with men, "Boers" and "British," fighting for their rights in the famous engagement of Spion Kop. A good-sized cannon was used to heighten the effect, and the kinetoscope was in position taking the moving pictures when, through some blunder, the gun was discharged prematurely, and the "officer in command" and two of his men were struck by the wad and burnt by the powder. They were carried off the field on ambulances, and the incident added considerably to the success of the series of pictures, but during future engagements more reliable men were placed in charge of the ordnance, and thus realism was kept within reasonable bounds.

The main building of the Edison laboratory is 250 feet long and three stories high, while the four small buildings are each 100 feet by 25 feet and one story high. The laboratory is being constantly added to, and each year sees some improvement or enlargement. At the present time immense factories are being erected for the manufacture of the storage battery, but these buildings can hardly be included in the laboratory proper.

On first entering, one is ushered into a fine library, 100 feet square and fully 40 feet high. It has two spacious galleries containing a magnificent collection of minerals and gems which Edison purchased in Paris many years ago. The books which have been gathered together in this spacious room number close upon sixty thousand volumes, and include every magazine and journal dealing with scientific research published during the last forty years. They are in French, German, Italian, and English, for though Edison only speaks and writes his native tongue, he can read these foreign languages with considerable fluency.

The library is plainly but comfortably furnished. There are few rugs on the polished oaken floor, for Edison does not believe in carpets — they collect microbes and are, in consequence, far from healthful. The oak chairs are leather-seated, and carved on the back are Edison's initials in monogram form — T. A. E. There is a large table for "Board Meetings," as well as two roll-top desks, an immense clock which takes up almost one entire side of the room, various alcoves furnished with little tables for the convenience of those who desire to study, portraits of various famous scientists, a bust of Humboldt, and a statuette of Sandow. Edison's desk is situated in a corner of the room, but he is very seldom to be found at it, for he prefers to

LIBRARY AT THE EDISON LABORATORY, ORANGE, N.J.

spend his time in the chemical laboratory or the workshop. Beside the desk is a "corresponding phonograph," into which the inventor sometimes dictates his letters, which are afterwards transcribed by his secretary, J. F. Randolph.

The principal object of interest in the library is a life-sized statue entitled "The New Genius of Light," which Edison bought at the Paris Exposition of 1889, where it occupied the place of honor in the department devoted to Italian art. It is the work of A. Bordiga, of Rome, and Edison was so delighted with the subject as well as the treatment of the statue that he purchased it. Perhaps it was made for the express purpose of attracting Edison, and, if so, the sculptor succeeded admirably. It is an allegorical figure typifying the triumph of electricity over every other kind of illumination, represented by a youth with wings half spread leaning upon the broken fragments of a street gas lamp. High above his head he holds an incandescent lamp, while at his feet are grouped a voltaic pile, telephone transmitter, telegraph key, and gear wheel. The statue is mounted on a pedestal three feet high, and the electric lamp which is held aloft is one of fifty candle-power.

Near Edison's desk is an alcove containing a small table and a chair, and here the inventor was accustomed to take his modest lunch. On one occasion, the writer was present when the meal was brought in, and it may interest the reader to learn that it consisted of some bread, a piece of cheese, and a portion of fish. There was, apparently, nothing to drink. Less than a year ago Edison also kept a little cot in the library, where he used to sleep for half an hour during the day or when stopping late at night. This bed, however, has lately been removed to another room in the laboratory, as the inventor found that during the cold weather the library was not sufficiently heated to satisfy his love of warmth. Edison can drop off to sleep at a moment's notice, and has frequently been slumbering quietly while the writer has been busy near by examining the thousands of papers bearing on his work which the inventor placed at his disposal. Edison sleeps as gently as a child, and invariably lies with his right cheek resting upon his hand. No sound disturbs him, and he could probably find repose quite as profound were he to seek it in a boiler factory. He never suffers from insomnia, and has frequently taken his rest on a pile of sawdust or even a deal board. He has the ability to accommodate himself to circumstance, and if he had to sleep on a fence or a telegraph wire he would probably secure a very refreshing rest and awake fully recuperated.

Speaking of sleep recalls an interesting story which Edison is fond of relating about a man who called upon him once asking for work, and in the course of conversation stated that he was a martyr to insomnia. Edison was delighted to hear it, and told his visitor that he was just the man he had been looking for. As he didn't require any sleep he would be able to work all the longer, and might get busy right away. "So," says Edison, "I put him to work on a mercury pump, and kept him at it night and day. At the end of sixty hours I left him for half an hour, and when I returned there he was, the pump all broken to pieces and the man fast asleep on the ruins. He never had an attack of sleeplessness after that."

Near the library is the stock-room, where everything necessary to scientific experimenting may be found, and in quantities which will possibly last for years. At one time there used to be a reward offered

THE LABORATORY AT ORANGE

to the employee who succeeded in mentioning any substance used in science which could not be found in the Edison stock-room. At first the "boys" earned a few dollars unearthing rare materials, but finally they gave it up, and now it is only the greenest of new hands who can be prevailed upon to enter for the prize. The stock-room is long and narrow but of considerable height, and contains thousands of small drawers, reaching from the floor to the roof, labelled with a hundred queer titles, such as ores, needles, shells, macaroni, fibres, inks, teeth, bones, gums, resins, and feathers. A peep into an old order book is in itself a revelation, for there you will find invoices for ten thousand different kinds of chemicals, as well as every kind of screw made, every sized needle, every kind of rope, wire, twine and cord, skins, human and animal hair, silk in every process of manufacture, peacocks' tails, amber, meerschaum, hoofs, varnish and oils, every kind of bark and cork, resin and glass. Visitors frequently ask in wonder what all these queer materials are useful for in the way of scientific work, and, if the question is put to Edison himself, the inventor will smile and answer: "You are evidently not a man of science, or you would know that almost every substance known can be brought into use in a chemical or experimental laboratory. At one time I was seriously hampered in my work by not having the materials necessary to enable me to carry out my investigations, but now I am happy to say that any experiment may be conducted here, if necessary, at a moment's notice." Some of the substances preserved in the stock-room are so rare and so minute that they are kept in small folds of tissue paper, like diamonds, which they probably equal in rarity.

One of the most interesting sections of the laboratory is the galvanometer building, which stands by itself about 30 feet from the library. It is really one long room of heroic size, and lighted by a dozen immense windows. In its construction not a speck of iron was used, everything being of brass. The cost, which was great, subsequently proved to be so much money wasted, for it had not been erected more than a few months when the electric cars were run past the very door, thus rendering futile Edison's costly endeavor to banish "magnetic influence." This room contains many things of interest connected with Edison's early inventions. There are the first models of the vote recorder, the gold and stock ticker, the picture telegraph (a device for transmitting photographs over the wires), the duplex and quadruplex telegraphs, the microphone, the mimeograph, and the like. Then there is a costly and rare collection of galvanometers, electrometers, photometers, spectrometers, spectroscopes, and chronographs. There is also a wonderful set of acoustic instruments, which were used in connection with the perfecting of the phonograph, as well as a number of anatomical models of the ear and throat. Neither the first phonograph nor the first incandescent lamp is shown, both these interesting records of Edison's most famous inventions being preserved in the South Kensington Museum, England. The writer asked Edison why he allowed these incomparable mementos to go out of his possession, and he explained that some years ago an Englishman paid him a visit, and seemed so anxious to have them that he cheerfully gave them up. He appeared rather surprised that people should take so much interest in such things.

The galvanometer room is furnished with massive stone tables built on solid brick foundations and capped with slabs of polished slate. On these tables the instruments are tested with absolute correctness, for perfect immobility is insured. The room is also provided with a constant flow of hot, cold, and distilled water, every kind of gas, live steam, hydrogen, electricity of different pressures, waste pipes, and electric lights.

At the head of the galvanometer room is Edison's private chemical laboratory — the *sanctum sanctorum* — where the inventor spends most of his time, and where many of his inventions have either originated or been perfected. It is probably the smallest room in the laboratory and almost destitute of furniture. A table and two chairs (one broken), with a kind of dresser running around the room with shelves above on which are piled innumerable bottles, constitute the contents of this historic apartment. Very few are permitted to enter this room — only those who are closely connected with the inventor in his experimental work — though when he is seated at his table (in all probability occupying the more rickety of the two chairs) solving some scientific problem, he is so absorbed as to be perfectly unconscious of any one who might enter. It is in this room that Edison used to spend days and nights without taking any rest, and often so engrossed in his experiments as even to forget to eat. Busy men sometimes can only find time to board at home, but Edison didn't even do that, until one day young Mrs. Edison put her small foot down and insisted on her husband returning to the house at a reasonable hour, and in order that he should not have the excuse of saying that he had nowhere to work, she had a laboratory built and furnished at the Llewellyn Park home, where the inventor now prosecutes his scientific investigations during the "small hours" as diligently as he desires.

Besides the private chemical laboratory there is another and a larger apartment fitted up on similar lines and presided over by Fred Ott, Edison's right-hand man in experimental work. This room is lofty, spacious, and splendidly lighted, furnished with every contrivance necessary to scientific experimenting, and replete with filters, stills, "muffles" (used for carbonizing or reducing chemicals), fume chambers, test tubes (for testing the solution of the storage battery), every kind of chemical, numerous charts, and so on. Experiments take place every day in this room, and occasionally they are conducted by scientists who visit Edison, and who are desirous of showing him a few things of interest. Edison likes to see others making experiments, and in 1900 he was much interested in watching Louis Dreyfus, of Frankfort-on-Main, melt a bar of steel in a temperature of 5400 degrees Fahrenheit, generated by what was then a new process, invented in Essen, Germany. The process consisted, briefly, in the combustion of a certain chemical compound in connection with powdered aluminium. Mr. Dreyfus placed in a crucible a bar of steel six inches in length and half an inch in diameter. Around it he scattered a teacupful of his chemical, and pouring on this a small quantity of powdered aluminium, he touched a match to it and in an instant it blazed up, throwing out an intense heat. In less than ten seconds by the watch the steel bar was completely melted. Edison was highly delighted with the experiment, said that the process was one which he had been in search of for a long time, and ordered a quantity of the chemical for his own use. It was one of the most successful and interesting exhibitions ever given by an outsider in the laboratory, and Edison extended a cordial invitation to the German scientist to come and show further wonders whenever he had the opportunity.

EDISON IN HIS CHEMICAL LABORATORY, ORANGE, N.J.

THE LABORATORY AT ORANGE

The "X-ray" room, which is in charge of E. Dally, is a small apartment on the first floor, and contains the identical machine which Edison sent down to Buffalo at the time of President McKinley's assassination, in order to locate the bullet. Curiously enough it was never used, and by a combination of circumstances its errand of mercy was rendered futile. The story of its journeyings is worth relating, for the question is still asked whether the President's life might not have been saved had the X-ray machine been used.

Almost directly after the President was shot a telephone message was received at the Edison laboratory asking if a machine might be held in readiness, should it be considered desirous to send one to Buffalo. Edison himself was consulted, and replied that the instrument could be forwarded at a moment's notice; and on the Saturday afternoon, about 2.30, another message was received asking for the apparatus to be forwarded at once. Two young men from the laboratory accompanied it — Charles W. Luhr and Clarence T. Dally.

They arrived in Buffalo Sunday morning, and were busy installing the plant in the Millburn house, when a message came to say that the machine would not be required for at least a week, as it was considered unwise to search for the bullet just then owing to the condition of the patient. As a matter of fact the doctors had come to the conclusion that the spent missile was located in a spot where it might safely be allowed to remain without any danger of decreasing the President's chance of recovery. A few days later Mr. McKinley had so far rallied that the Vice-President (Mr. Roosevelt) rejoined his family, Senator Hanna left for Cleveland, and two of the doctors took train for New York. Charles F. Luhr returned to the laboratory, and only Dally was left with the machine. Every one was hopeful, and the President continued to improve for some days, when there was a sudden and alarming change for the worse. One of the doctors took it upon himself to inform Dally that neither he nor his machine would be needed, but the young operator continued at his post waiting for a possible summons. Finally, the end came, and apparently the X-ray was destined to take no part in the tragedy.

The following day Dally left for Niagara Falls, which he was very desirous of viewing before returning to New York, firmly convinced that there was no use in his remaining any longer in Buffalo, and the machine was taken down. The autopsy on the body of the late President was to be held the same day, when it was confidently expected that the bullet would be found, but, after a search lasting an hour and a half, it had not been recovered. Then a call was made for the X-ray as the only means of locating the mysteriously hidden bullet, but it had been taken apart, and the operator could not be found. An hour was spent trying to find him, and then the doctors decided that the programme of arrangements did not permit them to expend any more time over the autopsy, and as a result the bullet was never recovered and the X-ray never used. To those interested in the progress of Professor Roentgen's discovery it was a great disappointment that circumstances had so contrived that the machine was not even given a chance of assisting in the effort to save the Chief Magistrate's life; and by no one more than Edison was regret felt, for he had had high hopes that it would have helped materially in prolonging the life of the President.

THE LABORATORY AT ORANGE

Four years later the young man who had taken the X-ray apparatus to Buffalo, and who had stood to his post so faithfully, if uselessly, died from the rays of the very machine he had assisted in conveying on its merciful errand. For some considerable time Dally had suffered from a mysterious skin complaint generated by experimenting with the X-ray, and his case had attracted the attention of medical and scientific men in all parts of the country. The disease began with small red patches resembling scalds but devoid of pain. Six months later his hands began to swell, and he had to relinquish his work in the Edison laboratory. But he was not altogether incapacitated, and spent his time setting X-ray machines in hospitals and colleges. At that work he remained for two years, though his hands became more and more affected. Then the burns commenced to smart and tingle, and finally great agony set in. Indeed, so intense were his sufferings that at night he was obliged to lie with his arms in iced water in order to gain sufficient relief from the fiery torment to allow him a few intermittent periods of sleep. Photographs of his hands were published, and the disease was followed with absorbing interest by scientists in Europe as well as America.

Then cancer attacked the left wrist. Grafting was advocated, and 150 pieces of skin were taken from his legs in an endeavor to patch up the tissues, but granulation refused to follow, and the operation proved a failure. The disease now made rapid progress, and the left arm was amputated a few inches below the shoulder. It was hoped that the progress of the malady had been checked, but three months later the little finger of the right hand became affected, and the knife was again brought into use. The right wrist was next attacked, and after skin-grafting had again been tried and failed, the arm was amputated four inches below the elbow. In spite of all Dally was in high hopes that at last he was free from the terrible, mysterious disease, and had artificial arms made, but almost immediately afterwards his entire system fell a victim to the strange malady, and the doctors gave up hope. To within a week of his death Dally was optimistic, then his brain became paralyzed, he lost consciousness and died martyr to a disease for which no cure has yet been found. But his death was not one to be entirely and solely mourned as a useless calamity, inasmuch as it drew attention to the dangers of the X-ray, and served as a warning to all operators against bringing their hands too frequently into the flood of the mysterious light. Edison was deeply grieved at his co-worker's death, and did all in his power to effect his recovery by obtaining expert advice and treatment, but the malady was one which defied the whole medical world. To-day the death of Dally is a sore subject with the inventor, and one which he absolutely refuses voluntarily to discuss.

Near the X-ray department is a small room which apparently contains nothing of interest save a table, a chair, some lumber, and a lathe or two. But it has "associations," for here it was that Edison perfected the phonograph. Many days and nights of experimenting have been spent in this room, but Edison never enters it now, for it is small and gloomy; it has performed its duty, however, and deserves to be preserved. There are two machine shops, both spacious and excellently lighted by twenty-four windows apiece. One is known as the heavy machine shop, while the other is where all the light experimental machinery is made. The latter is presided over by John F. Ott, who superintends the making of all the small models.

In the heavy machine shop, in charge of Robert A. Bachman, is turned out the big machinery used in the cement works and elsewhere, as well as the large battery trays.

Another interesting room is known as the Precision Room, where all the instruments are perfected. It is also in charge of Mr. Ott. Here the most delicate parts of the machinery used in the construction of the various inventions are made. There are many remarkable machines in this room, all of an automatic nature, such, for example, as the device by which the body of a phonograph is made in one operation. The metal box on which the phonograph is mounted is placed on the machine, and simultaneously eight holes are drilled, the box is milled, and the holes are reamed to size. This takes but a few minutes, and one man is able to turn out a hundred a day.

Perhaps the room having the greatest amount of interest to the ordinary visitor is "No. 13," or the Phonograph Experimental Department. Formerly it was in the charge of A. T. E. Wangemann, who, unfortunately, was run down and killed by a train during the summer of 1906. Everything connected with the "talking machine" is shown here — hundreds of records, forests of horns ranging in length from a few inches to eighteen feet, phonographs of all sizes and shapes, machines twenty years old and brand new, diaphragms, musical instruments, a grand piano, an organ, and piles of music. No mechanical parts of the phonograph are made in this room, for it is purely and solely used for experimental work directed towards obtaining better all-round results and superior records.

"All the work done in this room," Mr. Wangemann remarked on the last occasion that the writer met him, "is concentrated on making better apparatus for recording and reproducing, better raw materials for cylinders, and better records, both blank and moulded. In fact, it is here that every effort at improving and advancing the present way of phonographic production and reproduction is made. We are constantly experimenting with new records, new speakers, new horns or funnels, and there is nothing we do not try in order to obtain absolute perfection of sound reproduction."

Edison has a small room partitioned off from this experimental department, where he sits and listens to new records for many hours at a time, scribbling on scraps of paper his opinions of the various reproductions. In 1903 he spent the best part of seven months here endeavoring to render the phonograph more perfect. He devotes much of his time to finding out the reasons for poor work, for he believes that more can be learned from things going wrong than from things which go well. "As is well known," said Mr. Wangemann, "there is no substance of which we have at present any knowledge that is proof against influence by sound vibrations, or which will not transmit sound at some velocity. If it were possible to find a substance which would be absolutely dead to sound, and yet solid enough to be used in mechanical construction, then one could obtain far superior reproductions of sound waves, both vocal and instrumental, than is at present possible. Such a substance will be found sooner or later, and then we shall be able to reproduce sound so perfectly that it will be impossible to distinguish the voice of the man who makes a record from the record itself."

The legal department of the Edison laboratory is under the charge of Frank L. Dyer, who employs a numerous staff and who is, perhaps, one of the hardest-worked individuals in the building. Although a mem-

LEGAL DEPARTMENT, EDISON LABORATORY, ORANGE. N.J.

ber of a prominent firm of patent lawyers in New York, he spends practically his entire time at the laboratory, and there is little in regard to Edison's numerous inventions with which he is not acquainted. The writer had an interesting conversation with Mr. Dyer recently regarding his department, in the course of which the patent lawyer said:

"Mr. Edison's work being based almost entirely on new inventions, a large part of my work has to do with patents and suits based thereon. Not only has Mr. Edison been by long odds the most prolific inventor and patentee of any time, but numerous and frequent applications for patents are being filed by experimenters connected with the several companies that are identified with the Edison interests, such as the National Phonograph Company, the Edison Manufacturing Company, the Edison Storage Battery Company, the Edison Portland Cement Company, and about twenty others. Consequently there are always several hundred active applications for patents pending in this country and abroad, the special details of which have to be remembered in order that they may be properly prosecuted.

"It is, of course, physically impossible for me or my department to attend personally to the many suits against infringers of the Edison patents all over the world, although they are conducted under my own direction and some by me personally. In this work, however, I have the assistance of other lawyers in New York, Washington, Chicago, London, Paris, and elsewhere. In addition to the patent suits, there are many other legal actions of which this department has charge and many of which it directly conducts, such as the usual damage suits for personal injuries, actions based on contracts, matters of insurance, real estate, and so on."

Edison has no great appreciation of the protection afforded to inventors by the Patent Office, though he has generally been treated with great consideration by the officials. He thinks the system is all wrong. He does not believe in the life of a patent being as brief as it is, or that it should be possible for an inventor to be "held up" by any one who likes to bring in the most shadowy claim of priority. When such a claim is brought forward, declares Edison, the inventor should be given the benefit of the doubt, and allowed to continue manufacturing his invention until the courts give their verdict. But as the law now stands the benefit lies entirely with the claimant — the work of the real inventor being held in abeyance while the former is given unlimited time to make good his case, which he is very seldom able to do. Edison has on more than one occasion stated that he would have been many hundreds of thousands of dollars better off had he never taken out a patent. The best thing a man can do when he believes he has invented something which the public wants is to go ahead and manufacture the particular article and then flood the market with it. This is the only hope for him. He will then possibly make money before the pirates come along.

Three years ago Edison had an interesting case on with the United States Patent Office. The inventor had made application for a certain patent, and while this was pending the examiner, it was stated, had allowed some one else, who had sent in an application along somewhat similar lines, to take out his application for the purpose of inserting facts which were covered by the Edison application. This was quite irregular, for according to Patent Office laws no one is permitted to withdraw an application and insert something which may afterwards have occurred to him. When Edison's attorney heard of these irregularities he asked the Commissioner for a new hearing, which was refused. The attorney made a second application to the Commissioner with the same result, and then he carried his case to the President. Mr. Roosevelt listened attentively to the facts, and then replied: "What Mr. Edison asks is not unreasonable. He occupies a peculiar position in this inventive age, and he shall be given an opportunity to be heard." The President then wrote to the Commissioner directing that Edison be given a new hearing, which subsequently took place.

Employed in the Edison laboratory are about a hundred men, consisting of electricians, skilled mechanics, mathematicians, photographers, draughtsmen, and musicians, each of whom has his own particular line of work to attend to, and in the accomplishing of which he can always count on suggestion and encouragement from Edison, who is ever ready to advise. There is one thing, however, which Edison certainly is not, and that is a lightning calculator. This trait is very well indicated by a story told having reference to the occasion when he gave evidence in the Kemmler case already mentioned. He had asserted that the temperature of a tube of water the height of a man would rise 8 degrees Centigrade under the application of a certain current of electricity. Mr. Cockran, cross-examiner at the time, asked him how many degrees that meant on the Fahrenheit scale.

"I don't know," responded Edison, who had been admonished by Mr. Cockran a little while before only to tell what he knew as absolute facts.

"You don't know!" exclaimed Mr. Cockran. "Well, surely you could compute it for us?"

"I don't compute such things," replied the inventor.

"Well, how do you find it out, then?" queried the lawyer.

"I ask somebody," answered the electrician.

"Whom do you ask?"

"Oh, I have men to do such things," said Edison, stifling a yawn.

"Are there any here now?" questioned Mr. Cockran, looking around at the crowd, among whom were several of Edison's assistants from Orange.

"Yes, there is Mr. Kennelly," and straightway all eyes were fixed on Arthur E. Kennelly, Edison's head mathematician, who subsequently became President of the Institute of Electrical Engineers, and was generally believed to be the only man in America who was ever able to interpret the intricate system of mathematics evolved by the English electrician, Oliver Heavysides. Edison turned over the question of converting degrees Centigrade into degrees Fahrenheit to his associate, and Kennelly, after looking up at the ceiling in a meditative kind of way for a moment, performed the necessary mental calculation, and then gave the answer.

Kennelly is but one of the clever men who gathered around Edison in his earlier days. Perhaps it is not generally known that Nikola Tesla served his apprenticeship with Edison, and learned much that afterwards proved useful to him when he became an inventor and experimenter on his own account. Tesla called on Edison one day and asked for work, and, liking the look of the keen-faced, handsome Bohemian, Edison sent him to his foreman, a man named Fulton. The latter offered to give the young foreigner a position on condition that he would work. Tesla swore he would slave until he dropped, and he almost kept his word. Fulton put him to the test, and kept him hard at work for a couple of days and nights, seldom giving

THE LABORATORY AT ORANGE

him a chance to close his eyes. At the end of a fortnight if Tesla had secured forty-eight hours of sleep it was about as much as Fulton allowed him, and then the foreman magnanimously declared that he must have a rest. Moreover — feeling in a fairly generous mood — he invited Tesla to supper, and entering a café, ordered a steak — the biggest they had — with lots of vegetables and potatoes. When the steak came on the table its proportions were so huge that Fulton gasped, and declared four men couldn't finish it. However, they went ahead, and in time the steak vanished. Then Fulton turned to the young man and asked if there was anything else he would like. "You are out with me, you know," said the foreman, "and whatever you want just order it." Tesla looked vaguely around for a minute, as if cogitating over the matter, and then in a somewhat embarrassed voice he said, "Mr. Fulton, if you don't mind, I would like another steak." To those who know Tesla this story is doubly amusing, as the electrician is particularly tall and thin, and gives indication of rather a poor appetite than otherwise.

Among others who have worked with Edison mention should be made of Francis R. Upton, mathematician, who solved many difficult problems in the transmission and distribution of electricity; Charles Bachelor; John Krusei; Stockton L. Griffin and Samuel Insull, who looked after Edison's financial and business interests; Charles L. Clarke, whose name will always be remembered in connection with the economy test on the incandescent lamp; Charles T. Hughes, who worked on the Edison electric locomotive; Luther Stieringer; J. H. Vail, in charge of the dynamos at one time; Francis Jehl, who worked long and arduously on the Edison meter; Martin Force, who assisted in the perfecting of the loud-talking telephone;

John Ott, the expert mechanician, who thought nothing of making moulds for lamp filaments to the ten-thousandth part of an inch, and who secured several patents for ingenious mechanical devices; and Ludwig K. Boehm, who prepared the delicate bulbs for the lamps and the mercury pumps for exhausting them.

An amusing story is related of Boehm when he was working on his pumps, which may be recalled here. He had met with a series of mishaps in his work, and was considerably discouraged, when a bright youth who was assisting him said, "Couldn't we put the lamps in a balloon and send them up high enough to fill them with vacuum and then seal them off up there?" Boehm gave a contemptuous grunt, but Edison, who was standing near, said, "Good idea; we'll have to take out a patent on that, sure." "But," queried another, "how can we seal them off if there is no air to use in the blowpipe?" Edison regarded the objector with a fixed stare for a moment, and then, in a voice of assumed disgust and with a long-drawn sigh, answered: "That's always the way. No sooner does a man bring out a brilliant and practical idea but some ignoramus must needs interfere and try to show a reason why the scheme is impractical. There's no chance for a real bright inventor nowadays."

Others who have worked in the Edison laboratory, and whose names will long be remembered, are: E. H. Johnson, one of the earliest of Edison's associates, who, among other things, took the electric light to England; S. Bergmann, who was left in charge of the Newark factory after the inventor went to Menlo Park, and who subsequently became the largest manufacturer of electrical apparatus in the United States, and now owns very large works in Germany; Frank Sprague, who resigned from the navy to go with Edison, and while with him invented the "Sprague Electric System"; Frank MacGowan, whom Edison sent to South America to look for bamboo suitable for lamp filaments; James Seymour, who took the telephone to England, and afterwards became famous for solving ventilating and lighting problems in connection with skyscrapers, tunnels, and subcellars; W. K. L. Dickson, who interested himself in the kinetoscope, biographed the Pope, and wrote an interesting history of Edison and his inventions; Acheson, whose work is well known at Niagara Falls in respect to electric power; H. Ward-Leonard, the inventor of a system for moving turrets on war-ships by electricity; Philip Seubel, who installed the first electric plant ever put on a war-ship; and August Weber, who invented a new kind of porcelain and made a fortune out of it.

Edison has always shown consummate skill in choosing as his associates and workpeople men capable of withstanding long hours of continuous labor, and even when a very young man possessed the faculty for inspiring them with his own enthusiasm, determination, and boundless energy. When he told the writer a short time ago that he had on several occasions spent from three to five days and nights in succession over an invention, he added: "But there are many men here who become so absorbed over any new discovery that they cheerfully give up their rest and sleep for the same length of time to help me work out my ideas. They are great boys." Perhaps there is something more to account for the affection with which the employees, from the highest to the lowest, regard their chief than that which his genius and powers of endurance engender. And it is not far to seek. Edison will never allow any of his men to be "called down" by an outsider if he can help it, and Mr. Dickson gives a good example of this characteristic by relating an incident which took place twenty years and more ago, when one of his electricians was summoned to give the bearings of some intricate electrical problem before a Board of Inquiry.

In giving his evidence the man made several misstatements, which were taken exception to by some of the members before whom he was testifying, but the general verdict was waived in consequence of Edison's authoritative support of his employee. No sooner, however, was the room cleared than the inventor turned to the young man and said: "Now, see here, you were wrong about the whole affair. I saw that at a glance." "You did, Mr. Edison?" stammered the other, amazed. "Then why did you endorse me?" "Because I was not going to let that crowd have the satisfaction of crowing over you if I could help it," was the reply. Is it to be wondered at if the man afterwards declared that he would go to the ends of the earth and further for such a chief?

A quality which Edison admires most in a workman is his ability to keep silence. Any employee who talks outside about things which he has no right to mention he has no use for. On one or two occasions a workman — smart and ambitious, perhaps — has obtained a position in the Edison laboratory, and soon after been "fired" through his insatiable fondness for gossip. When given a fortnight's money and shown the door he has felt aggrieved, not realizing that he possesses every sense but common sense, and has yet to learn the value of silence. There are in the Edison laboratory, more perhaps than in any other, secrets which have to be guarded, and did his workmen talk the results of Edison's investigations would, of course, become known long before he desired to take the public into his confidence. Hence the value the inventor places on a man's ability to "hold his tongue."

Edison is always affable and genial with his workpeople, calls them by their Christian names, and never fails to note if any man is away sick and to inquire for him. He chats and jokes with the humblest of them, and the writer has a vivid recollection of seeing the inventor seated on a table in the chemical laboratory listening to a funny story related to him by the youngest boy in his employ, laughing heartily and unaffectedly, and apparently in no way thinking that there was anything strange or out of the ordinary in conversing thus intimately with what elsewhere would be called the "office boy." But no one takes undue advantage of such familiarity, and Edison probably gets better results out of his people by the exhibition of this geniality and good-humor than if he cultivated a sternness and aloofness which he does not feel.

Edison himself has played many a practical joke upon his employees, and in the early phonograph days he enjoyed many a laugh on them with the aid of his "talking machine." Sometimes, however, the joke was on him, as was instanced by the "fake cigar" story, which was a popular Edison anecdote twenty odd years ago. Edison was always an inveterate smoker, and used to keep a number of boxes of cigars in his room, and these were a constant object of interest to his associates. First one man, then another, would enter the room, ask Edison some trivial question, and when leaving would manage, unseen, to insert his hand in one of the boxes and annex three or four choice cigars. Edison began to suspect something of the kind, and one day he called on his tobacconist, explained things, and got the man to fix up some fearful "smokes," consisting of old bits of rag, tea leaves, and shavings, and worth about two dollars a barrel. These were done up in attractive-looking boxes, and delivered to the laboratory. Nothing happened, however; there was a falling off in the number of Edison's visitors, but no casualties were reported. Then one day Edison again called at the store, and inquired of his dealer if he had forgotten to send up the fake cigars. "Why, Mr. Edison," replied the amazed tobacconist, "I sent up ten boxes of the worst concoctions I could make two months ago. Ain't your men through with them yet?" Then Edison made a rapid calculation, divided the number of cigars by his daily allowance, and was forced to the painful conclusion that he had consumed those "life destroyers" himself. There and then he gave a big order for his usual brand, and his cigars disappeared once more with their accustomed celerity.

Occasionally the men get up a joke on their chief, and they much enjoyed themselves about the time that Edison's daughter Madelyn was born — some eighteen years ago. The technical assistants got together and declared that something should be done to celebrate the event, and at first it was proposed to serenade the happy father. The suggestion, however, was vetoed at a committee meeting, and instead it was decided to draw up plans for a mechanical cradle intended to save Mrs. Edison worry and trouble in managing the baby. "Several ideas outside cradles," wrote one of the plotters some years later, "were submitted to the committee; but the thought of the Wizard ambling up and down the room in the dead of night, occasionally stepping on a semi-submerged tack, was too much for us, so the cradle was decided upon. It was called the 'Automatic Electric Baby Tender,' and the plan showed an ordinary cradle with ingenious devices for the child's comfort and correct training attached.

"Immediately above the spot where the baby's head would lie was a diaphragm somewhat resembling a telephone receiver. If the infant should start crying, at the first wail communication was established between the diaphragm and an electric clock, and the cradle was set rocking by means of a small motor. If the remonstrance continued beyond a certain time, the clock released a lever and an arm attached to the side of the cradle, operated by a crank carrying a nursing bottle, was swung over the baby's mouth. If hunger was not the trouble and the wails continued, another arm on the opposite side swung over the child's mouth with paregoric, at the same time the electric current was turned into a set of magnets placed around the cradle, and any pin which might be causing the trouble would be at once removed. If the yells continued, the 'thirty-third degree' was applied. Two arms, lying flat in the cradle under the baby, were slowly raised and the child turned over. Then an electric spanker fastened to the foot-board proceeded to do its work with neatness and despatch." Although no model accompanied the plan, Edison was, nevertheless, delighted with the thoughtfulness of his associates, and declared that he was sure a patent would be granted to them if they applied for one. Some nervous mothers might not care to trust their offspring to the tender mercies of the "Automatic Electric Baby Tender," but doubtless, he said, a sufficient number would risk it and thus make the proposition a going concern. The plan of this remarkable cradle is still preserved, or was until a few years ago, and both Mr. and Mrs. Edison enjoyed many a good laugh studying its ingenious details.

At the time, it was not his associates alone that took so great an interest in Edison's baby, but the entire world seemed excited over the event. Leading articles appeared in almost every newspaper, and the comments were interesting, amusing, astounding, or ludicrous. Naturally all these sallies afforded Edison considerable amusement, for though the joke was on him, he could still see the humor of it. Some kind friend collected a lot of the published stories and sent them to him in a batch, and a few the inventor read to his wife, who, however, scarcely appreciated to the full the attention her baby was attracting. Even Edison thought the joke had gone far enough when visitors to the laboratory began to inquire after the various inventions which the electrician was reported to have created in order to make easy his baby's path through infancy. Finally, when one of these inquisitive and wholly gullible persons asked if he really had evolved a means whereby a baby's crying could be muffled without injury to the infant, Edison got very tired and decided to bring the interview to a conclusion as soon as the opportunity offered. It was not long coming.

Suddenly the visitor espied a peculiar-looking structure standing in one corner of the experimental room, and in a voice of intense interest inquired, "What's that?" "Why," replied Edison with a look of profound gravity and in a low tone, "that's the patent cradle that every one's talking about. It will be a great success, and I hope to make a lot of money out of it. It's not altogether perfect as yet, but I can tell you privately (though of course you won't say anything about it, as I don't want some smart fellow to get the idea and take out a patent before I have filed mine) that when finished there will be a motor attached which runs by sound, so that the louder the baby cries the faster the cradle rocks. It's a great scheme, and you must come and see it when I have it working." The visitor, somewhat suspicious at last, but murmur-

THE LABORATORY AT ORANGE

ing that it was wonderful, soon after took his departure, and that was the last of the patent cradle joke.

One more story and this long chapter may well come to an end. It has to do with a boy who came to the Edison laboratory full of determination to become a famous inventor, but who, owing to a sensitive nature and an unfortunate incident, failed in his ambitions when on the very threshold of his career and abandoned invention in favor of an occupation less distinctive. The anecdote is here given as related by an interviewer some years ago, whose name the present writer has been unable to trace, and who will, perhaps, forgive being accorded the customary credit under the circumstances.

"Six or seven years ago a new boy was employed in the Orange laboratory, and forced Edison to give an account of himself. It happened in this way. The boy was first of all told all about the man for whom he was to work. Then he was informed of the traditions of the establishment. He was told that the main building contained a piece of every known substance on earth, and that if he could name any substance not in the building he would be awarded a prize of $2.50. He was also told that his especial duty would be to guard the room in which Mr. Edison worked, it being important that the inventor be not disturbed by curiosity-seekers or schemers who often tried to reach him. Then the boy was placed on guard, full to the brim of the importance of his position. But one serious omission had been made by his instructor: he had not told him what Mr. Edison was like. So when, soon after he took up his post, the boy was approached by a somewhat shabbily dressed man who attempted to brush past him, he grabbed that man in such a way that the man stopped and gasped in astonishment.

"'What is the matter with you, boy?' demanded the man indignantly.

"'You can't go in there,' retorted the boy with just as much spirit.

"'Why not?' said the man.

"'Because no one can go in there without written permission, or when Mr. Edison sends out for him.'

"'I see,' said the man, and then he turned on his slippered heel and walked off, while the boy looked after the dirty yellow duster which the man wore, and said several things to himself not at all complimentary to 'blokes wot would try to bluff past him.'

"But the boy was surprised about five minutes afterwards to see the man in the yellow duster coming back accompanied by the 'instructor,' who looked very, very serious, and who said —

"'Don't you know who this gentleman is?'

"'No,' said the boy; 'but he didn't have any pass, and Mr. Edison wasn't with him.'

"'Why, this *is* Mr. Edison,' gasped the instructor.

"The boy collapsed.

"'Can I go in?' said the inventor with a twinkle in his eye. But the boy hung his head, while the instructor started to berate him for his mistake. Then Edison turned around and stopped that instructor on the spot, while he at the same time commended the boy for his vigilance. It was the fault of the teacher, not the boy, he said.

"Nevertheless the effect of the incident on the boy was such that he never could enter the same room without a visible tremor. Edison, who is fond of a joke, sought to reassure him by winking at him tremendously every time he came in, but that didn't seem to mend matters. One day he was very sick, and an investigation showed that he had been endeavoring to increase his courage by chewing tobacco. It nearly killed him, and he resigned his position in consequence."

CHAPTER XVII

NOTION BOOKS

OF the many thousands of volumes in the library of the Orange laboratory none have a greater fascination for the visitor than the famous "Notion Books," a series of folio volumes containing the results of Edison's investigations covering a space of nearly thirty-five years. They constitute the documentary evidence of original invention, and have, on more than one occasion, been produced in a court of law to bear silent witness in suits based on Edisonian patents. In these books will be found minute details of every invention patented since the quadruplex made Edison's name famous in telegraphy, besides which there are hundreds of ideas, or "notions," for inventions which have never materialized. Yet Edison does not keep these precious volumes under lock and key, but on the open shelves of his library, where they are at the service of any visitor who has the *entrée* to the laboratory.

Edison calls these volumes his "Day Books," for they contain the daily records of his experiments, together with sketches of machines drawn by him in pen and ink. Each and every page is dated, and the date attested by three witnesses chosen from the assistants who happened to be with the inventor at the time of making the entries. Every illustration is also initialled by the witnesses, as well as every paragraph of importance and every formula. The object of so much care and detail was, of course, to provide evidence in possible lawsuits affecting patent rights, and their usefulness in this respect has been proved over and over again, both in Europe as well as America, for they have crossed the ocean more than once to appear as witness against plagiarists of the incandescent lamp and other inventions.

An English scientist who called at the Edison laboratory some years ago and was shown these volumes, declared that they had impressed him more than the most remarkable of the electrician's inventions. "It is necessary," he said afterwards, "to look over these day books in order to have a clear conception of the patience and rigorous methods, the workmanlike probity, and thoroughness with which Edison hunts after means to ends aimed at. They have inspired me with the most profound respect for this great inventor."

The phraseology employed by Edison in his day-book records was a little too abstruse for the English scientist, however, and though he declared that the language used was "synthetic, strongly descriptive, and quaint," he was obliged to call on Dr. Moses and Mr. Lowry, Edison's representatives, who showed him the volumes, for some explanation of certain phrases. "He has clear terms," wrote the scientist to a friend, "which are probably current lingual coin at Menlo Park, but which would convey no scientific idea to a lecturer at the Royal Institution. A 'bug,' apparently (and it is frequently mentioned in these day books), is a difficulty which appears insurmountable to the staff, but to the master it is 'an ugly insect that lives on the lazy, and can and must be killed.' In one book I read the following remarkable paragraph: 'Awful lot of bugs still. Let Moses try what the following solution would do to rid us of them.'

Dr. Moses informed me that in this case the 'bugs' were difficulties in connection with the invention of the incandescent light."

In a series of these day books, extending over a period of thirteen months, the pages look like an inventory of a heterogeneous mass of subjects. Figures, notes, sketches, diagrams, are jumbled together in a way which defy solution by any one but the inventor himself, who can, marvellous as it may appear, interpret every diagram and every figure, though he made them thirty years ago. Before each entry in these particular day books there are, for many columns, the letters "N.G." and a little mark made by Edison's pen, which indicates that he has done with the various items thus "ticked off." "N.G." stands for "No Good," and the substances named after these signs are the materials he tried and which he found useless in his attempt to make a perfect carbon button for the telephone. Turning over the pages one comes to other columns, on the left side of which are the letters "L.B.," "N.B.," "D.B.," "E.," which means "Little Better," "No Better," "Deuced (or any other word beginning with D) Bad," "Encouraging." All these "notes" have to do with the telephone and Edison's efforts to make a perfect receiver. For thirteen months these entries show that he experimented with different materials daily without being able to place beside the records any sign more favorable than the letter E. During those thirteen months he got "cold" and "warm" in turns, but never "hot," and then came the incident of the smoky kerosene lamp, the scraping away of the soot which covered the inside of the glass, and the employment of it in connection with the carbon button. All these experiments with lampblack are carefully detailed in the day book, some being marked "V.E."

("Very Encouraging"), success being thus qualified by reason of the fact that the soot was not pure, but the final entry is endorsed with the triumphant word "Eureka!" written in printed characters. He had found success in the application of soot of the highest quality.

The records covering the invention and perfecting of the incandescent light fill many volumes. The hundreds of experiments which Edison made in his search for a suitable filament are fully detailed, and each record is marked with some initial which tells him whether he is on the right track or getting farther away from it. A portion of every substance he tried is also affixed to the records of these experiments, and scattered through the pages you will find filaments of platinum, iridium, silicon and boron, as well as specimens of different qualities of thread coated with plumbago, coal tar, cardboard, millboard, linen, from the finest to the coarsest, grape stalks, wood splints, cornstalks, and a hundred different varieties of bamboo. By these day books one learns that there are 1400 varieties of bamboo, of which about three hundred only are useful for any purpose. At least two hundred varieties were experimented with by Edison. There is an interesting account of one kind of bamboo which grows in certain parts of Japan. Beside this record is the word "Eureka" again, for it was exactly the fibre that Edison wanted in order to make his electric light an absolute success. There is a brief description, too, as to the manner in which the bamboo must be treated in order to make the best filament. Not all the cane must be used, but only a certain minute portion, and it is important that the fibrous material be taken from the interior of the bamboo when it has reached a certain growth. There is also a "recipe"

EDISON EXAMINING A STATEMENT RENDERED BY ONE OF HIS
WORKPEOPLE

for the correct carbonizing of the fibre in order that the filament shall be of a very high resistance. All these records are, of course, signed and dated, so that it is possible to follow the inventing and perfecting of the incandescent light daily and almost hourly from the moment when Edison made his first experiment to that historic occasion when the trees of Menlo Park were strung with some three hundred glowing bulbs — the pioneers of a new and brilliant illuminant.

As samples of other notations which appear in these remarkable books, the following items may be quoted as giving some idea of the varied character of those which have at different times flashed through Edison's brain:

"The matter in butter-nut shucks gives a color with sulphate of iron. Try butter-nute."

"Chloroform is a test for iodine."

"Experiment with the instantaneous formation of metallic tin-flake by chemical composition in glass and on paper to form metallic dots and dashes in paper for repeating."

"Experiment on the speed, strength, current, and form of coil which is best to work by induction. It may be a primary of 20,000 ohms R. and a secondary of 10,000 ohms will work with very delicate current."

CHAPTER XVIII

BANQUETS

EDISON has been the recipient of many banquets, and doubtless the number would be considerably greater had it not been for his modesty and his frequently expressed request not to be "lionized." He has a real and very strong objection to public dinners, and openly acknowledges that after attending one he feels more done up than if he had worked ceaselessly at some new invention for the better part of a week. As a consequence it must be something very important that will lure him from his quiet home and cause him to break his invariable rule of declining all banquets even when given in his honor.

During the last few years two Edisonian dinners may be recalled, both being of so unique and interesting a character that some description appears almost necessary. The first of these was given on February 11, 1904, at the Waldorf-Astoria, New York, by the American Institute of Electrical Engineers, in celebration of Edison's fifty-seventh birthday and the twenty-fifth anniversary of the invention of the incandescent electric-light system. In additional commemoration of the "double event" the "Edison Medal" was founded for the best thesis on current improvements in electricity, to be given annually by the Institute. Seven hundred of the most distinguished men and women in

America attended to do homage to the inventor, and the banquet was one of the most notable ever given in New York.

The tables were so arranged that every one could see the guest of honor as he sat, much to his own embarrassment, in front of a brilliant display of flags and beneath a pyramid of fifty-seven electric lamps. A painting of the little house where he was born in Milan, Ohio, had been placed on the wall above his head, together with the shield of the "Buckeye State," the coats-of-arms of New Jersey and the Empire State. In front of him were miniature models in sugar showing many of his inventions. Wires stretched across the room connecting poles from which ran cables to a Marconi apparatus. At the inventor's right hand was the original duplex-sender, and at the receiving end the quadruplex which was being used at the Baltimore office of the Postal Telegraph Company at the time that the operators were forced to flee from the approaching fire. Thousands of electric bulbs were strung along the galleries, festooned about the walls, and placed upon the numerous small tables.

When all were seated, the inventor, smiling and happy, sounded "73" — "Congratulations and best wishes" — on the Morse code, and the room shook with a mighty cheer. And after silence had been restored a number of messages addressed to the guest of the evening were read, among them being the following:

"I congratulate you as one of the Americans to whom America owes much, as one of the men whose life-work has tended to give America no small portion of its present position in the international world. — THEODORE ROOSEVELT."

"It is most unfortunate that I cannot be present when

the 'King of the Telegraphers' is to be crowned with the medal crown. Though absent, yet I here profess to the monarch loyal and unfaltering allegiance, swearing to render him at any time and all times such service as the most potent head of the clan that ever ruled his people ever received from his humble and devoted subject. To which I hereby pledge our life, our fortune, and our sacred honor. Long life to 'King Edison the First.'— ANDREW CARNEGIE."

"Hearty good wishes to Mr. Edison. I look back with greatest interest on his brilliant inventions in electric lighting and telephony, which I had the great pleasure of successfully maintaining in all the courts in England. — ALVERSTONE."

"I join heartily with the American Institute of Electrical Engineers in gratitude to Edison for his great electric work and for the phonograph, a most exquisite and instructive scientific discovery, and for his many other useful and well-worked-out inventions for the public. — KELVIN."

"I enthusiastically join in the honors paid to my dear and illustrious friend Edison, whose system I am proud to have introduced into Italy. — COLOMBO."

"Admiring your great inventions, Hungarian friends send sincerest congratulations. — ETIENNE DE FODOR."

"Honor to your illustrious guest. Fraternal greetings to the American Institute of Electrical Engineers. — ASCOLI, President Italian Society of Electrical Engineers."

After this came Edison's own message, which read:

"I want to thank you and all my fellow-members of the American Institute of Electrical Engineers for the great honor done me in thus celebrating my birthday, associated with the twenty-fifth anniversary of the complete development and successful introduction of the incandescent lamp. Your expressions of good-will gratify me greatly.

"The early days were enough to tire out any one's courage and persistence, but you stood it all and put up with me into the bargain. Now, in noble revenge for the burdens I put on you, and in addition to all the evidences of friendship in the past, you add this unusual token of continued affection. I should not be human if I were not profoundly affected and deeply grateful.

"This medal is founded to encourage young men to devote their best thought and work to electrical development. God bless them and you, my dear friends, and this American Institute of Electrical Engineers."

Then followed this fine toast, proposed by the toast-master:

"As I am about to propose the health of our guest, let me say there should be encouragement in the founding of this medal to-night for every struggling, ambitious youth in America. Let our sons recall and applaud the cheery little newsboy at Detroit; the half-shod, half-frozen operator seeking bravely a job along the icy pikes of the Central States; the gaunt, untutored experimenter in Boston taking eagerly much-needed fees for lectures he was too modest to deliver; the embryonic inventor in New York grub-staked by a famous Wall Street man for his first stock-ticker; the deaf investigator at Menlo Park who wreaked novel retaliation on his affliction by preserving human speech forever with his phonograph; the prolific patentee who kept the pathway to the Patent Office hot with his footsteps for nearly forty years; the genius, our comrade, who took this little crystal bulb in his Promethean hand, and with it helped to give the world a glorious new light which never was before on land or sea — Thomas Alva Edison."

In his reply Edison telegraphed his speech, which consisted merely of a few words of thanks, by means of the Western Union Edison quadruplex instrument which was on the table beside him. The message was received on a "Postal" portable "quad" placed at the right of the speaker's table. The telegraph circuit was looped on a wireless set of instruments, of which the transmitter was at the left of the speaker's table. It was so arranged that when Edison operated the key a spark was transmitted over the repeating sounder to the aërial transmitter, which conveyed a wireless message to the other end of the table. It was at 10.18 that Edison placed his finger on his original Western Union quadruplex and proceeded to telegraph his message of thanks to Colonel A. B. Chandler, president of the Postal Telegraph Company. At least half those present understood the Morse code, and as soon as the instrument began to click there was complete silence, while the band softly played the opening strains of "Auld Lang Syne." A moment later, however, it was evident that there was something wrong, for the instrument clicked intermittently, and Mr. Chandler asked Edison to repeat several times. Finally Edison rapped out, "It's not up to me," and there was a hearty laugh from those who understood the Morse signals, but immediately afterwards the apparatus was adjusted and Edison successfully telegraphed his brief message.

One of the prettiest and most interesting features of this unique banquet was the procession of waiters — over a hundred — bearing ices contained in models of motors, phonographs, switchboards, automobiles, incandescent apparatus, dynamos, megaphones, and

BANQUETS

batteries, the ices themselves being in the form of incandescent bulbs. To each guest some souvenir was presented, either a small ivory box bearing a model of the "Genius with the Lamp," or a pin made in the miniature of an incandescent lamp. The menus were elaborate and beautiful, and bore a reproduction in raised medallion of a bronze bust of Edison, beneath which the inventor had inscribed his autograph.

The second notable banquet to which special reference may be made is remembered as the "Magnetic Dinner," and it was given in honor of Edison, April 15, 1905, at the Hotel Astor, New York. It was arranged by the Magnetic Club, an important institution whose members consist of the officials and employees of the telegraph, telephone, electric-light, and electric-manufacturing companies of the American metropolis. The president of the club, Colonel A. B. Chandler, presided, and acted the part of toast-master in a unique and original way, his speech being punctuated by prearranged illustrative incidents, which, though they delighted those present, almost brought a blush of embarrassment to the modest cheek of Edison.

"I desire," said Colonel Chandler, "to call attention to the most noteworthy achievements of this great old telegrapher. First I shall mention the quadruplex transmitter."

An instrument which had been concealed in a corner of the room suddenly began to "dot" and "dash" in a highly excitable manner, the orchestra commenced playing the air of "My grandfather's clock," and the three hundred guests sang:

"When they tell their stories now of the way they used to send,
    And the record-breaking work they used to do;
And the way, every day, they would roast the other end,
    We are sorry that those happy days are through."

Edison beamed with delight and even hummed the old melody a bit himself; but before he had time to express his thanks for the novelty of the idea, Colonel Chandler said: "I think that the telephone should be mentioned next." This was the signal for the ringing of a dozen 'phone bells, a chorus of "Hellos," and the singing of a verse of "Hello, my baby!" After that the phonograph was mentioned, and from the huge funnel of a "talking-machine" came the martial strains of "The Stars and Stripes Forever." The last note had scarcely died away when Colonel Chandler said: "But the greatest of all, perhaps, was electric lighting." Members of the club who knew their cues touched various buttons, and every light in the room winked out — all save the wax candles on the tables. And in the semi-darkness the excited guests sang this parody of a popular song:

> "It was just like this in the olden days,
>   Which have passed beyond recall;
> In the rare old, fair old golden days
>   It was just like this, that's all:
>
> Then we studied hard by the candle-light,
>   With our visions of future gold;
> And some have realized all right
>   Since the days of old."

Edison was called upon for a speech, but with his usual modesty he declined, though he bowed his thanks with a smile that was brighter even than one of his own electric lights.

Before closing this chapter mention should be made of another dinner which was given to Edison also during that year which saw the twenty-fifth anniversary of his invention of the incandescent electric-light system. It was of the simplest kind, and, therefore, one which, perhaps, appealed more to Edison and pleased him better than a more gorgeous banquet would have done. It was given in his honor by the General Electric Outing Club, and the members hit upon the altogether delightful plan of holding the dinner almost on the very spot which had seen the inventing and perfecting of so many Edison wonders — Menlo Park.

It was a Saturday — June 14 — and the inventor joined his entertainers about four o'clock in the afternoon, arriving at the Park in his automobile. After shaking hands with every one, Edison said he would like to have a look round — to renew his acquaintance with those well-remembered spots to which he had been so long a stranger. The buildings in which he had labored so many years are still standing, including the very room in which the first commercially successful incandescent electric lamps were manufactured — a tiny room providing accommodation for barely a dozen men. As Edison walked about the grounds with various members of the club he talked of his early struggles, of the long nights he had spent endeavoring to solve some difficult problem, of the stern fights he had had with Nature to compel her to yield the secrets she so jealously guarded, and of the final triumph of the carbon telephone transmitter and the carbon filament for the electric lamp. He recalled the fact that it was many years since he had visited his old haunts, and he declared with a smile of unusual sweetness that he was glad to return in such good company and on the quarter-century anniversary of his most important invention.

Then he went into the old workshops, and for some moments stood there thoughtfully, saying nothing, but gazing with interest on the very benches where he had frequently labored for sixty hours at a stretch. The men who were his hosts remained outside during these moments devoted to "looking backward," and were themselves silent as they recalled the impressive fact that the "Wizard" was revisiting places which had seen the birth of innumerable wonders evolved from his own brain.

Every part of the grounds was visited, and when the tour of inspection was completed Edison, who had been a little grave, was his own cheerful self again and chatted and joked with his friends in his old familiar way. The meal was ready at six o'clock. It was a lovely evening, and a noble banqueting-hall was formed by giant trees, green grass, and a cloudless sky. A great log was relegated to Edison as the seat of honor. He took it modestly and was immediately helped to a leg of cold roast chicken. This he held in one hand and a piece of bread in the other, and it was a pleasant sight, declared the members, to see the great inventor straddling the log, taking alternate bites at the browned leg and the bit of bread while relating stories of his early days. All his stories were not humorous, though a great number were. He told the younger members how he had to struggle and "hustle" before he received any encouragement or recognition, but he did not let this cast him down or lessen his determination to "get there" some day. And his advice to them, given in a semi-serious voice, was to go ahead and never give up. A path, he said, sanely laid out and honorably followed, always led somewhere — usually to success if not great riches. Some one referred to the big dinner which had been given to Edison in New York a few days previously, and added in tones which clearly indicated a desire to be contradicted: "I suppose you liked that better than this?" And

Edison replied, as every one hoped he would reply, by saying in a very earnest way: "No, sir, I had a good deal rather be here. I get tired of big banquets and seldom attend them if I can help, but a picnic like this — well, that's the way I would dine every day if I had my choice. The outdoor air whets the appetite and helps digestion. I'm glad to be here."

It was not until the sun had set and twilight had fallen that Edison bade his hosts good-by, and, entering his car, finally took his departure from the Park which his genius had made famous, and where he had so long reigned as "Wizard."

Should the reader ever be in the vicinity of New Jersey he might spend a less interesting hour than visiting Menlo Park. He will, it is true, find an air of melancholy brooding over the once famous village — as though the very atmosphere were mourning some dead and gone glory — but there is still much remaining which will repay him for the trip. Two furlongs from the railroad he will see an old, dilapidated and disused trolley-car at which he may possibly cast a contemptuous glance should he be ignorant of the fact that it is the first car of the kind which ever ran in America, and, in fact, the world. How many famous people it carried in the heyday of its youth who can say? Certainly few noted personages — and some who were not noted — who visited Edison in those "Wizard" days, failed to take a ride in the wonderful electric trolley-car before bringing their tour of inspection to a close. That car is not occupied now, at least during the day, though on cold nights, or when a storm rages, an old cow occasionally wanders in and takes her repose where the giants of the scientific world once stood. When Edison had built this car he laid down three miles of rails, and the miniature electric trolley system attracted thousands of visitors to Menlo Park. "From this little line," says a writer, "sprang the huge network of trolleys which covers country and city, in which hundreds of millions of dollars are invested, and on which billions of passengers are carried yearly." At Menlo Park you may still see some of the trolley wires, but they hang with a melancholy sag, for it is many years since they were "alive." The rails were torn up soon after Edison removed to Orange.

Having inspected the trolley-car you will probably notice a two-story building which is in a good state of repair. Inhabitants of Menlo Park take pride in informing you that it is Edison's first experimental laboratory, and that in this building were invented and perfected the incandescent electric-light system, the phonograph, the carbon telephone, and many other important inventions. The building is inhabited — the lower story by a volunteer fire-brigade and the upper by an amateur theatrical company. Then there is a little brick building which, twenty-five years ago, was the "main office," and where Edison used occasionally to attend to his correspondence. An old man lives there now — or did until quite recently — who was popularly regarded as a hermit, and who, when questioned by interested visitors, would disclaim any knowledge of his distinguished landlord. And this, perhaps, is scarcely to be wondered at seeing that he pays no rent.

Behind the old laboratory is the machine shop built by Edison, and which has seen the creation of those electrical wonders which shed a glory on the name of Menlo Park. Now that machine shop stands vacant and deserted and crumbling into decay. There are, however, heavy brick foundations remaining in good preservation whereon Edison built his first dynamos —

gigantic affairs weighing nearly thirty tons, and which were the astonishment of the world. These dynamos are no longer in existence — they performed their duties, and years ago were reduced to scrap-iron and sold to the junk shop.

Though it is almost twenty-five years since Edison removed his laboratory from Menlo Park, his name is still mentioned with pride by the villagers. He was known to every one, and would chat and crack jokes with the humblest just as readily then as he does to-day. The stranger to Menlo Park hears many anecdotes about how the inventor would remain days and nights at his work without sleep and with very little food, and how he showed irritation only when disturbed while engaged in solving some problem which had defied every one else. Stories of his good-heartedness and geniality are numerous, and there are few who have not some incident to relate to the credit of the inventor. Meet the "oldest inhabitant" and ask him if he knew Edison, and he will answer: "What, Tom Edison? Well, I should say. Me and him was like brothers. Always affable he was, and very free with his money. Yes, he's got on since he lived here, and I guess he's as well known the other side of the world as he is in Menlo Park. That talking-machine was a wonderful thing, and made a great name for him. I remember the folks coming from New York to see the first electric lamps, and how astonished they were. But we weren't, for there was nothing, we thought, that Tom Edison couldn't do. He was a wonder, sure!"

Many people to this day suppose that Edison still resides in Menlo Park, and the post-office there is constantly forwarding letters to the inventor which have been addressed to the once famous locality under the impression that the "Wizard" is still its chiefest inhabitant. It was, indeed, a bad day for Menlo Park when Edison removed his laboratory to Orange, and the village never recovered from the shock. When the inventor left, all the glamour and mystery which had made the little place famous the world over faded away and the town rapidly began to decline in popular favor. Each year saw some decrease in its population until to-day it is little better than a deserted village. The railroad trains drop very few passengers now at Menlo Park, and these are for the most part pilgrims anxious to visit the place where Edison invented those innumerable devices which have made his name a household word. And after visiting the laboratory they seldom fail to view the Edison homestead a few hundred feet distant, and which was occupied for some years after the inventor left Menlo Park by his daughter, who now lives in Germany. The property still belongs to Edison, but is now tenanted by an Italian family who live there on the same terms as the old hermit, — rent free.

CHAPTER XIX

IN EUROPE

EDISON has not made many visits to Europe, and gives as his reason that he cannot stand all the kindnesses which are showered upon him. But he has stated on more than one occasion that he contemplates a return visit in the near future, when he hopes to meet many of those interesting people who have paid his laboratory visits at various times. Edison's most noted trip to Europe was in 1889, when he went across especially to visit the Paris Exposition at which he was so prolific an exhibitor. His preparations for the display of his inventions were of a very elaborate nature, and a small army of men were engaged for months preparing the various exhibits. No fewer than three hundred immense cases of goods were shipped to Paris, the freight alone costing $2500, while the total expenses of the Edison exhibition reached $75,000. One-third of the space allowed the United States in the Machinery Temple was allotted to him, and without doubt his exhibit was the sensation of the Exposition.

Edison did not visit Paris until long after the Exposition was open to the public, but on the 27th of April the following cable appeared in the New York papers: "President Sadi-Carnot has been profuse in courtesies and attentions to Thomas Alva Edison, the American inventor, since the latter's arrival in Paris for the purpose of superintending the establishment of his exhibit of electrical apparatus on the Champs de Mars. Mr. Edison has been received at the official residence with the utmost cordiality by the President, and has had several interviews with him, in which M. Carnot has manifested the greatest interest in the inventor's work."

It so happened that a New York *Evening Sun* reporter had been in communication with Edison's secretary at his Orange laboratory the day before, and his surprise when the item met his eye was great. As the announcement was not confined to one paper, but had appeared in nearly all the morning papers, it was obvious that there was a mistake somewhere. Doubtless the French President had been imposed upon. The reporter, who was anxious that his paper should maintain its reputation for correct news, immediately travelled down to Orange for the purpose of finding out whether Edison had secretly invented some method of crossing the Atlantic during the night and had really arrived in Paris, or whether he himself had been deceived in what he had been told regarding the inventor the day before. The minuteness of the despatches in describing the manner in which M. Carnot was fraternizing with the great American inventor on the Champs de Mars made them appear as truth personified. The following amusing description of the reporter's "search after facts" appeared in a late edition of his paper:

"The newspaper man carried a pocketful of the strange despatches down to Orange, in order to show Edison's private secretary how irreligiously the latter had imposed on the reporter's credulity when he declared yesterday that Mr. Edison was upstairs in his workshop undergoing a process of incubation on another electrical discovery.

"'Is Mr. Edison in?' the reporter inquired of the office boy, very authoritatively.

"'He has just gone to New York with his private secretary,' the boy replied.

"'He is in this country, then, not in Europe — not in Paris?'

"The boy appeared dazed. He looked around him once or twice as though about to call for assistance, when the reporter assured him that everything was all right.

"'Has Mr. Edison a representative at hand?'

"Mr. Bachelor was summoned. The reporter produced the despatches. Mr. Bachelor hastily scanned one of them and smiled.

"'Well, all that I have got to say is that he was here this morning. If he is now in Paris he must have gone by the air-line.'

"Mr. Bachelor smiled again as he spoke, and called the attention of several in the office to the articles. All laughed heartily.

"Mr. Bachelor stated that Mr. Edison was in the city for the day, and would return to Orange that night. He had no idea how it was that such insane despatches had been cabled from abroad, but thought that some one had been impersonating Mr. Edison in the French capital and had imposed himself upon the President."

The sequel to this story never appeared. Undoubtedly some one had endeavored to pass himself off as Edison, but as soon as it became known that the inventor had not left Orange, the French papers made a joke of the matter and no action was taken. The impostor, whoever he was, did not go to the extent of "touching" the President for a loan, and therefore his object in passing himself off as some one else was not very clear. Edison laughed when he heard the stories, but did not consider it worth while to make inquiries regarding them when he did reach Paris. He thought the President might feel sore on the subject.

A brief description of Edison's exhibit at the Paris Exposition of 1889 may not be without interest, for many readers possibly did not see it, while those who had that good fortune will not be averse to recalling the wonders of the great electrical display. The exhibits of Edison were classed as follows: Telegraphic, telephonic, phonographic, physical electric lighting, underground conductors, the manufacture of incandescent lamps, electric motors, and the magnetic separation and analysis of metals.

The most striking feature of the display was a monster incandescent lamp, 40 feet high and mounted on a pedestal 20 feet square. The American flag was shown in red, white, and blue lamps on one side, the French escutcheon on the other, while in front the flags of the two republics with the name "Edison" above, and the date, "1889," below, appeared; all these features were made of opalescent electric lamps. Twelve steps of vari-colored lamps led to the top of the pedestal, where there was a niche in which was placed a bust of the inventor surrounded by tiny lamps. The pedestal was surmounted by a perfect model of the standard Edison lamp and socket magnified 20,000 times. In other words, the great lamp was composed of 20,000 perfect 16-c.p. lamps which, although not lit, acted as a medium through which the light of the immense carbon might shine.

Inside the base was the switchboard, where an operator was stationed, who could produce varied and dazzling effects by the quick manipulation of the switches. The different devices were independent of the others, but could be lighted in rapid succession, and the crowd was never tired of watching the bottom light run up the base, step by step, and illumine the various designs until it reached the carbon of the great lamp above.

In front of this monument were arranged tables on which were set out working models of many of Edison's most famous inventions, including the duplex and quadruplex telegraphs, the phonoplex, stock telegraph, printing telegraph, automatic telegraph and perforator, and the harmonic telegraph. There were also shown in other parts of the Machinery Hall voltmeters and indicators, galvanometers, the pyromagnetic motor and generator, the vote recorder, the water-bridge, etheroscope, odoroscope, electric pen, vocal engine, megaphone, and many other wonderful inventions. In the room containing these models an operator sat at a type-setting and distributing machine, setting up matter from a phonograph, which was afterwards printed by a press run by an electric motor.

Besides all these interesting things there were shown the Edison system of underground conductors, a sectional view of Edison tubes laid in place and connected, comprising feeders, mains, taps, junction and distributing boxes — in fact the whole paraphernalia necessary to the correct working of a genuine electrical central station. The methods adopted in the manufacturing of the tubes were also shown. The dynamo plant installed comprised a complete three-wire system run from 500-light machines; also a No. 56 dynamo having a capacity of 2500 lights, and a 1200-volt dynamo running the 100 big lamps surrounding the entire exhibit. The working of the Edison meter system was also exhibited, together with a magnetic ore separator in operation, showing the crushing of the quartz and the separation of the ore from the silicates by means of powerful magnets. A glass case which attracted universal attention was one containing, besides specimens of every incandescent electric lamp made, a wonderful collection of bamboos and fibres, used in the manufacture of the filaments.

But more popular even than the electrical display was the "Phonographic Temple," where dozens of machines speaking every European language were a constant source of delight and astonishment to the thousands who crowded around them, all anxious to hear their own native tongues. There was a small pavilion where visitors could make records for themselves, and afterwards experience the novelty of hearing their own voices. It must be remembered that there were thousands who had never heard a phonograph before, and so some idea can be obtained of the interest which this Phonographic Temple created. The mechanism of the machine was explained by operators who spoke in several languages, and, for the benefit of those who desired to know more of the wonderful "talking-machine" than that to be obtained from a brief description, lectures were delivered by various scientific experts at different hours of the day and night.

It is little to be wondered at, therefore, if after exhibiting so many wonders, Edison's arrival in the French capital created excitement. He was more popular, more mobbed, more run after than all the royal visitors put together. And his striking personality pleased the crowds, who constantly broke into cheering when it was known that he was paying the Exposition a visit and his form was recognized. Edison was accompanied by his wife, and Miss Marion Edison, the inventor's eldest daughter. Every scientific society in the capital gave a dinner in honor of the celebrated inventor, and the Municipality of Paris presented him with a banquet which was attended by every notable person in the city. The *Figaro* gave him a great dinner at which nearly all the theatrical artistes and litterateurs in France were in attendance. In his speech, the editor said: "Never can a sufficient tribute of honor be paid to him who, by the telephone, transports speech from pole to pole; who, by the phonograph, repeats to our ears the blessed words of dear dead ones, giving them to us with their charm of intonation; who has illuminated the world with a new and dazzling light. He has merited well of all countries."

Some years previous to this, however, the *Figaro* came out with a somewhat remarkable description of Edison and one of his inventions, and in the course of a long and startling article it solemnly declared that Edison did not "belong to himself." "He is the property," so the writer said, "of the telegraph company, which lodges him in New York at a superb hotel, keeps him on a luxurious footing, and pays him a formidable salary, so as to be the one to know of and profit by his discoveries. The company has, in the laboratory of Edison, men in its employ who do not leave him for a moment, at the table, on the street, in the workshop. So that this wretched man, watched as never was a malefactor, cannot give a second's thought to his personal affairs without one of his guards saying, 'Mr. Edison, of what are you thinking?'"

This interesting description was copied into a good many American papers, and created much fun among Edison's associates and those acquainted with him. A few days after the translation appeared, a Cincinnati paper came out with the following account of the "Wizard," which in turn was copied in several French journals. Its sarcasm, however, was probably lost on those readers who had read and digested the *Figaro* article.

"Edison, the phonograph man, is wretched unless he invents half a dozen things every day. He does it just for amusement when regular business is not pressing. The other day he went out for a little stroll, and before he had gone a square he thought out a plan for walking on one leg so as to rest the other.

"He hailed a milk wagon and told the driver of a little invention that had popped through his head just that moment for delivering milk without getting out of the wagon or even stopping his horses. A simple force pump, with hose attached, worked by the foot, would do the business. Milkmen who dislike to halt for anything in their mad career, because it prevents them running over as many children as they might otherwise do, would appreciate this improvement. Edison isn't sure but that sausage and sauerkraut could be delivered in the same way.

"He then stepped into a hotel office, and, observing the humiliation which guests encounter in seeking to obtain information from the high-toned clerk, he sat down in the reading-room, and in five minutes had invented a hotel clerk to work by machinery, warranted to stand behind the counter any length of time desired, and answer all questions with promptness, correctness, and suavity — diamond pin and hair parted in the middle, if desired.

"Lounging into the billiard-room he was struck with the endless amount of cushions to each table. Quick as lightning he thought of a better and more economical plan — cushion the balls. He immediately pulled out a postal card and wrote to Washington applying for a patent.

"When Edison started to go out he had to pass the

barber shop of the hotel, and as he did so he sighed to think that, with all his genius and creative imagination, he could never hope to equal the knight of the razor as a talking-machine. This saddened him, so he went home and invented no more that day."

But to return to Paris. The French Society of Civil Engineers gave a dinner for Edison on the first landing of the Eiffel Tower. The builder of the great structure was in the chair, and at the close of the many speeches delivered in honor of the distinguished guest, M. Eiffel suggested that coffee should be taken in his private room on the highest landing of the tower, to which the public was not admitted. Elevators took the guests to the room, which was large and commodious, easily accommodating the seventy-five gentlemen who made up the party. Among the guests was M. Gounod, who sang and played for Edison's especial benefit, and afterwards composed a piece of music which he sent as an autograph to Mrs. Edison, who had expressed a desire for the famous composer's signature. M. Eiffel, not to be outdone, wrote on a slip of paper, "Notre belle journée serait complète si nous avions en le plaisir d'avoir avec nous Madame et Mademoiselle Marion Edison," and sent it with his compliments.

Before he left Paris a gold medal was struck in honor of the inventor, and Edison acknowledged the kindnesses which had been showered upon him by drawing a check to be given to the poor. Edison had thought that possibly he might have received some valuable suggestions in electricity while abroad, but he was disappointed. Apparently there was nothing any one else could teach him in that line. He was interested, and somewhat amused, to discover that scientific men abroad were greatly surprised that he was not more of a scientist in the higher sense of the phrase. They could not understand that he was between the scientific man and the public, as it were. However, their admiration for him was none the less.

On his return Edison thus humorously described his experiences in Paris: "Dinners, dinners, dinners, all the time," he said. "But in spite of them all they did not get me to speak. Once I got Chauncey Depew to make a speech for me, and I got Reid, our Minister there, to make three or four. I could never get used to so many dinners. At noon I would sit down to what they called *déjeuner*. That would last until nearly three o'clock, and a few hours later would come a big dinner. It was terrible. I looked down from the Eiffel Tower on the biggest dinner I ever saw, given to the mayors of France by the Municipality of Paris. I saw 8900 people eating at one time. I ate one American dinner while abroad, given by 'Buffalo Bill.' Depew, Reid, John Hoey, and lots of other Americans were invited. We had, among other things American, an immense pie, Boston baked beans, and peanuts. John Hoey had brought some watermelons, which we ate. Now I feel I must starve for a few months in order to get straight again after all those dinners. I wonder they didn't kill me."

From Paris Edison visited other European cities, where he was accorded an equally enthusiastic reception. At Heidelberg the German Association of Advanced Scientists gave a dinner in his honor at which twelve hundred guests sat down. The Grand Duke of Baden was there with all his guards, and delivered an address through the phonograph in German. He was gifted with a powerful voice, and the phonograph repeated his words in such clear and thrilling tones that the speech was heard and understood by hundreds of people who were standing outside. In Heidelberg the inhabitants go to bed at 10 o'clock as a rule, but on that occasion the "Advanced Scientists" were still making merry at 3 A.M.

While in Italy Edison was fêted with equal enthusiasm, and he received letters of commendation from King Humbert and Queen Margherita for his phonograph, which Chevalier Capello had exhibited before them. It was on this occasion that the report was circulated that Edison had been made a count by the Italian monarch. So persistent was this rumor, and so eagerly was it believed in America, that when Edison returned to his native country he and his wife were addressed as "Count and Countess Edison," to their amusement and embarrassment. The inventor said that the story was first circulated by a French reporter, who took the personal letters of the King and Queen to mean a title at the very least.

Edison then crossed over to England and paid a brief visit to London, where he was the recipient of a very hearty welcome. The Lord Mayor entertained him at the Mansion House, and various dinners were given in his honor. One of the British institutions which he tried was the beer, and it didn't agree with him at all. He afterwards declared that it sank to the bottom of one's stomach and there stayed for an indefinite period. "It must be a good thing to ballast ships with," he said on one occasion with a smile.

One of the things in London that surprised Edison was the obvious fact that the Metropolitan and District railway trains were not driven by electricity. "Nothing could be simpler," he protested, "than to substitute electricity for steam." He had offered to do it long ago, and stated that if he got the order then he could carry it out "almost offhand." And he gave to a reporter a glowing picture of what the underground would be without its steam and its choking sulphur fumes. "The underground atmosphere," said Edison, "must be bad for the lungs. With an electric motive force there would be no more smoke. And the motion of the trains would keep the air of the tunnels pure. The companies might also light them with electric lights throughout." Those remarks were made by Edison nearly twenty years ago. How long was it before London took the advice of the man who knew what he was talking about?

CHAPTER XX

HOME LIFE

EDISON'S home life is an exceptionally happy one. He lives in a beautiful house called "Glenmont," in Llewellyn Park, at the foot of the Orange Mountain, with his wife and children. This residence Edison purchased soon after his second marriage in 1886, though at the time he scarcely had the intention of occupying quite so large a house. It happened, however, that "Glenmont," which had been built at a cost of an immense sum of money, as well as an expenditure of much artistic effort, was placed on sale to satisfy the creditors of the absconding owner, and the inventor bought the place outright — house, furniture, library, artistic treasures, which it had taken ten years to collect, thirteen acres of park and garden, an acre of glass houses, several horses and cows, and a well-filled poultry run. At the time Edison, in showing his newly purchased paradise to a friend, said, "It's a great deal too nice for me, but — well, it isn't half nice enough for the little wife here," placing his hand gently on the arm of the beautiful girl who stood beside him.

The house — a handsome structure of brick and wood — belongs to the Queen Anne period of architecture, and was built with a view to comfort as well as elegance. The porch, covered with purple wistaria in the spring, is massive in its proportions and hospitable in appearance. Inside is the comfort one finds in an old English country house. The square hall is furnished with oak tables, a finely designed open fireplace, where in winter a log fire is always burning, and cosey window seats generous with soft cushions. Japanese jars filled with flowers from hothouse and garden occupy every corner, and the air is laden with the odor of blossoms. At night the hall is illuminated by electric lights cunningly concealed, which produce a soft glow infinitely preferable to the brilliance of the more usual cluster of incandescent lamps. On the east wall hangs the original of Andersen's famous "Le matin après le bal."

To the right of the hall is the library, full of nooks and corners, where readers may pass the hours in quietude with their favorite authors. One entire side of the room is taken up by an immense fireplace, furnished with old-fashioned andirons, while the logs are piled high, ready for the cold weather or a chilly evening. Though the room is lighted by a double window there is a certain sombreness about the apartment, partly due to the outside vegetation, and partly to a third window of stained glass through which the light filters in a rather solemn and religious way. Dante's head glows from this window, which was designed by Edison, who is a great admirer of the Italian author's writings. A bronze bust of Edison stands on one of the small tables, and a bronze equestrian group between the two windows. The room is distinctly a library — plain and severe — and its principal furnishing consists of books. You will not find a great number of scientific works here, for they are kept down at the laboratory, but those dealing with modern thought are numerous. The works of the standard authors of England, America, and France occupy the shelves of the home library, for the inventor likes to vary his reading at times by a masterpiece of Dumas or Scott or Hawthorne.

Whenever his wife recommends him a book, and Edison is in the humor for reading an unscientific work, he will commence it right away and not lay the volume down until it is finished. He is not a very quick reader, but absorbs what he reads very thoroughly. For Dumas's works he has a very great admiration, and he thinks "The Count of Monte Cristo" probably the finest romance that was ever penned. He read it fifteen years ago and under somewhat interesting circumstances. One evening, on returning from the laboratory, his mind busy with some problem which defied solution, the inventor entered his library, closed the doors, and walked up and down for hours trying to solve the difficulty. Finally Mrs. Edison entered the room, and with a desire to divert her husband's thoughts she picked up the first book that came to her hand and inquired of the inventor, "Have you read this?" He stopped in his walk and looked at the title. It was "The Count of Monte Cristo." Opening the book a moment, Edison answered, "No, I never have. Is it good?" Mrs. Edison declared that it was a great work, and she was sure he would enjoy it. "All right," he replied, "I guess I'll start right away." He settled himself comfortably, and a moment later was absorbed in the fascinating story. He read on and on and through the night and never laid the book aside until the sun shone through the window. Then he took his hat and went down to the laboratory, and after many hours solved the difficulty which had been worrying him. When he returned home he declared that "The Count of Monte Cristo" was a fine fellow, and had certainly aided him in discovering a solution to a very difficult problem. After that he always took Mrs. Edison's advice with regard to fiction.

One of Edison's favorite authors is Gaboriau, and he was very sorry when that king of detective-story writers died. What pleased Edison with regard to this writer was the fact that he didn't waste any time getting down to business. The story was commenced at once, there were no irritating preliminaries, you became absorbed in a very intricate plot from the first page. Another favorite is Edgar Allan Poe, and he derived considerable pleasure from reading "The Murders in the Rue Morgue" and "Arnheim." Among less exciting writers he has a fondness for Ruskin and Dickens. Flammarion and Jules Verne he has read over and over again.

But to return to "Glenmont." Mrs. Edison's drawing-room, on the side of the hall opposite to the library, is a beautiful and spacious apartment with an archway in the centre supported by onyx pillars. The hangings are crimson and the furniture carved rosewood. A grand piano stands at one corner, and near it is a comfortable easy-chair where Edison very often sits while his wife plays to him from his favorite composer — Beethoven. No music appeals to Edison like that of Beethoven, and the very name of the composer will bring into his eyes an expression very much resembling adoration. Edison at one time played the violin himself, but put it aside when he found it was occupying rather more of his time than he could very well spare. He also sang, and had a good voice, but experimenting in acoustics affected his larynx and he soon gave up all attempts in vocal music. He still finds, however, some of his greatest happiness in listening to the performance of other musicians.

EDISON'S "DEN" IN HIS HOME AT LLEWELLYN PARK, N. J.

The dining room, on the same floor, is simply and severely furnished; the sideboard, occupying a recess facing the window, displays one or two pieces of silver only. Edison probably spends less time in this room than any other in the house, for he is not fond of remaining long at his meals.

The most interesting room in the house is on the second floor, and generally known as the "den." It is a big room, with a great window at one end looking over the Jersey Hills. There are interesting portraits on the walls — portraits of Edison when he was a little fellow of four in a plaid dress, and when he was a newsboy on the Grand Trunk. And at one end of the room a small alcove is devoted to photographs of the inventor taken at different ages — a sacred spot which is guarded jealously by Mrs. Edison. There are two special portraits, one showing the inventor in his favorite holland "over-alls," which is his wife's favorite portrait, and the other taken when a young man of twenty-four or so, at the time when he was, as he says, a "hustler" of the most hustling kind. This photograph is the favorite one of the inventor himself.

Then there is a businesslike-looking roll-top desk where Edison sits occasionally and replies to his private correspondence — where he writes to his daughter Madelyn, at Bryn Mawr College, or to a particular friend. On his desk are portraits of his wife and his children — a particularly charming one of his daughter with her chin on her hand and her father's serious expression in her eyes. Above the desk are two interesting items of Edison's early days: a copy of the paper he published on the train and a bill for ten dollars signed by Edison about the same period of his life. There is also a "tin-type" of the inventor, which is some forty-eight years old, and shows the boy in a jersey and cap, and, wearing that engaging, frank smile which always attracted strangers.

In another corner of the room, beneath a strong electric lamp, is a comfortable easy-chair furnished with a reading-desk on which are a couple of books. This is where Edison invariably sits after dinner and smokes a cigar or a couple of cigars and — thinks. One of the books is a treatise on chemistry, while the other is an ordinary exercise book about half an inch thick and contains a hundred or more pencil drawings made by the inventor himself. It is one of Edison's note-books, though not strictly speaking a "notion" book. The little volume contains diagrams of inventions already conceived, and some of them are very carefully drawn. Seldom does an evening pass without Mr. Edison contributing some drawing to his notebook, for, as a rule, his pencil is as active as his brain. He loves to explain his meaning with a pencil illustration, and when he is doing this for a visitor it always amuses him to hear the inevitable request, "Oh, Mr. Edison, would you mind signing this and putting the date?" There must be a great number of these interesting autographs in existence.

In this room is a large glass case containing Edison's collection of medals and decorations. Few men have had more honors of the kind showered upon them during their lives; and though Edison treasures them a good deal for what they represent, he places little value on the medals themselves. This was shown a few years ago when some one called and asked the inventor if he would allow his decorations and medals to be put on exhibition. Edison had no objection, if any one were sufficiently interested in them — which he very much doubted. The case was produced, but Edison had lost the key. It was not to be found, so the box was forcibly opened. Then a greater difficulty still presented itself. The visitor wished for some description of the different medals, and wanted to know for what each particular trinket had been awarded. And Edison couldn't help him! He had totally forgotten the circumstances under which he had received at least half his honors, and no effort on his part could recall the facts. So they were all put back in the case and, though they were subsequently shown, the exhibit was hardly as interesting as it might have been.

But among the medals in the den are one or two which deserve a word. There is, for instance, the Albert Medal, which was presented to Edison by the Prince of Wales in honor of his father, the Prince Consort. With the medal is a series of letters, including one from the Prince, and one from Sir Julian Pauncefote, who took the medal to America. The latter is a document showing much grace of composition and quite Chesterfieldian in style. The third communication is from Secretary of State Foster, and amused Edison not a little when he received it. The medal was entrusted to Mr. Foster for delivery, and after informing Edison of his charge and explaining how delighted he was to present the medal, he concludes by saying that Edison can have it "by paying express charges"!

There are also among these medals the three degrees of the Legion of Honor — Chevalier, Officeyr, and Commander. The highest degree was conferred on the inventor during the Paris Exposition of 1889, when he paid his memorable visit to the French capital. At about the same time a cable was sent to the United States announcing that Edison had been created a count by the King of Italy. The democratic nation was flattered at the honor conferred upon their countryman, but of course hoped the inventor would refuse the title. The rumor was incorrect, and when Edison returned after his European tour, the first thing the reporters asked was, whether he were really a count, and much to the disappointment of the interrogators he replied that he was not. "But," said Edison apologetically, as some of those present seemed rather hurt that he hadn't received a title, "I've come back decorated with the red ribbon of the Legion of Honor of France. I have been made Commander, the highest title they confer on a foreigner." Then, with a smile, he added: "When I first exhibited the old phonograph over there, France made me a Chevalier of the Legion of Honor. At the time of the electrical exhibition they advanced me a grade, making me an Officeur. This summer they raised the ante again [Edison plays poker] and made me a Commander, I believe they call it. At all events, it's the highest decoration of the Legion of Honor. Over in France they think a great deal of these decorations. A great many privileges go with them. The Minister of Foreign Affairs gave me this one through Ambassador Reid, sending a very nice letter with it. At Mr. Reid's house they wanted to put the ribbon and cross around my neck, but I would not have it there."

The "very nice" letter to which Edison referred is kept in the case with the decorations and, translated, is as follows:

"SIR, — I have the honor of announcing that, upon my suggestion, the President of the Republic desires to confer upon you the Cross of a Commander of the National Order of the Legion of Honor. In awarding you to-day this high distinction, the Government of the Republic wishes to recognize the services, exceptional in every sense of the word, which you have rendered to science by your marvellous inventions, all of which have been admired and envied by the visitors, French and foreign, to the Champs de Mars. We are happy in offering to you a souvenir of your visit to Paris and your participation in the national exhibition in which the great Republic of the United States has taken so brilliant a place, thus proving again the indissoluble ties which attach it to France.

"You, yourself, Sir, in becoming our visitor have endeavored to ally yourself with these sentiments of cordial sympathy. It is particularly agreeable to me in recognizing this fact, to assure you of our appreciation of it. Accept, Sir, the assurance of my highest consideration.

"Spuller."

Many other decorations, medals, and interesting letters does the case contain, but they are seldom taken out unless a visitor expresses a special desire to see them. Mrs. Edison looks after them, keeps the trinkets in order, and is proud of them, but were it not for her care the probability is that they would have been lost or stolen long ago.

Mrs. Edison's boudoir is a pretty and home-like room, furnished in light colors, contains plenty of books, and is always generously supplied with flowers. Many portraits hang upon the walls, prominent among them being those of her father and husband, and, of course, several photographs of her children taken at different periods of their lives. The windows command most magnificent views of the Orange Valley, and the room is so bright and cheerful that Mrs. Edison and her children spend a great deal of their time here.

From this room a door leads to Mrs. Edison's bedroom, another pretty apartment, containing many interesting pictures and photographs. There is a portrait of Edison at fourteen, another of Mrs. Edison at sixteen, and a very fine painting of the first Mrs. Edison. A door opens on to a roof garden, over which an awning is spread in summer and where many pleasant tea-parties are given.

Of the other rooms in the house it is needless to speak, for all are characterized by the same good taste and simplicity, whether it is a guest-chamber or little Theodore's play-room. The grounds are extensive, beautifully kept, shady with well-grown elms and other trees, contain croquet and tennis lawns, five or six glass-houses, pasture for several Alderney cows, and an extensive fowl-run. Edison keeps horses, but has no great fondness for them, as he regards the "friend of man" as a poor motor. As a matter of fact, both Mr. and Mrs. Edison are a little afraid of horses, each having been in one or two bad accidents. Several motors are kept at the Glenmont garage, and Charles Edison, the inventor's seventeen-year-old son, is an expert chauffeur. All the family are keen automobilists, and are by no means afraid of exceeding the speed limit, even Mrs. Edison herself delighting in covering the Jersey roads at thirty miles and more an hour.

The present Mrs. Edison is the inventor's second wife, and still a young and very beautiful woman. She is the daughter of Lewis Miller, the founder and President of the Chautauqua Assembly, who died in 1899. Mr. Miller was himself an inventor of considerable note, his reaping, binding, mowing, and thrashing machines being known to every farmer. He was also the founder of a model Sunday School, a millionaire, and the father of ten sons. Mrs. Edison met the inventor in Akron, Ohio, the home of her father, and it is generally believed to have been a case of love at first sight. They were married within a year of the meeting. Mrs. Edison takes considerable interest in her husband's work, and she has watched the development of many of his inventions with considerable pride. She frequently goes down to the laboratory and has even assisted at an occasional experiment, much to the inventor's amusement. Up to quite recently Edison would have his lunch at the laboratory, and Mrs. Edison either sent the basket, which she herself prepared, by a special messenger, or took it herself in the automobile. Now she generally calls for her absent-minded husband about 1.30 and insists upon his accompanying her back to the house, where the inventor enjoys a modest meal and afterwards smokes a cigar. He objected at first, but Mrs. Edison, who has a will, was firm, and finally he laughingly capitulated, and now takes his meals more regularly.

Of this happy union there are three children — Madelyn, a very pretty girl of eighteen, who is shortly to graduate from Bryn Mawr; Charles, who is still at college; and Theodore, the pet of the family, who is not quite nine. The family life of this brilliant and simple man is an ideal one, and he has certainly reaped the reward of his labors in happiness and contentment, which are not always the lot of those who strive.

CHAPTER XXI

HIS PERSONALITY

MANY readers doubtless know Edison best from the portrait published twenty years ago which shows him listening to the phonograph. Although taken so long since, the inventor still resembles this photograph to a remarkable degree. He is older, of course, but his face wears that same youthful expression which will, without doubt, always be its chief characteristic, whatever age he may reach. He is of medium height, powerfully and compactly built, and, when at work in his laboratory, usually wears a well-worn coat, much stained with chemicals, a pair of trousers which have seen better days, spotless linen, and an old-fashioned white string tie. His head is massive, the forehead high, and the deep-set gray eyes extraordinarily keen. Indeed, the latter are startlingly luminous, and, when he is interested, light up his entire face. The nose is straight, the mouth tender and humorous. He is somewhat deaf in his right ear, and, through constantly placing his hand behind the left orifice in order to catch what is being said, the organ has been pressed slightly forward.

Edison does not regard his deafness as an affliction, and on more than one occasion he has declared that it has saved his listening to much nonsense which could only have resulted in the waste of a lot of valuable time. His wonderful powers of concentration

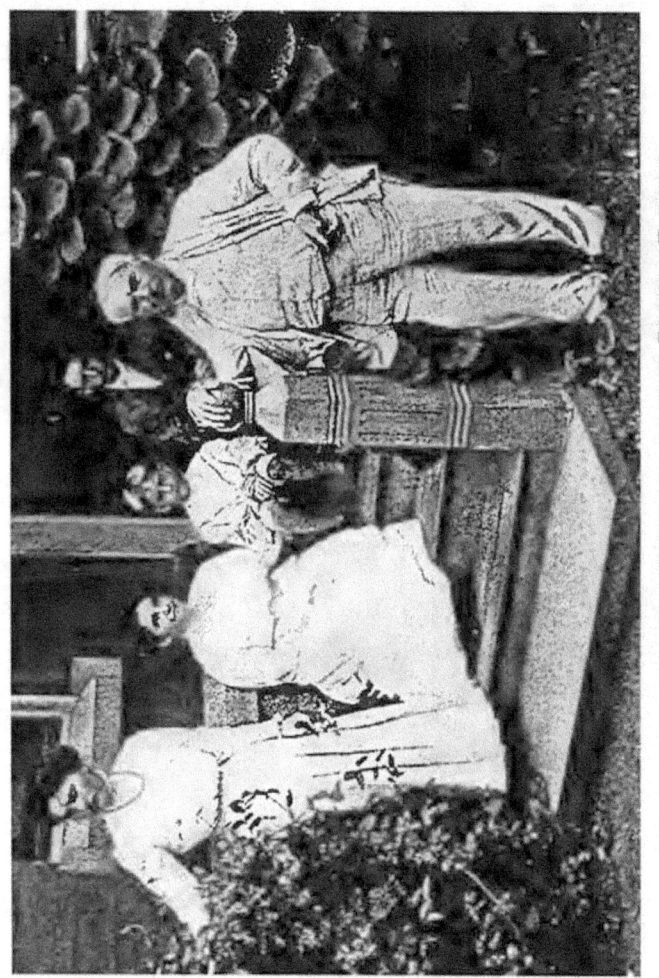

MR. AND MRS. EDISON AND FAMILY ON THE PORCH OF THEIR HOME AT LLEWELLYN PARK, N.J.

have been ascribed to this partial deafness, and certainly it has enabled him to pursue his investigations undisturbed in the midst of hammerings, conversation, and a hundred-and-one noises which might have distracted him had he possessed unimpaired hearing. If Edison does not look upon this deafness as a blessing in disguise, he at all events regards it with that cheerfulness which prevents it in any way detracting from his full enjoyment of life. People who know Edison well have declared that his deafness is more a psychological phenomenon than a physical condition, for he can very easily hear that which interests him while being perfectly oblivious to that which does not. Edison has always been a celebrity of especial interest to aurists, and many have called upon him firm in the belief that they could restore his hearing. One visited the Orange laboratory quite recently, and after explaining a method which he declared would bring about a speedy cure, begged the inventor to submit himself to treatment. Edison, however, declined, and being asked for a reason said, "I am afraid you might succeed." And then, with his humorous smile, he added, "Supposing you did? Think of the lot of stuff I'd have to listen to that I don't want to hear! To be a little deaf has its advantages, and on the whole I prefer to let well enough alone."

Apropos of his deafness a story is told illustrative of his ability to hear when least expected. A number of visitors had called at the laboratory, and though Edison, as usual, was extremely busy, he made them welcome, was polite and genial, and never expressed any irritability even when foolish questions were shouted at him in unnecessarily high-pitched keys. Every one had evidently been told that the inventor was very deaf and they adjusted their tones to suit a conversation which might have been carried on at a distance of a mile or so. Then the humorist of the party said to a companion in his ordinary voice, "I guess he would hear if we asked him to take a drink." Edison smilingly turned and, looking the young man squarely in the eye, he said, "Yes, perhaps I should; but no, thank you, not to-day."

Some one has described Edison as "thoroughly comfortable and undeniably human." It is a queer form of description, and yet it suits the inventor admirably. Those portraits or drawings which show him with head resting upon his hand, and a solemn, dreamy look in his eyes, are all wrong. Edison is the exact reverse of a dreamer, and always has been — he never gives himself time to dream, and his chief characteristics through life have been marvellous alertness, indomitable determination, and mercurial energy. His eyes are more often laughing with suppressed humor than solemn with thought. When he was a young man, and no one knew him, he was shy in disposition and seldom spoke of himself or his doings. When he became famous he did not "grow out of proportion to himself," but was the same simple, unaffected, *human* being that he had always been. He has about as much conceit and self-esteem as there is air in one of his own electric globes, and the thing he fears most in life is a "swelled head." His kindliness is unfailing, and he never loses his temper. No man in the laboratory has ever seen Edison "let himself go"; and though his eyes may take on the sternness of a Napoleon, his anger never expresses itself outwardly. One of his workmen declared to the writer that the thing that surprised him most about the "old man" (as he is called in all affection) was the way he kept his temper. "When he would lie down to take an hour's sleep," said this assistant, "after working, perhaps, on something for a couple of days or more, and, for some important reason, we had to wake him up, and nearly shake the life out of him in doing so, he never showed any irritability, but would merely tell us to 'go easy,' and not knock quite all the stuffing out of him." Probably if Edison had been born with less patience he would not have been enabled to accomplish so much, for temper uses up more energy than the most strenuous hard work.

One of Edison's chief personal characteristics is a disregard for the conventionalities of dress. From the days when he spoiled a new suit with a bottle of chemicals he has had rather a contempt for fine clothes. "He's the poorest man at dressing," said an aggrieved assistant on one occasion, "that ever lived, and doesn't care what he wears. He'll buy a suit of clothes and come into the laboratory with it just as it came from the store, and the first thing he does is to throw the coat in a dusty corner and sit down where some chemicals have been spilt." Not so long ago Edison always wore a long linen duster — a masculine "Mother Hubbard," as some admirer once called it — and a dilapidated straw hat, but within recent years he has discarded both these articles of dress, and, greatly to his wife's relief, appears somewhat better clothed. But still, as telegraph operators, who regard Edison as one of themselves, are proud to state, the inventor is no "dude." He still wears mighty plain clothes, but they are less noticeable for hard usage than formerly.

In spite of his peculiar ideas regarding dress, however, Edison has theories about correct clothing and its bearing towards health which, coming from a thinking man, may very well be considered. He never wears an overcoat, for the simple reason that it fails lamentably to keep out the cold. The wind gets up the sleeves, he declares, and between the folds, rendering the garment useless as a protector against the attacks of an American winter. Much better, he says, to turn one's attention to the underclothing. This, if properly made, will stick to the skin and defy the elements. If it is unreasonably cold Edison will wear a double set of undergarments, and if a death-dealing blizzard sets in he may put on a third, but he never gives in to the overcoat. Moreover, his suits are all made of the same weight of cloth, summer and winter, and he never by any chance suffers from respiratory complaints. Whether this is due to his mode of dressing is, perhaps, a question, but the fact remains that on his trips to Florida he can take off his coat, roll it up for a pillow, and sleep on the wet grass without contracting a twinge of rheumatism or emitting a single sneeze. He has scarcely ever had a day's illness in his life, and he himself ascribes this happy state of affairs to common sense regarding dress and the capacity for hard work.

Edison never wears a silk hat — even on Sundays. — and on few occasions has he been known to carry a pair of gloves. Should he attend a dinner given especially in his honor, he does not appear in evening dress. Indeed, he has a particular aversion to this mode of costume, and nothing will persuade him to adopt it. Some years ago he so astonished the footman at a mansion where he had been invited to dinner by arriving in an ordinary Prince Albert that the man showed some reluctance to allowing him to enter. At the moment, however, the host came forward and smoothed things out by conducting the visitor to his room and summoning a valet. This man was also a little surprised at Edison's appearance, and delicately inquired if the inventor desired to dress, and if so, where he had left his dress-suit case. Edison replied that he was dressed already, and that he wouldn't detain the valet, who finally departed. Afterwards he sat down to dinner in his comfortable Prince Albert, and cracked jokes about the affair with his host and hostess.

Edison has strong opinions regarding diet. He firmly believes that half the ills to which flesh is heir are due to incorrect and excessive eating. He himself is very abstemious, and often does not consume a pound of food during the day. Yet he is no faddist regarding what he shall eat, taking everything he fancies, but in very small quantities. He believes in change of food, and declares that nature requires it, and so when he has been eating meat for any length of time, and begins to feel a little run down, he turns vegetarian for a spell, returning to meat again when he finds it is necessary. In this way any normal man or woman may keep in perfect health. In regard to wines and liquors Edison is equally abstemious. "Much liquor," he says, "is a bad thing for any one who wants to go through life and work in earnest. Unless taken in very moderate quantities it deadens all your nerves and makes you feel listless. A fellow in that fix isn't worth anything but to sit around and wait for the end to come. He just does everything mechanically." Total abstinence, however, does not appeal to Edison. He does not think it a good thing, and declares that total abstainers are usually pale, with sallow complexions and abnormally large shoulders, and have a greater tendency to consumption than people who take a little wine or spirit. A small quantity of "cordial" is not harmful; it is only when taken in excess that the mischief is done. An occasional sip of champagne Edison enjoys, and he can even appreciate an occasional bottle of beer, but not the English kind, which is too heavy. With regard to smoking, he has never felt any ill effects from the habit, though at one time he consumed each day twenty of the strongest cigars he could obtain. If he had found that his nerves suffered he would have stopped smoking altogether, but he never experienced any inconvenience from them. To-day he smokes less than he used to and his average is five a day — one after each meal and two in the evening.

Eighteen years ago, when Edison was in England, he was interviewed regarding his ability to get through so much work, and he then ascribed his wonderful powers of endurance to correct diet and "sleeping when he wanted to." "If," he said, "I spend sixty hours at an invention, there must, naturally, be a loss of physical force, but I regain this by afterwards taking a slumber which may last from eighteen to twenty-four hours. In this way tired Nature reasserts herself, and both of us are satisfied." At that time Edison appealed strongly to the British interviewer, and during his visit was probably the most popular man with the press that ever came to England's shores. He has known newspaper men so well throughout his life that he is more than ordinarily genial with them and ever ready to give all the information in his power. Said one English interviewer who spent an hour with him:

"It is worth going a long way to chat and shake hands with Edison. The greatest practical electrician that ever lived is not more interesting than the man himself. We can realize from the strong, resolute look how the boy, whose regular schooling scarcely extended to half a year, succeeded in educating himself by stray reading at newspaper stalls and haphazard studies in telegraphy at the railway signalling station. With all its strength Mr. Edison's face wears a gentle expression. The suggestion of strength comes out when he is interested in a discussion and driving his argument home. A noteworthy characteristic of his face is the attractive smile and the mixture of shrewdness and kindliness of the gray eyes. There is no simpler, more open, more unaffected man than Edison living. He seems as if he had no notion that he was anybody in particular. His shrewd, ready common sense is apparent even in the smallest things."

Edison's greatest happiness is found in his laboratory and his home, for, though appearances seem against it, the inventor is rather a domestic kind of man. True, he does not care for social life, and it is only by great diplomacy on the part of Mrs. Edison that he can be persuaded to attend any functions or friendly gatherings. He does not like society, as the word is usually interpreted, but he is always glad to see interesting people — especially scientists — in his own home, and if his visitor is amusing and can tell good stories Edison is quite willing to stop up half the night or longer listening to them. The writer has a vivid recollection of calling upon him many years ago at the Orange laboratory by appointment one morning at eleven o'clock, and being informed that the inventor had been up throughout the night and was then sleeping. He had left instructions that he was to be called at ten, but Mrs. Edison had refused to disturb him, taking upon herself any risk which might attend the breaking of an engagement. Edison never moved an eyelash until three o'clock, when he awoke and got up, scolding every one within earshot for having let him sleep so long. He came down to the laboratory accompanied by a Japanese friend in native costume, and apologized for the lateness of his appearance by explaining that the Oriental gentleman had kept him up until two in the morning telling funny stories. The Japanese, a highly cultured diplomatist in the service of the Mikado, smiled with good humor and some pride, and declared that everything would have been all right and the appointment kept if Mr. Edison had not at two o'clock commenced a full day's work and never gone to bed until eight. Hence the profoundness of his slumbers at the time when he should have been on his way to the laboratory.

Visitors to the Edison laboratory occasionally arrive in such numbers that unless they are well known to the inventor he finds it necessary to decline giving them an interview owing to something more pressing occupying his attention. Some of these visitors plaintively state that they have known "Tom Edison" since a boy, and they feel much aggrieved when the gateman informs them that it is impossible to see him that day. On one occasion a *bonâ-fide* friend who had known Edison from his childhood called at the laboratory with a companion, and was extremely offended when informed that Mr. Edison was very busy and could not receive visitors. "What!" said the caller indignantly, "do you mean to say that Thomas Edison won't see me? Why, I have known him intimately all my life." "Oh, no, I don't say he won't see you," replied the man, "but Mrs. Edison waited here for two hours this morning and had to go away without seeing him, and I don't suppose you know him any better than she does."

Edison is remarkably practical. This was shown years ago when he declared that he never wasted any of his time upon inventions which would not prove useful or which would not pay for the time spent in perfecting them. When the phonograph was in its infancy he was complimented by a well-known scientist upon the wonder he had achieved, when the inventor somewhat startled his admirer by replying, "Yes, but it doesn't bring in any money." Another story illustrative of the practical side of his nature is also connected with the phonographic days. It was after he had made the cylinders of wax, and when a fine, delicate brush was necessary to keep them free from dust. The brush he used cost a dollar, and he made up his mind that it must be possible to obtain one equally serviceable for half the money or less. The hair, of course, had to be exceedingly fine, so as not to scratch the record, and he had been told that what he required was costly, and a dollar was the lowest price at which the brushes could be manufactured. Edison thought otherwise, and after he had obtained specimens of hair from almost every known animal, he found that the red deer provided a hair so fine that it could scarcely be seen without the aid of a microscope. This was just what he had been looking for, and henceforth his phonograph brushes cost five cents instead of a dollar. On another occasion a visitor found Edison one Sunday morning deeply occupied with his phonographic dolls. One was in pieces beside him, and the inventor was busy scribbling figures and line diagrams in a pocket-book. When asked to explain what he was busy on, Mr. Edison said:

"The idea suddenly hit me at breakfast this morning that I might cheapen the cost of this doll, and I couldn't rest till to-morrow to put my plan to the test. It occurred to me that I could make the framework that holds this tiny phonograph cheaper by changing its shape and thus saving metal. The change in shape will permit me to substitute a small brass screw for this large one, and so I can save several cents that way, too."

From these little stories it must not be supposed that there is anything "close" about Edison. As a matter of fact he cares little for wealth, and when experimenting or perfecting a new invention he never sits down to consider the cost. If it should take his entire fortune to attain his end he would spend it, and never since he has had the handling of big sums has he allowed expenditure to stand in the way of success. Towards his workpeople he has always been known for his liberality and generosity. He believes in paying a good man a good salary, in encouraging him by a liberal wage to give the best that is in him, in "raising" him as his usefulness increases. The employer who pays his men poor wages and then expects good results he considers a fool, and strikers under such circumstances have his sympathy. But he can be stern when he thinks he is being imposed upon, and when he knows himself to be in the right he can act with the grim determination of a Napoleon. Years ago outside agitators got among his men employed at Edison, Morris County, and as a result eighty of his workpeople in the machine-room formulated a demand for time and a half for working Saturday nights, and double time when Sunday work was necessary. A petition to this effect was drawn up and presented to Edison by a committee of four. His reply was that the rate of wages paid was liberal, but he would consider the matter. The committee arbitrarily told him that he could have four days to decide. Then Edison's eyes lost their genial expression and took on a glint that indicated some of the determination which dominates him. He informed that committee he could reply immediately and give them all the summer to think it over. "Go back to Edison," he said, "and the reply will be there by the time you are." He then telegraphed Superintendent Conly to close the works at once, as the demand, in view of the wages received, was unreasonable. The following morning the men returned in a body and begged to be taken back on the old footing, which was permitted. Since that day there has been no strike among Edison's employees.

If the inventions of Edison are remarkable, he himself is no less a physical wonder. For forty-five years he has labored incessantly regardless of the ordinary laws of nature. In the pursuit of some desired end time has been forgotten, sleep ignored, food left untouched, rest abandoned. Yet he has not suffered. To-day he looks twenty years younger than his age, and he can still work twenty or thirty hours at a stretch without feeling unduly fatigued. His juvenility is remarkable, and his capacity for recuperation is equally astonishing. Perhaps the secret of his tireless activity is his determination never to worry. "Don't worry," says Edison, "but work hard, and you can look forward to a reasonably lengthy existence — barring accidents, of course." Edison's passion for work has been likened to some men's love for strong drink, and the comparison is not at all bad. Recently the inventor stated one Saturday night that he intended to quit work for a spell, and his manager need not expect him for a few days. That manager smiled, for he had heard the same thing before. Monday morning at eight Edison was hard at work as usual. It is probably the only thing that the inventor cannot do — give up work, and until he can invent something to make the task easy he probably never will.

Edison is absent-minded, and even now, when absorbed in any deep problem, matters of importance slip his memory very speedily, and if he were not reminded from time to time complications might arise. European celebrities frequently visit the laboratory at Orange, and Edison is always glad to see them, but more than once some idea has struck him while in conversation, and he has left them with a hurried word of apology, and, an hour later, he has been discovered hard at work in his chemical laboratory — everything and every one forgotten in the pursuit of some elusive clew. On one occasion at least he forgot his name. This was in the early days when he went to pay his taxes, and, as was customary then, got in line to await his turn. Moving on monotonously as the man ahead paid his dues and passed out, Edison became deeply absorbed in the mental solving of some problem, and by the time he reached the cashier's window he was oblivious to his surroundings. The clerk asked him his name. He looked blankly at the man, tried vainly to recollect his baptismal cognomen, and was about to pass out when the tax commissioner, who was standing near and who knew him, said, "Hello, Mr. Edison," and memory returned. He afterwards declared that, had his life depended on giving his correct name, he could not have done so. At one time he had serious thoughts of studying some memory system, but he never did, and consequently he is as forgetful to-day as ever he was.

The following incident is another good example of his occasional lapses into absent-mindedness, and has the additional interest of being vouched for by one of his co-workers. During his experimental work in connection with the invention of the incandescent electric-light system, when the inventor had been up several nights in succession and was very much worn out, he entered one of the workrooms at four o'clock in the morning (having previously left instructions to be called at nine, when breakfast was to be brought to him) and was soon locked in profound slumber. Meanwhile one of his co-workers — Mr. Bachelor, I believe — had arranged to have breakfast in the same room at 8.30, and when he came in and saw the inventor peacefully taking a much-needed rest, the idea of playing a joke upon him came as an inspiration. So, learning from the young man who brought in his meal that Edison's breakfast would be ready at nine, at which time he, the young man, would arouse the "boss," Bachelor leisurely proceeded with his meal and read the paper. At nine o'clock the assistant, prompt to time, entered to awaken his master. After a good deal of shaking and pummelling — for Edison is rather a heavy sleeper — the "old man" got up and sat down to the table to await the coming of his breakfast, which, the youth declared, was "on the way." It took a few minutes, however, and during the interval the inventor was so sleepy that he dozed off again. Then, when it finally did arrive, Bachelor quietly appropriated it and put in its place the *débris* of his own meal. A moment later Edison awoke, gazed at the fragments before him, looked into the empty cup, thought a moment, and then, taking out a cigar, he lit it and proceeded to enjoy his usual "after-meal" smoke, quite content in the belief that he had eaten his breakfast and forgotten all about it. When his co-worker enlightened him on the point he gave an amused grin and merely remarking, "Well, that's one on me" (a favorite expression of his), he proceeded to do good justice to a substantial meal. He afterwards declared that though it never occurred to him that he hadn't eaten anything, he certainly had an inward feeling that he could have done with another breakfast.

Though Edison thus suffers from absent-mindedness, in common with many other great men, he is possessed of a memory which is remarkable for its keenness. He can keep in mind a dozen inventions, and remember the smallest details in connection with each without any effort at all. Moreover, in his experiments he frequently hits upon some phenomena which, while of no use to him at the time, are remembered for future inventions, and invariably taken advantage of. This has clearly been shown in connection with the telephone, the phonograph, and the chalk battery, to which reference was made in earlier chapters. He has a well-stored mind, the capacity for absorbing knowledge is strong with him, and he never forgets a principle once learned. He is said to have thoroughly digested the substance of his entire library, comprising what is probably the most complete collection of scientific books in the world, and is more familiar with past and present literature dealing with science than any other man living. He is also extraordinarily quick to catch on to the principles of a thing. Years ago some English capitalists visited America to see if they couldn't organize a typewriter trust, and they thought it would be a good plan to interest Edison in the matter. So they went out to the laboratory and took all their legal documents with them, hoping that he would pass judgment on them. At the time Edison knew nothing whatever about typewriters, and he asked if there was any book that would enlighten him upon the subject. One of the men had just such a book in his pocket, and he handed it to the inventor. Mr. Edison glanced rapidly through it, spent about ten minutes over the work, and then surprised the experts by his knowledge of the subject. Had they come about flying machines or incubators or submarines it would have been the same. Given a comprehensive book on the subject, Edison would have grasped the principles with the same facility and rapidity as any one else would have turned the pages; but he takes no credit to himself for this faculty. "It is partly a gift," he explains, "and partly cultivation. It is wonderful how one can accustom one's self to absorbing facts when necessary. Most people could do it if they wished."

One writer recently said of Edison, "He has a most retentive memory and enough imagination, but not too much, for practicality. Imagination in an inventor is a dangerous quality. An inventor must have it, but if he has too much of it he is sure to become a dreamer. That is where Edison is strong; he has just the requisite amount of imagination to make him conceive great things, yet not enough to make him a dreamer. He is astonishingly practical in all his ideas." Few dreamers possess retentive memories, for dreams themselves are but fleeting things. Edison himself has no use for a dreamer, and none has ever found a footing in his laboratory. All must be "hustlers," though they may never hope to "hustle" as Edison does; people who "hustle" generally remember things.

Edison never forgets a face. He will regard a man newly introduced with great keenness, and after that his features apparently are indelibly impressed upon his brain. At a recent dinner given in Edison's honor, the most striking thing in connection with it was the number of men who renewed their acquaintance with the inventor and found that he had not forgotten them. Guest after guest was brought up with scarcely a hope that Edison would recollect him, and went away marvelling at his memory for faces. A characteristic incident occurred when Marion H. Kerner, of the Western

Union Telegraph Company, was brought up by W. S. Logue, of Mr. Edison's staff.

"I don't suppose you remember this man?" said Mr. Logue, by way of introduction.

Edison peered into his face. "To be sure I do," he replied promptly; "it's Marion Kerner," and a cordial hand was extended.

The two men had not met for thirty years or more, when both were experimenting in Sigmund Bergmann's little shop in Wooster Street, where Edison found greater conveniences for working upon the phonograph, then in the tin-foil record stage, and Kerner was working upon a burglar alarm system.

After that the two men drifted apart, yet less than half a minute was required to bridge the gap of thirty years.

This characteristic of Edison to remember faces was once the cause of an amusing incident which was related a short time since in the pages of the *Sun*, and which I quote by permission. It has the additional value of being true, and on the occasion that the incident occurred no one enjoyed the joke more than Edison, who was the unconscious cause of much mental perturbation in the mind of at least one of the actors in the little comedy.

"In a certain great machine-manufacturing plant devoted to electrical appliances visitors are constantly being received from all quarters of the globe. The guides who take these visitors through the works have all kinds of experiences. It often happens that the visitor who knows the least about electrical matters will ask the stiffest questions and make the most disconcerting remarks. It is rather staggering, for instance, after you have made your clearest and most concise explanation of the phenomenon of electricity as you understand it, to be met with the comforting remark —

"'After all, Mr. ——, you don't really know what electricity is!'

"The average working electrician worries no more about the nature of the force he handles than he does about the doctrines of Confucius. One of the linemen demonstrates the idea by the recital of a past experience.

"'When I worked on a third rail at Hartford, the boss says: "You fellows don't care where the juice comes from or where it goes to; all you care about is where to get it and where not to get it. So you, Hennesy, keep your crowbar off that third rail or you'll have a beautiful short circuit and a pirate-technical display that'll make you so blind that you'll not be able to tell bad whiskey from ice water for six months."'

"One engineer at the factory, who may be called Steve because his name is something else, is frequently detailed to take visitors about on account of his fund of information and his clear, lucid manner of explanation. On one occasion he escorted a guest from the West — a light-haired little gentleman, who seemed duly impressed with all he saw, but made no comment. He was apparently drinking in and criticising every word which young Steve uttered, and that usually confident gentleman grew nervous and suspicious.

"'This fellow,' he thought, 'must be some smart electrician, and he is just taking all my statements with a huge grain of salt.'

"At last, when they arrived back at the office, and Steve was feeling limp and tired, the little gentleman held out his hand and said —

"'I am exceedingly obliged to you. I don't know much about the electrical trade. I am a barber. If you ever come to Chicago, look me up.'

"Steve had recovered from this, and was beginning to look and feel like himself once more, when he was again detailed to escort a visitor through the works. This was a silent and undemonstrative man, who paid considerable attention to rather insignificant machines and details. Consequently, Steve rather hastily concluded that he had another barber to amuse. Moreover, as the quiet visitor showed little or no surprise at, or appreciation of, the many really remarkable machines and operations, Steve was aggrieved, and for the honor of the works determined to shake some enthusiasm out of him. So he proceeded to load him up with many wonderful stories.

"He pointed out a dynamo so powerful that it never had been and never could be run up to full capacity, it being utterly impossible to control the current. He gave a dissertation on the incandescent lamp and its manufacture, asserting that its discovery was due to the accidental observation of a lightning flash playing on a two-pronged fork in a pickle bottle. Waxing eloquent, he rose on his toes, stretched out his right arm, and exclaimed —

"'And so, that inestimable boon to mankind, the incandescent lamp, was born!'

"At this moment the visitor stepped up to a workman, who was winding coils, slapped him on the back, and said —

"'Hello, Dan!'

"The man started, looked up, and his face flushed with surprise and pleasure as he grasped the outstretched hand.

"'God bless my soul! It's my old boss,' he exclaimed. 'Mr. Edison, how are you?'

"Steve staggered back and sat down on a casting. He tried to think it over, to recollect some of the stuff he'd been telling — but his mind was a blur. One thing only stood out distinctly: he had told the 'Wizard of Menlo Park,' the inventor of the incandescent lamp, that it was the evolution of a pickle bottle and a two-pronged fork! Then he disappeared.

"A week or two later he received from Mr. Edison a book on electrical wonders, written for juveniles, on the fly-leaf of which was a pen drawing of a fork in a pickle bottle, and below, the inscription:

"'And so that inestimable boon to mankind, the incandescent lamp, was born.' Sometime in the future, perhaps, that little book may fetch a round sum of money. At present no money could buy it."

Edison himself occasionally likes to take a rise out of a visitor, but he would never let himself go to the extent that Steve did. It is, of course, but natural that many interviewers should call upon him whose acquaintance with electricity is not very profound. When this is the case — and Edison can tell in about two minutes whether a man knows a dynamo from a galvanic battery — the inventor is very considerate, and endeavors to make his language as untechnical as possible. Perhaps this has something to do with his immense popularity with newspaper men who all delight in getting an assignment to call at the laboratory. On one occasion, however, a particularly unscientific journalist was accorded a few minutes by Edison, the object of the visit being to "write up" a new and extremely intricate machine which the inventor had recently perfected. Edison was very anxious that the interviewer should get his facts correctly, and whenever he noticed a look of despair come into his visitor's face, he would pause and ask: "Do you understand?" Receiving a faint affirmative, he would proceed again with his rapid and fluent description, only to pull up once more and repeat the question: "Now, do you understand?" The journalist, who kept getting hotter and hotter and more fogged in his frantic efforts to grasp the meaning of this and that, would occasionally venture to stop Edison's flow of eloquence by declaring that he wasn't quite clear on such and such a point and would be glad if the inventor would explain a little more lucidly. Whereupon Edison would heave a profound sigh and commence all over again.

Finally the journalist, in an apologetic tone, said he was afraid he knew very little about machinery and was almost ashamed of his ignorance regarding electricity, upon which Edison brightened up and with his customary kindness declared that the young man knew much more than many who called at the laboratory. And in order to put his visitor completely at his ease he inquired if he had ever told him the story about the fireman he once met in Canada.

"No," replied the journalist, thankful for the chance of at last hearing something that he could understand. "Please tell it me."

"Well," replied Edison, "in a certain Canadian town where I was running a telegraph office in my youth, a new factory, with a fine engine-house, was put up. I visited this factory one day to see the engine. The engineer was out, and the fireman, a new hand, showed me about. As we stood admiring the engine together, I said —

"'What horse power has this engine?'

"The fireman gave a loud laugh. 'Horse power!' he exclaimed. 'Why, man, don't you know that this machine goes by steam?'

"Another fellow," continued Edison, "who used to assist me in the early days was almost as green, and

HIS PERSONALITY

with less excuse. He helped me once to erect a miniature electric-light plant, and when the job was complete he was so pleased with his part of the work that he said to me with a smile of pride on his face: 'Mr. Edison, after working with you like this, I believe I could put up an electric-light plant myself.'

"'Could you?' said I.

"'I believe I could,' he answered. 'There's only one thing that beats me.'

"'What is that?' I asked.

"'I don't quite see,' he answered, 'how you get the oil along the wires.'"

Lady interviewers have occasionally bearded Edison in his lair, but the inventor prefers the masculine species, even if they are sometimes less attractive. Some years ago a lady on a religious paper thought it would be highly interesting if she obtained from Edison his opinion on the "Christianizing of the world" and some facts regarding the best way in which it could be speedily and permanently accomplished. She was an intelligent and bright young woman, but worried a little bit too much about the betterment of that part of the globe where, we are told in the hymn, "the heathen in his blindness bows down to wood and stone." She was very courteously received by Edison, who submitted quite quietly to a perfect fusillade of questions respecting his religious beliefs and disbeliefs. After stating that all scientific men, he thought, believed in God, that he hadn't any particular creed, that he considered all religions had some good points, and that he went to church when he felt inclined and not oftener, he was requested by his interviewer to pass judgment on the great question, "Was the world becoming Christianized? If not, would it ever become Christianized?" Edison thought deeply, his brows contracted with the profoundness of the problem, until the young woman began to fear that the question was beyond him. And then his brow cleared, a smile rose to his lips, his eyes lost their profound expression, and he replied: "Not only do I think that the world in time will become Christianized, but I believe we shall both live to see it." Then, as the young woman gave an ecstatic upward glance, he added: "Just look at the way these big improved machine-guns are wiping out the heathen."

As appropriate to the conversation, Edison then proceeded to show his visitor plans for a new collection plate of a very novel make, which he felt sure would prove highly successful in drawing substantial contributions from any ordinary congregation. "You know," he said with a smile, "how modest people are in dropping money into the collection plate? They don't want it to be known how generous they are, so I have thought out a device furnished with slots. The silver coins — half-dollars, quarters, and dimes — would fall through their respective slots into a velvet-lined compartment, but the nickels and pennies, falling through theirs, would ring a bell like a cash register."

CHAPTER XXII

PHOTOGRAPHING THE WIZARD

The present writer has had Edison photographed so often that a few words regarding the inventor as a poser before the camera may not, perhaps, be without interest. The first occasion was many years ago at his laboratory, Silver Lake, New Jersey, and though the pictures were really excellent Edison did not think so. But there was a "reason," which will subsequently appear. We had taken with us a snapshot camera fitted with films, and invited the inventor to step out into the sunlight to have his picture taken. He had no objection, though he looked a little askance at his well-worn and chemical-stained coat. He even tried to rub away some of the dust, but immediately afterwards remarked with great philosophy that he "guessed it wouldn't show in the picture."

We guessed it wouldn't either, and, leaving his laboratory, Edison took up his position near the door of his office and the shutter was snapped. Then one of his men brought a chair, and a sitting position was taken, after which Edison examined the camera with some minuteness. On making the discovery that we had used films he said he was afraid the pictures wouldn't turn out very good, as he did not believe in anything but plates in portraiture. "Films," he said, "are bound to stretch more or less, and when they do — well, what becomes of your features?" However, the photographs turned out very well — excellent, in fact — and those in the laboratory who saw the prints vowed that we had got the "old man" to a dot. When we showed them to Edison, however, he recollected that they were the ones we had taken with films and immediately handed them back, saying they were very bad.

On another occasion, when visiting the Orange laboratory for photographic purposes, Joseph Byron, the artist, together with an expert assistant, accompanied us, and we photographed the laboratory from end to end. Edison happened to be away at the time, but he returned at four o'clock in order to give us the promised sittings. Naturally we wished to show the inventor in his own chemical laboratory, as being the scene where he evolved those wonders with which from time to time he startled civilization. First of all, however, we met him in the library, and it was suggested that a picture should be made of the inventor "attending to his correspondence." Nothing loath, he seated himself at his desk, took out one of his famous notebooks, and was soon so absorbed that he never knew when the photograph was taken, or raised his head when the flash was fired. We were obliged to remind him that he had promised to pose for us in the chemical laboratory, and he roused himself with a start, regarding us for a moment in some astonishment. He laughed as soon as his thoughts returned, and said:

"Yes, I'm a bit absent-minded at times, but I'm not so bad as I used to be. Some years ago I remember one of the boys from a New York paper came down to take some pictures of me, and made some very funny ones. The fact was I had been up all night and several nights, and was pretty well tired out, but I had promised him a sitting, and, as I always try to keep my promises, I told him to go ahead. Well, before he had time to arrange his camera I was sound asleep in my chair. When I woke up he had vanished and I went to bed. A few days later he came down again and showed me the photographs — half a dozen of them — depicting me in various stages of sleep. We had a hearty laugh over them, and I gave him another sitting."

When we reached the chemical laboratory Edison immediately fell to work and began experimenting with phials and retorts and other mysterious-looking things, and again forgot all about the photographer. However, as soon as he took on a characteristic pose Byron would say, "Just a moment, Mr. Edison," and he would remain in position until the picture was made. As the laboratory was not very bright, for the day was cloudy, a mixture of daylight with a small flash was used, which gave most excellent results. Some one, however, seeing smoke issue from the windows concluded that a fire was in progress, and informed the day watchman, who came running into the room in great excitement.

After a few minutes the inventor left his table and walked to the outer laboratory, where Mr. Ott was busy watching some queer compound bubbling over an electric spark. Edison, noting his tense expression, declared that his chief assistant would make an excellent study of an "Alchemist," and in spite of Mr. Ott's modest protestations that he didn't want to pose, the plate was exposed. While this picture was being made Mr. Edison, who had found a bottle containing some soft compound and was extracting it by the aid of his penknife, had struck another characteristic attitude, which was also transferred to a plate. On being asked what the bottle contained, he replied, "Liquid glass," and seemed much amused when the assistant innocently remarked that he didn't know one could preserve glass in bottles like pickles.

A few days prior to the twenty-fifth anniversary of his invention of the incandescent light we photographed the inventor again. He was in the highest spirits, and was on the eve of going for a holiday to Florida. He loves fishing, and was as pleased at the prospect of having a "good time" as a schoolboy might have been. He came down specially to the laboratory to give the promised sittings, and we took him in a variety of interesting poses. While in the chemical laboratory Mrs. Edison entered and whispered to her husband that a certain well-known daily newspaper had sent down a representative. Would he spare him ten minutes? "Not on your life," replied the inventor, as though too excited over his approaching holiday to wish to talk. Mrs. Edison was too tactful to press the matter, and retired to give the disappointing message. Presently she returned, and was consulting with her husband over some subject, when one of the photographers whispered that a picture showing the two together and in the laboratory would be unique. Mrs. Edison's permission was asked for the making of the negative, but she begged to be excused as she had a great objection to being photographed. Edison at once took in the situation, and with great presence of mind remarked to his wife: "My dear, don't mind those gentlemen, they will soon be finished." Then turning to the operators he screwed his left eye into a very palpable wink, as much as to say, "Go ahead," and immediately returned to the discussion he was having with Mrs. Edison. No other hint was required, and we "went ahead" at once, with the result that we obtained one of the most interesting photographs of the inventor and his wife ever taken.

MR. AND MRS. EDISON IN THE CHEMICAL LABORATORY

CHAPTER XXIII

SOME ANECDOTES

As has been remarked before, Edison is an extremely modest man, and perhaps one of the best examples of his modesty was given a few years ago when he was making out an application blank for membership in the Engineers' Club of Philadelphia. Among other particulars it was necessary to give his qualification for membership, and in the space reserved for that piece of information the inventor wrote: "I have designed a concentrating plant and a machine shop, &c." A very big volume indeed would be required to contain all that that " &c." included.

One of Edison's stanchest admirers was Pasteur, the noted bacteriologist, who was not afflicted with modesty, as is evidenced by the following little anecdote. An American journalist of some note was interviewing Pasteur when the discoverer of the cure for hydrophobia remarked: "Your Edison is a great man. When the history of our generation comes to be written two names that will stand out most prominently in science will be his and — mine!"

Apropos of Edison's drastic opinions on the subject of diet, the inventor is fond of telling a story illustrative of how great a slave a man may become to meal hours if he chooses. "You know, of course," he would say, "all about the Ohio man who went to New York for the first time, and, having taken a room at a good hotel, unpacked his grip and then went to the desk to inquire about the meals.

"'What is the eatin' hours in this yere hotel?' he said to the clerk.

"'Breakfast,' the clerk answered, 'seven to eleven; lunch, eleven to three; dinner, three to eight; supper, eight to twelve.'

"'Jerusalem!' exclaimed the astonished farmer, 'when am I goin' to git time to see the town?'"

Edison, as has frequently been stated, takes little notice of the flight of time. He never carries a watch, and there is no clock to be seen in the chemical laboratory where he works. With him it is time to knock off when a task is finished — the hour has nothing to do with it. His workpeople, of course, disperse at a fixed hour each day, but nothing is more likely to irritate the inventor when engaged in some interesting experiments with a close associate than to be reminded that time is passing. An English admirer recently wrote to Edison to ask if he might bring his little son to see him, for he was visiting America and would not like to take the child back without his having spoken to the inventor. Edison, ever agreeable, wrote back to say that he would be glad to see them both. After a cordial greeting the visitor bade the boy look upon the inventor, and recollect that he had met one of the great ones of the earth. Edison, somewhat embarrassed, disclaimed any claim to greatness, whereupon the visitor begged that he would say something to the boy which he would carry away with him and which would help to influence his life. Edison looked down upon the lad, patted his curly head, and then, with a smile of unusual kindliness, said, "My boy, never watch the clock."

Edison has strong opinions on cigarette smoking. Some years ago he said to an interviewer: "Smoking tobacco is a pretty good working stimulant. But cigarettes, they're deadly. It is not the tobacco, it's the acrolein produced by the burning paper that does the harm, and let me tell you —" his voice betrayed some feeling and his face grew grave— "acrolein is one of the most terrible drugs in its effect on the human body. The burning of ordinary cigarette paper always produces acrolein. That is what makes the smoke irritating. I really believe it often makes boys insane. We sometimes develop acrolein in the laboratory in our experiments with glycerine. One whiff of it from the oven drove one of my assistants out of the building the other day. I can hardly exaggerate the dangerous nature of acrolein, and yet that is what a man or boy is dealing with every time he smokes an ordinary cigarette. The harm that such a deadly poison, when taken into the system, must inflict upon a growing lad is horrible to contemplate."

"The other day," he continued, "I found a package of cigarettes which some one had dropped on my office step. The very sight of it gave me a feeling of disgust, and I went back into the office and wrote this sign: 'A degenerate, who is retrograding toward the lower animal life, has lost his tack.' And I nailed the package with the sign up in a conspicuous place. I was mad at first, but I carried the thing through as a joke. The fellow, whoever he was (and I never found out), must have been a facetious scamp, for he confiscated his cigarettes and nailed a cigar up in their place. The point of the joke, of course, was that I smoke cigars down here in the shop nearly all day long."

Edison is a close student of the newspapers, and has a habit of cutting out any paragraph (not necessarily of a scientific nature) which appeals to him. In going through some of his papers one day the writer came across the following paragraph which happily illustrates what Edison has always asserted, viz., that it is worry that kills and not hard work. The inventor probably saved the cutting for the reason that it so succinctly puts into words his own thoughts, and for that reason I reproduce it here:

"It is well to be concerned about one's business sufficiently to look after it in all its details, but it is not well to be so concerned that one cannot sleep. It is a privilege to work, but that privilege should not be abused. It is not an indication of deep intelligence for a man to labor until his vital forces are exhausted. When a man works more than is good for him, sensible people look upon him as one who considers this the real life, instead of the temporal existence preceding the life which is to come. Thomas Alva Edison is a happy and healthy man. He does not worry. He is great as an inventor and great as a man, and the men of this and coming generations will do well to follow his example, remembering always that it is worry and not work which kills, and, furthermore, that all the worry in the world never helped to emancipate one from the thraldom of a bad business situation. On the other hand, worry has unfitted many a man for the task of meeting obligations, which caused the worry, when they came." These clever remarks — I wish I knew the name of their author — should be hung above the desk of every business man in the country — at least of every business man who makes a worry of his work.

And here may be given Edison's remarks on newspapers. It must be remembered that the inventor was once a newspaper man himself, and he has in his heart a very warm corner for the "boys" who follow journalism as a profession, though, sad to relate, he has not always been treated well by them, and has, indeed, on more than one occasion forbidden representatives of certain papers entering his laboratory. However, as he himself will cheerfully remark, there are black sheep in every flock, be they in the clerical, scientific, literary, military, or medical fold, and this fact has in no way changed the very high opinion he has of the press as a whole. "Looking over the whole country," he says, "I have come to the conclusion that the greatest factor in our progress has been the newspaper press. When one wants to do a thing the newspapers take it up. Everybody reads the newspapers, everybody knows the situation, and we all act together." On another occasion he said: "To let the world know through type who and what and where you are, and what you have which this great world wants, is the secret of success, and the printing press is its mightiest machine to that end."

For a great many years Edison had no great belief in the advantages of book-keeping — even that kind of book-keeping which comprises double and single entries and other mysteries — though his faith in its usefulness as well as necessity has long since been reestablished. And in support of this queer lack of confidence in what is generally regarded as the sheet anchor of every firm's successful career, he sometimes relates how in his early days, when he first started in business for himself, book-keeping ran him into an extravagance which, as it turned out, he could ill afford.

It was in the Newark days, and having opened his factory and engaged his men he was advised by his friends to hire the services of a capable accountant in order that the books should be correctly kept. No self-respecting firm, he was informed, could get along without a book-keeper, and so a book-keeper was engaged. For a year Edison directed the affairs of his business and never thought any more of the man of figures until at the end of the first twelve months the accountant drew up a statement and presented it to the inventor. That statement brought great joy to the heart of Edison, for by it he saw that the firm's status had improved to the extent of $8000 during the year. He gave a whoop, and soon every one in the building heard that the factory was making good money. Edison felt so pleased that he issued orders for a big dinner to be held in the stock-room, and the entire staff, from the overseer to the humblest member, was invited. They all had a good time; Edison was in the highest spirits, the eatables and drinkables were of the best, and every one voted the banquet a great success.

Then, after Edison had discharged the bill and the excitement occasioned by the knowledge that he had made a good profit had somewhat evaporated, he began to think. He really couldn't figure out how the profit had been arrived at, and, calling his book-keeper into his office, he spent an hour or two with that gentleman going over the accounts. As they proceeded in their investigations Edison's face became longer and longer, while the accountant himself showed some signs of nervousness. Finally, it became only too evident that a mistake had been made, and when the debits and credits were at last disentangled, it was found that instead of $8000 profit there had been a loss of $7000. Edison was very much upset, said some hard things about book-keeping in general and his own book-keeper in particular, but finally laughed and put his accountant a little more at his ease by declaring that it didn't matter, and perhaps they would do better next time. The following year there really was an excellent profit, but Edison celebrated the event more quietly, and the staff was obliged to do without a dinner at his expense. But even though the accountant made no more mistakes it was a very long time before Edison's belief in the infallibility of book-keeping was thoroughly restored.

Mr. A. A. Anderson, the well-known American artist, who painted a very fine portrait of Edison in 1903, relates some interesting facts regarding the inventor and refers to Edison's attitude towards mathematics. He said: "I tried to paint Edison as the scientist, for it is the artist's duty not only to study his subject well, but to consider for what purpose the picture is designed. I enjoyed painting Edison, though he is no easy subject. He is restless, until he gets his thoughts concentrated upon some scientific problem, and then he becomes quiet, and the expression upon his face is one that an artist loves to catch and transmit to the world. But it was not so easy to get him thinking, for his brain works best in a noise. He likes to be in his factory or workshop, with the hum and clatter of his machinery about him. But I know something of electricity, and am deeply interested in it, so I was able by conversation to lead him into a train of thought that would get him into the proper condition for sitting as a subject.

"In painting him I learned that he has the mind, not of a deductive reasoner, but of the man inspired, you might almost say. He arrives at his conclusions by intuition and not by mathematical reasoning. For instance, when he invented the ordinary pear-shaped glass bulb for incandescent electric lights he wanted to ascertain its precise cubic contents. He gave the problem to several eminent mathematicians and they figured it out. When they brought their answers he told them that they were all wrong. He could not tell exactly how he reached his own conclusion, but he knew what it was and wanted to prove it. His method of proving it illustrates the practicality of his ways. He had made a series of tin cubes, forming a nest, each one a minute quantity smaller than the one enclosing it. He filled a bulb with water and poured it from one cube to the other until he found which of them the contents fitted exactly."

Edison invariably refers to his genius for arriving at correct solutions without employing mathematics as "guesswork," and when engaged on the Central Station idea he had many a tussle with mathematicians, who endeavored to pit their mathematical deductions against his common-sense reasoning. "In all the work connected with the building of the first Central Station," he said in after years, "the greatest bugbears I had to contend with were the mathematicians. I found after a while that I could guess a good deal closer than they could figure, so I went on guessing." His first dynamos were built by guesswork, and when asked how it came about that they were generally up to the required power he would reply with a smile, "Well, I happened to be a pretty good guesser."

Edison, as previously mentioned, has a name for being very kindly disposed towards newspaper men, who come to see him on various subjects of interest — from his latest invention down to his opinion on nuts as a satisfactory form of diet. If the subject is of a technical nature, the inventor generally clothes his explanations in language which is easily understood by the very freshest reporter. On one occasion, however, so very green a young man called to question him regarding a new light which Edison had evolved while experimenting with the X-ray, that the temptation to treat him to something a little above his head was too great, and after showing him what the new light would do, the inventor unburdened himself of the following:

"Of course you will understand," he said, "that ammeters placed in the primary circuit show a mean current of two ampères when the lamp is giving one candle." Beads of perspiration began to ooze from the brow of the reporter, but he managed to get something down and declared that he fully agreed with what the inventor had said. "Well," continued Edison, "I need scarcely tell you that the drop of potential across the primary is three-tenths of a volt." The reporter faintly murmured he believed that that was about the usual percentage. "But you must not forget," went on his tormentor, "that the current is interrupted 250 times per second." The reporter said he would try to remember it. "And also that it is closed four-fifths of the time and opened one-fifth of the time." At this stage the newspaper man could only nod with the faintest appearance of sagacity. "The spectrum of light," continued Edison, "is a lower refrangibility than the arc light. Do you follow me?" The dazed man gave a more animated nod than he thought he was capable of, and the inventor drew a deep breath and went on. "A globe six inches in diameter will give eight candles. The best commercial lamp requires three and one-half times the amount of energy per second required in this lamp." The reporter began to breathe again. "But the best incandescent lamp requires 138 foot-pounds of energy per second for each candle-power. The new light requires but 39.6 foot-pounds. And therein," concluded Edison, triumphantly, "lies its value." Then he said good-by to the white-faced reporter, telling him to come again when he wanted another simple explanation; but up to the present he has not taken advantage of the invitation.

The last time that Edison acted in the capacity of telegraph operator was in 1896, during the Electrical Exhibition at the Grand Central Palace, New York. He had been asked if he would be willing to receive a proposed message to be sent around the world by Chauncey M. Depew. The inventor said that while he was perfectly willing to play operator for one night, he doubted his ability to do so. It was twenty-six years since he had tried to read a message over the wire. Several electricians and friends present also doubted his ability to receive, and some jokingly said that they did not think after so many years without touching a key that he would be able to distinguish a dot from a dash. A gentleman interested in the discussion thereupon asked Edison if he would try his hand as an operator in the telegraph room of the New York *Journal*, and to this the inventor smilingly agreed.

When he entered the room with the dozen or more instruments rattling off messages from all parts of the world, he glanced around, smiled, and said —

"Oh, I guess I'm all right yet."

A key was selected, and pen, ink, and telegraph blanks given to him.

"Good man at the other end?" asked Edison, as he tilted the cigar in his mouth at an angle of 45 degrees.

"Pretty fair," said the manager of the telegraph department, who had called up the main office and told the man in charge to send what he had on hand to a new operator.

The instrument commenced to click, and Edison to make the usual cabalistic signs that nobody but a telegraph operator knows the meaning of.

"It's easy to read. Good Morse," said the new operator. "Only afraid I cannot write as fast as I used to."

SOME ANECDOTES

Then, continuing to write with one hand, he struck a match and lighted the cigar that had gone out while he was talking.

> Nv 57 Cg — Collect nite press Eastport ny 110
>
> the Journal ny —
>
> The wind has again changed and is now blowing to the north the fire is coming rapidly towards the village It has already reached the Long Island Country Club grounds — The people are now massing to go to fight the flames will send in a later report if anything occurs of importance
>
> Penny
>
> first press recd in 26 years
> Edison

PRESS MESSAGE RECEIVED AND WRITTEN OUT BY MR. EDISON AFTER TWENTY-SIX YEARS' ABSENCE FROM THE TELEGRAPH KEY.

The crack operators, who expected to see the man who was boss of them thirty years ago "break" in his work, looked on as Edison wrote without a pause. When the signature was given, he commenced to repeat the message just to see how he could send.

"Wonder if that other fellow works a typewriter? I guess he has got the best of it," said Edison, as he turned loose on his man at the other end. "That is the first message I have received or sent in twenty-six years," he continued as he leaned back in his chair. "I think I could receive or send if I lived to be a thousand. I do not believe a man ever forgets it. It read just like copper-plate, but it kept me scratching to get it down. Now, if those fellows who are going to send that message around the world want to turn loose next Saturday night, why, I guess they can."

The operators declared the exhibition between Edison and the main office manager to be "bang up" work for anybody. As it happened, however, Edison was unable to spare the time to receive Chauncey Depew's message.

Senator Depew, by the way, tells an amusing story about Edison which I cannot refrain from quoting here. "During the exhibition at Chicago," he says, "Edison visited the Fair, and saw everything in the electrical line. One day, while down town, he happened to see the 'shingle' of an electric-belt concern — a belt you put around you, and which is supposed to cure any ailment you happen to be troubled with. Well, thinking that perhaps there was something in the application of electricity which was new to him he went up to the office. A very pert young lady immediately inquired what she could do for him.

" 'Well,' began Edison, 'I wanted to know how those belts worked, and I thought I might learn by coming up here.'

" 'Certainly,' said the young lady, taking up a belt. 'You see the current of electricity goes from the copper to the zinc plate, and then ——'

"'Just a moment,' said Edison, politely, 'I don't hear very well at times. Did you say the current went from the copper to the zinc plate?'

"'I certainly did. Then, as I was saying——'

"'Just one moment,' interrupted Edison again. 'Let me understand this. You say it goes from the copper to the zinc?'

"'Yes, sir, it goes from the copper to the zinc.'

"'But do you know, I always thought it went from the zinc to the copper.'

"'Well, it don't.'

"'But are you sure?' Edison asked, smiling.

"'Well, maybe you know more about electricity than I do,' snapped the girl, as she threw the belt down and glared at the 'Wizard.'

"'Perhaps I do,' Edison admitted, and he turned and left the place."

The incident, however, in no way ruffled his temper. Nothing, indeed, puts him out, and the fact that he possesses so even a temperament is doubtless due to his unfailing fund of patience. A story is told which aptly illustrates this trait in his character. He had been for some days carrying on a series of experiments in which he used a great many open-mouthed tumblers. In one experiment alone he had destroyed over four hundred tumblers, the experiment itself ending in complete failure. Then one of his assistants who had been helping the inventor for many hours and was somewhat weary of the work, said: "Well, Mr. Edison, what shall we do next?" fervently hoping that he would suggest his going home. Instead, however, Edison scratched his head for a moment, and then looking at the mountain of broken glass said slowly, "Why, I suppose the next thing to do is to get some more tumblers."

Scientific visitors to the Edison laboratory are often astonished at the number and variety of things which the inventor has worked at during his life and of which the general public knows nothing. One distinguished scientist — a celebrated German savant — becoming confidential, spoke of some experiments which he had himself made in a direction that he supposed was unknown and untried.

"Did you try this?" inquired Edison; "and did you get such a result?"

The visitor was lost in amazement on discovering that Edison had made similar experiments and had arrived at the same result. But, unlike his visitor, he saw that there was "nothing in it" — nothing of commercial benefit, that is — and had discarded it in favor of something more directly useful to the human race. The same visitor asked Edison to name his principal inventions, and with characteristic reluctance he replied: "Well, first and foremost the idea of the electric-lighting station; then, let me see, what have I invented? Oh, there was the mimeograph and also the electric pen, and the carbon telephone, and the incandescent lamp and its accessories, and the quadruplex telegraph, and the automatic telegraph, and the phonograph, and the kinetoscope and — and — oh, I don't know, a whole lot of other things."

Among the innumerable visitors to the United States who have desired to see Edison was Li Hung Chang, who, however, was disappointed in meeting the inventor. Almost as soon as he arrived on American soil the Viceroy sent for Edison's representative in New York, and scarcely giving the man time to breathe, the distinguished Chinaman said —

"Now about Edison. Where is he? How old is

he? How long have you known him? Where and when did you meet him?"

All these questions, with a great many more, came out in a perfect stream, and the interpreter had a hard job translating them without incurring his master's wrath. As it was he was several questions behind and had to miss a few in order to keep up with the impetuous Viceroy. The representative of the inventor replied that he had first met Edison many years ago on Broadway.

"He is the inventor of the telephone, isn't he?" asked the Viceroy.

"He is the inventor of the improvements which make it a practical machine," was the guarded reply.

"If I want to introduce it into China, he is the man to see, isn't he?" asked Li excitedly.

"Yes, he can introduce it," replied the representative.

"I want to see Edison. Will he go to China?" were the next sentences, uttered with some impatience.

"He will go there if he has work to do," calmly replied the much-questioned American.

"Can you arrange a meeting between us? I want to see him. I must see him. He is a great man. Can you bring him to me?"

"Yes, if he can be found," answered the worried representative.

The following morning, before five, the representative was hurriedly sent for by Li, who wished to see him at his hotel. When he arrived the Viceroy received him while in bed and anxiously inquired if Edison had been found. He was told that Edison was at Niagara Falls, and he expressed his determination to go there to meet the great inventor in a couple of days' time.

A week after a reporter hurried off to Orange and succeeded in buttonholing Edison, and inquired if he had had any dealings with Li Hung Chang during his visit. The Viceroy's anxiety to meet the inventor had become public. "I have not met Li Hung Chang," Edison replied. "He telegraphed to me here asking if I would meet him, but I didn't comply with his request, as I was in the country and did not care to leave my family alone. I have no idea what he wanted to see me about."

Meanwhile, a long article had appeared in the New York press stating that a gigantic deal was in progress between Li and Edison. Millions were involved, and Edison was going to China to be a guest of the Empress. He was to be entertained with Oriental splendor, and Li was to act as his guide through the celestial country. Edison was shown the article and asked if it were correct. The inventor smiled. "I have no deal on with the Viceroy," he replied. "Nor do I expect to have one. We have put in big electric plants in Shanghai and other Chinese cities and, if I remember correctly, have done work for Li. That is all there is to this foolish story."

So Li Hung Chang was obliged to leave America without seeing the man who is accessible to the humblest admirer. Probably if such a thing had happened in his own country he would have given orders for Edison's head to be brought to him if his body refused to accompany it. But, as has been stated before, Edison is no respecter of persons. He didn't want to see Li, and so Li didn't see him.

There is, however, one illustrious personage whom Edison would greatly like to see and chat with, and that is King Edward, for whom he has a very real and sincere admiration. "He is a great man," Edison declared to the writer recently, "and perhaps the best and wisest king that ever sat on the British throne. There are no 'frills' about King Edward, he is just as democratic as you or I, though of course there are certain ceremonies which he must keep up in order to safeguard the dignity of the Monarchy. In two years' time I hope to pay England a visit, and then, perhaps, I may have the happiness of meeting his Majesty. You know," he added, with a twinkle, "Mark Twain did."

Mr. Edison well recollects the visit of King Edward to America, now nearly half a century ago. "And no wonder," he humorously remarked, "for on that day I managed to get the biggest black eye I ever had in my life. It happened in this way. I was at school at the time, and there was bitter rivalry between our establishment and another school in the neighborhood. Well, the Prince of Wales, as he was then, consented to pay our town a visit, and all the schools were to take part in the general welcome. We were therefore lined up, commanded to 'quick march,' and were nearing the scene of festivities when our rivals loomed in sight. We met, and an instant later the fight was on. I felt that things were coming my way, and I was not wrong, for suddenly I received a terrific blow in my left eye which put it entirely out of business. When I recovered myself our assailants had vanished, order was restored, and we proceeded on our way. Yes," concluded Edison sadly, "I saw the Prince all right, but it was out of one optic only."

CHAPTER XXIV

HIS OPINIONS

As has been mentioned once before, Edison has probably been interrogated on a greater number of subjects than any other living scientist. Directly a discussion begins in the press — whether of electrical, scientific, or general interest — the newspaper men rush off to Orange to get Edison's opinion. Very often the inventor declines to say anything, but should he happen to be in the mood to talk and the subject is one which has attracted his attention — he follows the papers with as much keenness as he does Nature's secrets — he will discuss it with considerable freedom.

Fifteen years ago Edison was asked if he believed a ship would ever be constructed which would do the trip between Liverpool and New York in four days. He said that he was positive that such a vessel would be built and that he would live to see it. He also stated that the question was one of reducing the friction between the sides of the ship and the water. Perhaps, he declared, some means might be found whereby electricity could be employed to arrive at such an end. He had experimented a little in this direction, but not much. Then Edison, with a humorous smile which the interviewer did not notice, suggested that a possible means of rendering a vessel capable of slipping through the water more easily would be by greasing her sides, which might be perforated so that oil would be slowly but constantly oozing out. He hadn't tried it himself, but it was an idea which had occurred to him.

This suggestion was one which appealed to the reporter's imagination, and when he returned to his office he wrote an interesting account of how by merely oiling the sides of a vessel she might thereby double and even treble her speed. The article was sanely and reasonably written, and widely quoted both in the European as well as the American press, and Edison was credited with another remarkable "discovery." One newspaper, in a leading article heavily leaded, said: "It may be that the theory propounded by the ingenious Mr. Edison that greasing the sides of ships will so diminish the resistance of the water as to increase their speed by one-third is a correct one, and if so it will be another instance of the enormous economic advantage hidden in a simple appliance lying always ready to hand, and overlooked in the costly and laborious search for remoter ones.

"We can compute the millions which have been and still are being expended in increasing the speed of ships, fighting for hours and half-hours and minutes ever with a fervor of ingenuity which spared no cost and left no pneumatic or mechanical or constructive resources unexplored. It will be a startling disclosure to naval architects and engineers if the solution of their problem be found, not in improved wave lines or tubular boilers or triple screws, but, like truth in a well, at the bottom of the obscure and unregarded grease-pot. Perhaps Mr. Edison has made the greatest economic discovery of the century, and, except steam, the greatest ever applied to navigation since the launching of the Ark or the Argo. If it fulfil what are asserted to be his expectations, New York and London will be only four days apart, and the carrying trade of the world will be revolutionized. At the same time the price of oil will be likely to go up."

But experiments in this queer method of reducing the resistance of the water and enabling a vessel to slip through her element at treble her usual rate were not prosecuted with any real enthusiasm, and engineers and naval architects to-day still pin their faith to boilers and turbines. The four-day ship, however, is in sight, and Edison's prophecy will doubtless be realized during the next few years.

Fourteen years ago considerable excitement was caused by certain writers — who probably desired to "rig" the market — declaring that aluminium was to be the metal of the future. There was nothing that this mineral would not be useful for, and its strength and cheapness would render it a suitable material for either a table ornament or a battle-ship. Edison was again asked for his opinion on the question, and he was very emphatic in stating that "there was nothing to it." He affirmed that as a metal it was practically useless, and for machinery or construction one might just as well employ lead. Its extreme lightness would render it a suitable material for making ornaments, and that would be all. To be of any use for other things it must be alloyed with another metal — preferably copper. The coming metal, Edison thought, was nickel steel — steel with a five per cent addition of nickel. It would make splendid armor plates, for, unlike pure steel, it will not crack and is very difficult to bore.

"A burglar-proof safe," Edison further stated, while on the subject of metals and their qualities, "is as impossible to make as an unsinkable boat. You can make a safe of nickel steel which you may not be able to bore or crack, but there is no safe that is not at the mercy of a dynamite cartridge. A burglar can carry in his pocket power sufficient to break open a dozen safes. An absolutely burglar-proof safe is as difficult to make as perpetual motion is to find, for as soon as a material is invented which will resist the most powerful explosive known, chemists go to work and evolve some other substance which will destroy it. That is the whole history of armor-plating and big guns."

Edison has absolute faith in wireless telegraphy, and he believes that the man who will make it a success is Marconi. Two or three years ago Edison made a statement regarding wireless which is well worth recalling, for he indorsed that statement in June, 1907. "I think," he said, "Marconi will work across the Atlantic commercially. He will send messages around the world by repeating stations, but he will not do it in one jump. Great undertakings are not completed in jumps. The discovery of any fundamental principle, of course, always is a jump, but the working out of the details is another matter which involves laborious work in the field of experiment, especially if it is to be worked on commercial lines.

"Wireless is going to be the telegraph of the sea. The time will come when any one on the maritime exchange can send out a wireless message and catch any vessel afloat in any part of the world and change her routing. I don't think so much about the outlook for the wireless system on land. That field is practically occupied. But the ocean field is open. I think it will be only a question of a few years before wireless is developed to a point where it will be a practical and important factor in the industrial world."

Readers will perhaps remember how many years ago

the plague of rabbits in Australia became so great that the Australian government offered a big reward to any one who would suggest a means of dealing successfully with the pest. A certain American who had a desire to claim the reward but didn't quite see how he was going to do it, conceived the idea of calling upon Edison to get a few points which might be useful. Edison received the gentleman very courteously, and having learned the object of his visit did not "turn him down" immediately, but talked on the subject, and suggested several simple methods by which the rabbits in Australia might be got rid of. He did not think his visitor's idea of sowing fields of carrots and then injecting a poison into the vegetable was quite practical; neither did he believe the difficulty was to be overcome by inoculating a number of the rabbits and then letting them loose among their unsuspecting companions. "What do you think," said Edison, "of stringing loaded wires around the fields, so that when the rabbits bumped against them the circuit would be complete and the animals would be eletrocuted? It might be done." The visitor was excited over the suggestion. "Why," he said with the greatest enthusiasm, "we might hang carrots and lettuce and other rabbit food on these lines, and the creatures would be certain to receive shocks which would kill them by thousands." He asked if it would be possible to electrify the barbed wire which was much used in Australia, and when Edison declared that it might be done the visitor left the laboratory all aglow with the possibilities of such a gigantic scheme. Whether he made any use of the information obtained from the inventor never transpired, but Edison rather thinks that he must have "completed the circuit" himself while experimenting, for he heard no more of his inventive friend.

Edison has experimented long and successfully with the X-ray machine, and when it was a nine days' wonder he received many letters from unknown correspondents asking if the Roentgen discovery could not be applied in ways which were certainly the reverse of legitimate. Among these communications was a missive from a man living in what is known in American parlance as a "hat" town in the oil regions of Pennsylvania. The letter amused Mr. Edison very much at the time, and he put it away with a few other curiosities which had been delivered at his laboratory through the medium of the mails. The letter was addressed to Menlo Park, and had been forwarded on to Orange. The following is a copy of this curious document:

Mr. Thomas A. Edison, Menlo Park, N.J.
"Dear Sir, — I write you to know if you can make me an X-ray apparatus for playing against faro bank? I would like to have it so I can wear it on my body, and have it attached to spectacles or goggles so I can tell the second card of a deck of playing cards turned face up. If you will make it for me let me know what it will cost. If I make a success out of it I will pay you five thousand dollars extra in one year. Please keep this to yourself. If you cannot make it will you be kind enough to give me Professor Roentgen's address? Please let me hear from you.
"Yours truly,
"———."

Edison has received many other letters almost as curious, but he declares that that was the first and only occasion upon which he was asked to assist a gambler in beating faro banks. He would have liked very much to have sent for the imaginative card-sharper and administered a lecture, but thought it better to ignore his unique request. Should the smart Pennsylvanian have repented his ways it will, perhaps, be some satisfaction to him to see his letter published here and to learn why it was that he received no reply to his communication.

When America was engaged with her war with Spain, Edison was consulted by many reporters, hot on the trail of "copy," who desired to know his views on the outcome of the disagreement. One of them asked the inventor his opinion regarding the possibility of New York being "taken," and Edison declared that it would be more difficult for a fleet of war-ships to enter New York harbor than it would be for a dozen fishing boats to capture Gibraltar. He also made a statement to the effect that he believed the uses of huge war-vessels were growing less, and that torpedo-boats and torpedo-destroyers were the great thing. Other celebrities were interviewed regarding the best means of annihilating an enemy, among these being Nikola Tesla, General Miles, and Russell Sage, which emboldened a writer, who concealed his identity under the name of "The Farceur," to write a play, which he called, "Clank — Clank, the Cranks are Clanking," and published in *Town Topics*. The play was never performed or even put into rehearsal, though it was received with much favor and greatly amused the celebrities who figured in it. The author stated that it was a realistic representation of "War as it is carried on by high Privates in the Rear Ranks," and the opening "business" and chorus are well worth quoting:

"CLANK — CLANK, THE CRANKS ARE CLANKING

"(The scene is the Battery. All the cranks are assembled, and there is much excitement. Each one

is preparing to annihilate Spain and free Cuba at a
moment's notice. All the people who in time of peace
prepare for war, and who never felt a wound, are there
with their inventions. Rabid Jingoes are gnawing all
the bark off the trees. General Miles is posing on a
pedestal as a statue of Mars. Edison is engaged in
charging the lobsters in the Aquarium with electricity.
Nikola Tesla has his ear to the ground, and is talking
through the earth to Li Hung Chang. The bicycle
squad is getting ready to charge down the bay on
their wheels. Numerous war balloons are being
rapidly filled with gas by speech-makers, while the sky
takes on a lurid hue, and a flaming Cabbage Head,
rampant, appears in the heavens in the direction of
sou'-sou'-east.)

"Chorus of Inventors

"We've each a great invention
That we'd bring to your attention,
And we guarantee 'twill knock the Spaniards stiff;
It will shock 'em and surprise 'em,
It will simply paralyze 'em,
It will blow 'em all to purgatory — if —

"If it works all right —
If the fuse will light —
If you put it underneath 'em when the moon
shines bright —
If they stand just so —
If the wind don't blow —
If it don't explode and kill you accidentally,
you know!

"Now's the time to place reliance
On the wonders of our science,
And our country's foe we'll settle in a jiff;
Our plans are all perfected,

>   And it's generally expected
>   Our invention will annihilate 'em — IF —
>
> "IF it works all right, &c.

(At this moment Mr. Edison rushes to the front waving his arms.)

"Mr. Edison: 'Hooray! Victory is ours!'
"The Crowd (*breathlessly*): 'How now, O Wizard?'
"Mr. Edison (*proudly*): 'It is done! I have filled these lobsters so full of electricity that they buzz when they move. When the Spanish war-ships come in sight I will turn 'em loose in the bay, and then you'll see what you will see. These lobsters will establish a current with a line of electric eels that I have stationed at Sandy Hook, and the haughty hidalgos will get a shock that will make 'em look like twenty-nine cents marked down from forty.'
"The Crowd: 'Hooray! Cuba *libre!*'
"Mr. Tesla (*interrupting the demonstration*): 'That scheme won't do at all. Now, I have a fan here that is charged with four billion volts of Franklin's best brand of bottled lightning, and when this fan gets fanning the results are astounding. Not ten minutes ago I fanned a fly from off Emperor William's nose, and fluted the whiskers of the King of Siam. Now, when the Spaniards come up the bay I'll just climb a tree and pour a broadside of vibrations at 'em. Say, I'll fan 'em off the earth in not more than a minute and a half.'
"The Crowd: 'Hooroo! Cuba *libre!*'"

Edison laughed so heartily when he read the play that the author himself would have been satisfied if he could have seen him. However, he has long since become used to appearing in novels and plays, and at one time even seriously thought of writing a work of fiction in conjunction with George Parsons Lathrop. Edison was to furnish the electrical suggestions and Lathrop the plot. The writing was to be the work of both. The inventor was very enthusiastic at first, and Lathrop had a number of interviews with him, and Edison began to turn out suggestions quicker than the novelist could take them down. But after half a dozen of these "collaboration" interviews Edison's enthusiasm cooled very considerably. Lathrop was as keen on the novel as before, and had managed to collect from the inventor sufficient material to take him halfway through the book, when his collaborator met him one day with a bit of a frown on his smooth brow, and declared that he would have nothing more to do with the novel. He was very tired of the whole thing. He would rather invent a dozen useful things, including a mechanical novelist who would turn out works of fiction when the machinery was set in motion, than go any further with the electrical novel. He solemnly declared that there was no fiction in electricity, and he advised Lathrop to turn his attention to something else, which Lathrop, somewhat crestfallen, agreed to do. And that was the first and last incursion the inventor made into the realms of fiction.

Edison has on more than one occasion been interrogated regarding the writing of his autobiography, and questioned as to the reason why he has not put out such a work. In conversation there is no man more brilliant than Edison, and many of his associates have declared that when interested in a subject or describing the results, perhaps, of some experiments of which the general public knows nothing, he uses language which is not only forceful but dramatic. It seems a thousand pities that on such occasions there should not have been some one by — some Boswell, perhaps — to treasure and preserve such conversations. And could Edison write his life as he talks every day in his laboratory the result would be a volume equal to any biography or autobiography yet published. But this, it has been affirmed, he cannot do. It is said, though Edison has not verified this, that more than once he has taken pen in hand with the notion of writing the story of his life. "But when he does this," says an anonymous writer, "a curious thing happens. He becomes strangely self-conscious, and the resulting narrative — instead of being easy, flowing, and full of snap and vigor — is hard, formal, and unsatisfying. He seems, in fact, to be seized by a sort of stage fright, which prevents him from doing his best, exactly as a man who, sitting in private conversation, can talk intelligently and well by the hour, is sometimes forced to the baldest commonplaces the moment he gets upon his feet. This mental condition, by the way, is not peculiar to Edison. There are many men of great ability who seem mentally paralyzed the moment an attempt is made to direct their thoughts down the point of a pen in a thin stream of ink."

It is estimated that if everything that has ever been written and published about Edison were collected and republished in book form it would make a library of a thousand volumes — each volume containing an average of a hundred thousand words. And of these stories which would go to the making of such a library a very small proportion only would be found to have any real authority for their being. It is generally believed, for instance, by those outside the Edison laboratory that the inventor forgot his wedding day, or, rather, forgot that he had been married after the ceremony was performed. The story refers to his first marriage, and the writer asked Edison if the facts were as narrated. "It was nothing but a newspaper story," Edison replied, "got up by an imaginative newspaper man who knew that I was a bit absent-minded. I never forgot that I had been married. In fact, I don't believe any man would forget such an event unless he wanted to. But perhaps there was something to account for the story, and I think it must have been this.

"The day I was married a consignment of stock tickers had been returned to the factory as being imperfect, and I had a desire to find out what was wrong and to put the machines right. An hour or so after the marriage ceremony had been performed I thought of these tickers, and when my wife and I had returned home I mentioned them to her and explained that I would like to go to the factory to see what was the matter with them. She agreed at once, and I went down, where I found Bachelor, my assistant, hard at work trying to remedy the defect. We both monkeyed about with them, and finally after an hour or two we put them to rights, and I went home again. But as to forgetting that I was married, that's all nonsense, and both I and my wife laughed at the story, though when I began to come across it almost every other week it began to get tedious. It was one of those made-up stories which stick, and I suppose I shall always be spoken of as the man who forgot his wife an hour after he was married."

Another absurd story which gained currency some years ago, and is still flourishing very healthily, is one connected with the invention of the incandescent electric-light system. This story for about the thousandth time made its appearance in an English publication as late as 1907, and once more described how Edison invented the incandescent lamp in order to be revenged on the gas companies. His anger had been aroused by his gas being peremptorily cut off by a hard-hearted collector who wanted his bill paid. "That night," Edison is reported to have said, "as I sat in the darkness I swore I would make an electric light that would ruin the gas companies." This story always annoys Edison when his eye lights upon it — as it does every month or so — for he is the last man in the world who would seek to revenge himself on any one, let alone the man who merely demanded his rights. The story deserves by now to die a natural death — it is quite old enough.

Some years ago, when the four leading Edison companies consolidated into one General Electric Company, with a capital of twelve million dollars, a good deal was written about the man who had been the instrument by which such a great business enterprise was possible. Edison's "twelve-million-dollar brain" became a saying, and lessons were drawn anent the value of first-class brains. "Here," said one writer, whose words are well worth preserving and thinking over, "is a business aggregation that springs from the wits of one man. A few years ago Thomas Edison was a poor and obscure telegraph operator. To-day, by devising machinery of advantage to the human race, he is a millionaire and the means by which others acquire immense wealth. Yet no one is injured. The new fortunes come from traits of observation and mechanical wit that lay hid in the brain of one poor wise man. There are mines of the mind that are richer than any which the geologist finds in the mountains, and more precious gems lie hidden there than can be dug from the rocks or washed from the streams of the wilderness." This truism might be instilled in the mind of every growing youth who desires to gain a name and fortune by the cultivation of his brains. He may not be an Edison, and he may not possess genius, but perseverance will carry him a long way on the road to success. As a matter of fact, Edison does not think a great deal of so-called "genius." "Genius," says some wise man, "is an infinite capacity for taking pains," but Edison goes one better when he says: "Genius is two per cent inspiration and ninety-eight per cent perspiration." And let the man who believes that he is no "genius," or even particularly clever, take this wise remark to heart and he will find that Edison is not far wrong in his belief that it is hard work that tells and the virtue that will eventually land one on the topmost rung of Fortune's ladder.

Edison has an excellent ear for music, and the statement which one frequently sees made that he has a dislike to the phonograph and never listens to it is quite wrong. At one time he "passed" every record made in the Orange laboratory, and would mark them "Good," "Fair," "Bad," or "Very Bad," as he thought fit, in order to classify them for the trade. These distinctions, of course, did not refer to the quality of the record, but rather to the style of composition. Some of the "pieces" which he disliked most often turned out to be the very ones which the public liked best, and it became a kind of standing joke that when Edison ticketed a record "Very Bad" the factory had to work overtime in order to supply the demand.

When all records were made at the Edison laboratory (now they are made in New York), singers, reciters, and instrumentalists would come down from the city and give their performances in Edison's library. So long as the "talking-machine" was something of a novelty, the fees demanded by these artists were not very heavy, but later on the bills for "professional phonographic services" swelled considerably, the "services" of some singers being almost prohibitive. Edison was generally present when the records were made, and it surprised him to find that not infrequently the most capable singers made the poorest records. On more than one occasion when famous soloists had been engaged the records, when tested, proved utterly worthless. These performers had not the knack of singing into a phonograph, and had to go through considerable training before becoming successes in the phonograph line. Other singers have visited the laboratory, whose names were certainly not "household words," and who demanded but modest fees, yet their records have been among the best ever made. In other words, one must have a regular "phonographic voice" in order to make a good record, and if a singer is denied this then he or she must cultivate it — which it is quite possible to do. High sopranos are less successful on the phonograph than contraltos, while the violin and other thin, high-toned instruments do not sound so well as double basses, 'cellos, and harps. In men's voices baritones and basses reproduce better than tenors as a general rule, though there is no man living who makes a finer record than Bonci.

Edison, by the way, has a distinct objection to placing his own voice on record, and on two occasions only has he been persuaded to do so. When perfecting the phonograph he had, of course, to talk into the machine, but the records were afterwards scraped or destroyed. He says he has no desire to see machines adorned with notices announcing that by putting a penny in the slot you may "Hear Edison Talk." Once he sent his agent, who was in London, a "phonogram," and he also said a few words in a phonograph for a young man in whom he was very much interested.

Apart from these two, however, there is no record of Edison's voice in existence. He has been approached by numberless enterprising managers, who have offered him almost any sum if he would relate to the phonograph the story of how he created it, but to all such requests he has turned a deaf ear. And here it may be remarked that the statement so frequently made that when distinguished visitors call upon Edison at the laboratory they are requested to put their voices on record is a wrong one. There is no phonograph kept for this purpose. The only request made to visitors is that they shall sign their names in the "Visitors' Book" — a number of which may be seen on the shelves of the library.

Edison regards the art of inventing very much in the light of a profession which may be "learned" almost as successfully as soldiering, or acting, or even "doctoring." Thousands of men, he thinks, might have become inventors had they but cultivated their ideas, for the creative germ lies hidden in most brains. Observation is one of the greatest assets in successful inventing, and the man who sees what is wanted and then provides it is the one who makes good. Ideas increase as they are cultivated, and the brain must be exercised like any other part of the body, for the more one works that mysterious "gray matter" the more good will one get out of it. As a rule, authors who write a great deal improve their "style," and in the same way the more one cultivates ideas the more readily will ideas come and the better will be their quality. Some inventors are "born," of course, but a greater number are "made," and the man who says he is entirely lacking in ideas is generally the man who is too lazy to cultivate them.

Edison is now engaged on what he considers the

greatest problem of all — the generation of electricity direct from coal. The subject has occupied his attention for many years, and now that he has practically laid aside his work as a commercial inventor he is devoting all his time to the unravelling of this fascinating mystery. He has made some progress towards success, and has been enabled to get a little energy direct from coal, but, unfortunately, it has no great force. At present, as every one knows, electricity requires another power to generate it, and while this is so it cannot become the motor of the world. But when electricity is generated direct then steam will become obsolete, and the newer power will reign.

Of the force hidden in coal about 15 per cent only is available, the other 85 per cent being wasted. That is why it requires so many hundreds of tons of coal to propel a liner across the Atlantic. When the problem of generating electricity direct is solved, then two or three tons of coal only will be needed for the same purpose. Edison has been experimenting on these lines with his customary enthusiasm and determination for twenty years without any really satisfactory results, but he is not discouraged. His investigations have been sufficiently productive of good to spur him on, and the problem is one which he will never relinquish as long as life lasts. Possibly, he declares with great cheerfulness, it may not be his good fortune to discover the right means of thus obtaining the true force, and if this should be so, then he feels perfectly convinced the problem will be solved by some one else. Many other scientists are also working on the question, and Edison would not be surprised any day to learn that it had been solved by some comparatively unknown man. Should such an event happen, then Edison would be among the first to acknowledge him as the greatest inventor of all times.

INDEX

A

A, the letter, as pronounced backward and forward on phonograph, 152-153.
Absent-mindedness, Edison's, 289, 301-303, 344-345.
Accumulators in storage batteries, use of cobalt for, 215-216.
Acheson, assistant of Edison's, 241.
Adams, Milton, 53, 56, 57-60.
Albert Medal, the, 285.
Aldermen, New York, visit of, to Menlo Park, 113, 118-119.
Aluminium, Edison on uselessness of, 336.
Alumni Association telephone dinner, 93.
Anderson, A. A., portrait of Edison by, 323.
Anderson, Captain H. M., 56.
Animals, experimental electrocution of, 204-206.
Annealing of metals, 131-132.
Astronomy, invention connected with, 184.
Autobiography, question of Edison's, 343-344.
Autographic telegraph, the, 69-70.
"Automatic Electric Baby Tender," 244-245.
Automatic telegraph, the, 68-69.
Automobile, perfected storage battery for, 216-217; Edison family's expert use of the, 288.

B

Baby, and the phonograph, 145-147; interest in the Edison, 245-246.
Bach, Dr., quoted, 83-84.
Bachelor, Charles, 69, 104, 106, 239, 269, 303, 345; quoted, 69; assists Edison at Saratoga lecture, 78-81; puts first filament into an incandescent lamp, 107; Edison's tribute to, 107.
Bachman, Robert A., 233.
Baden, Grand Duke of, 276.
Baker, manager of Memphis office Western Union Telegraph Company, 52.
Bamboo, discovery of suitability of, for use in incandescent lamp, 96, 108; the search for the right kind of, 108-109, 252.
Banquet, a "long-distance," 93.
Banquets to Edison. See Dinners.
Barker, Professor, 77-78, 94.
Battle, a kinetoscopic, at Orange, 221.
Beebe, Grant, 93.
Beecher, H. W., phonograph record by, 156.
Bell, Alexander Graham, 73-75, 77.
Bell Telephone Company organized, 74.
Bergmann, Sigmund, 115, 240, 306.
Bijou Theatre, Boston, the first to use electric lighting, 120-121.
"Bingen on the Rhine" on the phonograph, 151.
Bishop, Mr., quoted, 88-89.
Bismarck, phonograph record by, 156.
Blue Mountain House the first hotel lighted by electricity, 121.
Boehm, Ludwig K., 240.
Book-keeping, Edison's distrust of, 321-323.
Bordiga, A., statue by, 223.
Borton, Professor, 77.
Boston, Edison a telegrapher, experimenter, and lecturer in, 53-61.

INDEX

Boursel, Charles, 72–73.
Bridge, the magnetic, 186.
Brown, Harold P., 203, 204, 206.
Browning, phonograph record by, 156.
Buddhists and the phonograph, 157–158.
Bugs, in electrical parlance, 87, 250–251.
Buildings, first illuminated by electric light, 120–121; use of solid concrete in construction of, 174–175.
Byron, Joseph, 314.

C

Callahan, Edison's first assistant, 63.
Calves, electrocution of, 205.
Capital punishment, Edison's views on, 212.
Carbon-button transmitter, 74, 81.
Carbon rheostat, 185.
Carman, foreman for Edison, 138.
Cats, phonographic study of, 159–162.
Cement, manufacture of, by Edison, 171–174.
Centennial Exhibition, the first practical telephone exhibited at, 81.
Central station in New York, 114–120.
Chalk battery, the, 186.
Chalk telephone receiver, 178.
Chandler, Colonel A. B., 258, 259–260.
Chemical telephone, the, 75.
Christie, George, 43.
Church, the first, lighted by electricity, 120.
Churches, telephones in, 93.
Cigarette-smoking, Edison on, 318–319.
Cincinnati, Edison in, 48–50.
City Temple, London, first church lighted by electricity, 120.
"Clank — Clank, the Cranks," etc., 340–342.
Clarke, Charles L., 239.
Coal, generation of electricity direct from, 350.

Cobalt, use of, in storage battery, 215–216.
Cockran, W. Bourke, defence of Kemmler by, 206; cross-examines Edison, 209, 237–238.
Columbia, first steam vessel lighted by electricity, 121–122.
Concrete, houses built of, 174–175.
Condenser telephone, the, 75.
Condensers in storage battery, material for, 215–216.
Conly, Superintendent, 301.
Cortlandt Street telephone office, 90–91.
Coster and the phonograph, 162–163.
Cotton filament, the carbonized, discovered, 105–106, 110.
Count, Edison as a, 277, 285–286.
Crystal Palace exhibition of phonograph, 153–156.
Curtis, William S., 93.

D

Dally, Clarence T., with X-ray machine at Buffalo, 229–230; death of, from effect of X-rays, 231–232.
Dally, E., 229.
Day books, Edison's, 249–253.
Deafness, Edison's, 49, 290–292.
Decorations bestowed on Edison, 284–287.
Depew, Chauncey M., 276, 326; story about Edison by, 328–329.
Dickens, Edison's liking for, 282.
Dickson, W. K. L., vii; quoted, 50–51, 57–60, 69; works on kinetoscope with Edison, 166; photographs Pope Leo XIII., 167–168; as an assistant in Orange laboratory, 241.
Dinner, given by American Institute of Electrical Engineers (1904), 254–259; Magnetic Club (1905), 259–260; General Electric Outing Club, at Menlo Park, 260–263; the *Figaro*, in Paris, 273; of

INDEX

French Society of Civil Engineers on the Eiffel Tower, 275; at Heidelberg, 276–277.
Discovery, distinction between invention and, 177.
Dog, electrocution of a, 204–205.
Draper, John W., 129–130.
Dreyfus, Louis, experiment by, 228.
Duplex telegraph, invention of, 66; description of, 67–68.
Dyer, Frank L., vii, 234–235.
Dynamite, Edison's handling of, 198–199.
Dynamos, 186.

E

Edison, Charles, son of Edison, 288, 289.
Edison, Madelyn, daughter, 244, 283, 289.
Edison, Marion, daughter, 272, 275.
Edison, Nancy Elliot, mother, 2, 5–8, 11–12, 13–14.
Edison, Samuel, father, 1–2, 5, 10, 34–36.
Edison, Theodore, son, 288, 289.
Edison, Thomas Alva, career of — Birth and parentage, 1–3; first seven years, spent at Milan, O., 5–9; at school, 6–7; removal to Port Huron, Mich., 10; life there, 11–14; receives most of his instruction from his mother, 11; early reading of, 13; at eleven becomes news agent and candy vender on Grand Trunk Ry., 14–15; laboratory and printing office on train, 15–16; publishes the *Weekly Herald*, 17–29; second paper, *Paul Pry*, 30; learns telegraphy at fifteen, 38–39; night operator at Port Huron, 39–42; operator at Sarnia, 43–44; in Western Union office at Port Huron, 44; at Stratford, Canada, 44–45; operator at Indianapolis (1864–1865), 45–47; leaves Indianapolis and goes from city to city, 48; in Cincinnati, 48–50; in Memphis, 50–52; in Boston, 52–61; goes to New York, 61–62; experience with Law Gold Indicator and engagement at $300 a month, 62–63; improves ticker and sells improvement for $40,000, 63–64; gains confidence of Western Union Telegraph Co., 66; resigns management of Gold Indicator and opens factory at Newark, N.J., 66; manufactures improved ticker and invents duplex telegraph, 66–67; invents quadruplex telegraph, 68; sextuplex telegraph, 68, 71; places Newark factory in charge of manager and settles at Menlo Park, 71–72; called "Wizard of Menlo Park," 71–72, 87; becomes interested in telephone and invents carbon transmitter, 74; compromises with Alexander Graham Bell after litigation, 74; further telephone appliances devised by, 75; invents incandescent electric light, 94–113; establishes central station in New York, 113–118; experiments with platinum wire, 126–133; invents the phonograph, 134–138; invents the kinetoscope, 165; masters photographic art in connection with last invention, 166; invents ore separator, 169–170; financial failure of ore-separating scheme, 170–171; manufacture of cement, 171–174; houses built of solid concrete, 174–175; war machine stories, 192–202; connection with electrocution, 203–204; a witness in Kemmler case, 206–209, 237–238; at Paris Exposition, 272–276; in Heidelberg, 276–277; in Italy, 277; in London, 277–278; home life of, at Llewellyn Park, 279–289; wife and family of, 288–289.
Characteristics of — Reading habits, 13, 69, 282; "curious but

INDEX

Edison, T. A. — *Continued*
lovable" as a boy, 16; carelessness in dress, 16, 50, 53, 57, 290, 293-295; "a good boy" and "a smart youngster," 28; skill and quickness in grappling with a difficulty, 42-43, 62-63; his deafness, 49, 290-292; handwriting, 51-52, 53; a rapid operator, 52; modesty and retirement of, 61, 147, 214, 330; description of, at Saratoga lecture, 80-81; newspaper tales of, 87-88; Mr. Bishop's description of, 88-89; the real man, 89; inexhaustible energy, 126; sleeping habits, 137, 177, 224, 241, 297-298, 303; dislike of lionizing, 147, 254; two preëminent qualifications as an inventor, 177; patience of, 177, 329; never boasts, but lets perfected product speak for itself, 214; as a reader of foreign languages, 222; eating habits, 223, 283, 289; not rapid at figures, 237; as a smoker, 243, 289, 296; treatment of workpeople, 243-244, 300-301; musical tastes, 282, 347; absent-mindedness, 289, 301-303, 344-345; control of temper, 292-293; drinking habits, 295-296; eminently practical, 298-300; does not care for wealth, 300; keenness of memory, 304-305; memory for faces, 305-306; as a writer, 343-344.

Inventions by — Vote-recording machine, 53-54; improvement of Gold and Stock Indicator ("ticker"), 63-64; duplex telegraph, 66-67; quadruplex telegraph, 68; sextuplex telegraph, 68, 71; automatic telegraph, 68-69; harmonic multiplex telegraph and autographic telegraph, 69-70; carbon telephone transmitter, 74; numerous telephone appliances, 75; fuse wire, 118-119; phonograph, 134 ff.; kinetoscope, 165-167; magnetic ore separator, 169-170; ore-milling machinery — crushers, pulverizers, conveyers, and presses, 170-171; cement formula, 171-174; concrete houses, 174-175; long list of lesser inventions, 176 ff.; motograph, 180; electric pen, 180-181; mimeograph, 181-182; "grasshopper telegraph," 182-183; megaphone, 183-184; phonomotor, 184; tasimeter, 184-185; odoroscope, 185; microphone, magnetic bridge, etheroscope, "dead beat" galvanometer, etc., 186; fake, ascribed to, 186-190; submarine torpedo-boat, operated by electricity, 192-193; storage battery, 213-220.

Opinions of, on — Work, 14, 262, 347; telephoning across the sea, 84-85; patents, 122, 236-237; possibilities of the phonograph, 141-142; phonographic record of Napoleon's voice, 156-157; combined use of kinetoscope and phonograph, 165-166; "discovery" and "invention," 177; wireless telegraphy, 182, 337; England and her wars, 198; use of electricity in executions, 204, 212; capital punishment, 206, 212; storage battery for vehicular use, 216-217; success and its achievement, 262; banquets, 263, 276; English beer, 277; electricity in London underground railways, 277-278; dress, 293-295; temperance and total abstinence, 295-296; worrying, 301, 320; cigarette-smoking, 318-319; newspapers, 320-321; book-keeping, 321-323; King Edward VII., 332-333; four-day ships between New York and Liverpool, 334; aluminium, 336; nickel steel, 336-337; battle-

INDEX 355

ships and torpedo-boats, 340; genius, 347; recording his voice for phonographic reproduction, 348; the art of inventing, 349.

Reminiscences of — Attempt to hatch goose eggs in person, 9; concoction for enabling hired girl to fly, 9; *Paul Pry* personal and its penalty, 30; peanut trick and its cure, 30–31; the dandies and the train-boy, 31–34; the 9.30 retiring rule and its remedy, 34–36; the cow and the telegraph wire, 36–37; the exacting train-despatcher and the young operator, 39 ff.; remedies break in telegraph line at Port Huron, 43; responsible for possible train wreck at Sarnia, 43–44; swindled by Western Union manager at Port Huron, 44; nearly shot as a thief by policeman, 48–49; mechanical work of telegraph operating illustrated by story connected with shooting of Lincoln, 49–50; experience at Memphis with rapid St. Louis operator, 50–51; a cockroach exterminator, 55–56; running to breakfast to save time, 56; a thirty-dollar suit and its ruin, 57; successful but dangerous home-made gun-cotton, 57; the mark-down sale of stockings, 57–58; first lecture, before young ladies' school, 58–60; Law Gold Indicator episode, 62–63; locating a break in the New York-Albany telegraph line, 65–66; cashing a $40,000 check, 64; the Saratoga lecture, 77–81; originates the expression "Hello!" 85–86; coins word "filament," 86; the phonograph bet, 138; the baby and the phonograph, 145–146; phonograph jokes, 151–152; the interview anent war machines and its results, 192–198; the troublesome ministers and the explosives, 200–201; other unwelcome visitors, 201–202; the martyr to insomnia, and his cure, 224; computation by proxy in Kemmler case, 237–238; support of a mistaken assistant before board of inquiry, 242; the fake cigars, 243–244; the Automatic Electric Baby Tender, 244–246; the new office boy, 247–248; remarks on "hustling," 262; *Figaro* story and American paper's parody, 274–275; Parisian experiences, 276; Count and Countess Edison, 277; "The Count of Monte Cristo," 281; the degrees of the Legion of Honor, 286; the advantages of being deaf, 291; "Ask him to take a drink," 292; forgetting his name, 302; story of the uneaten breakfast, 302–303; incandescent lamp and pickle fork incident, 307–309; the unscientific journalist, 309–311; the religious lady interviewer, 311–312; a novel contribution box, 312; "Never watch the clock, my boy," 318; cigarette-smoking story, 318–319; the book-keeper who figured wrong, 321–323; another green journalist, 324–325; experience in telegraphing after twenty-six years, 326–328; the electric-belt young woman, 328–329; an exterminator suggested for Australian rabbits, 338; the faro-gambler's request for X-ray apparatus, 339; the proposed electrical novel, with G. P. Lathrop, 342–343; false story of forgetting his wedding-day, 344–345; tale of invention of incandescent lamp to be revenged on gas companies, 345–346; proportional parts of inspiration and perspiration that go to make genius, 347; great

INDEX

Edison, T. A. — *Continued*
  man's taste in phonographic music not the popular, 347.
Edison, Mrs. T. A., vii, 17, 18, 272, 275, 287-289; making a photograph of, 316.
Edison, town of, 170-171; labor difficulty at, 300-301.
Edison Electric Light Company formed, 94.
Edison Illuminating Company, New York, 115.
Edison Medal, the, 254-257.
Edison Patent Shirt, the, 189-190.
Edison Tower, the, 12-13.
"Edison's hands," nickname of Charles Bachelor, 107.
Edward VII., King, Edison's admiration for, 332-333.
Eiffel, M., 275.
Eiffel Tower dinner, 275.
Electricity, generation of, direct from coal, 349-350.
Electric light, the incandescent, 94 ff.; interest in, in America and abroad, 99-100, 109-110; Edison's specifications for patent for, 110-112; vast litigation over, 122; effort to show use of, in thirteenth century, 122-123; mighty proportions in growth of, 124-125; number of patents covering, 186.
Electric pen, the, 180-181.
Electrocution, Edison's slight connection with, 203; experiments with animals at Menlo Park laboratory, 203-206; use of alternating current in, 204; methods used in Kemmler's case, 210-211; executions since Kemmler's, 211-212; Edison's views on, 212.
Electrolier, the first, 121, 179.
Electro-motographic receiver, the, 75.
Electro-motograph principle, 76-77.
Electro-motograph, the, 186.
Electrostatic telephone, the, 75.
Engines, procuring of, for electric lighting, 115-118.
England, views in, on Edison's experiments with electric light, 98-100; last country in general adoption of electricity, 122; first public exhibition of phonograph in, 153-156; Edison's jokes on war machines taken seriously in, 194-196; Edison's visit to, 277-278; newspaper men of, 296-297.
Etheroscope, the, 186.
Evening star and electric light story, 123-124.
Experiments in electrocution, 204-206.
Experts, telephone, 86-87.
Explosives, experiments, with 198-200.

F

"Faraday" anecdote, 82-83.
Farmer, Moses G., 94.
Figaro, dinner given Edison by, 273; story about Edison once published in, 273.
Filament, word coined by Edison, 86; the search for a perfect, for incandescent electric light, 95-96, 105-106.
Fish, F. P., quoted, 85-86; telephone facts given by, 89-93.
Flammarion, a favorite of Edison's, 282.
Force, Martin, 239.
Forests, telephones used in, 91-93.
Foster, Secretary, letter by, 285.
France, views in, regarding Edison's war machines, 196-198; Edison in, 272-276.
Fruit-preserver, the, 186.
Fulton, foreman at Orange laboratory, 238-239.
Fuse wire, invention of, 118-119.

G

Gaboriau, Edison's fondness for, 282.
Galvanometer, "dead beat," 186.
Galvanometer building at Orange laboratory, 225-227.
General Electric Company, 346.

Genius, Edison's definition of, 347.
Germany, the phonograph in, 147–151.
Gladstone and the phonograph, 153, 155–156.
Glenmont, Edison's residence, 17–18, 279–288.
Gounod, M., at Eiffel Tower dinner, 275.
Gout, discovery of drug used in cure of, 191.
"Grasshopper telegraph," the, 182–183.
Gray, Elisha, 73.
Green, Dr. Norvin, 65–66.
Griffin, Stockton L., 239.

H

Handwriting, Edison's, 51–52, 53.
Harmonic multiplex telegraph, the, 69–70.
Harvard University, Phonographic Archives at, 150.
Heidelberg, Edison at, 276–277.
"Hello!" origin and use of expression, in telephoning, 85–86.
Hoey, John, 276.
Hood, Thomas, believed to have predicted telephone, 143–144.
Horse, electrocution of, 205.
Hotel, the first to be lighted by electricity, 121.
Hotel Astor banquet (1905), 259–260.
Hughes, Charles T., 239.
Hughes, D. E., 82–83.
Huron Institute, 3, 4.
Hydrography, invention connected with, 184, 186.

I

Incandescent lamp. *See* Electric light.
Indianapolis, Edison a telegraph operator in, 45–47.
Inertia telephone, the, 75.
Ingelow, Jean, prediction of the phonograph by, 144.
Insull, Samuel, 239.

Interviews, newspaper, 188–189, 296. *See* Newspapers.
Inventing, Edison's opinion of art of, 349.
Inventions and patent laws, 236.
Inventors *vs.* discoverers, 177–178.
"Iolanthe" the first play in which electric lighting was employed, 120–121.
Italy, Edison visits, 277.

J

Japan, bamboo from, 96, 252.
Jeanette, the, lighted by Edison's system, 120.
Jehl, Francis, 239.
Johnson, Edward H., 81, 240.

K

Kelvin, Lord, 82, 256.
Kemmler case, 206 ff.; Edison as a witness in, 207–209; computation by proxy in connection with, 237–238.
Kennelly, Arthur E., 238.
Kerner, Marion H., 305–306.
Keyes, Dr. E. L., 101.
Kinetoscope, invention of, 165; finding suitable films for, 166; photographs for, 166–169; taking battle pictures for, 221.
Knapp, Alexander, 52.
Kruesi, John, 115, 137, 239; model of phonograph by, 137–139.

L

Laboratory, Edison's first, on train on Grand Trunk Ry., 16; sudden end of, 26–27; in Boston, 53; in New York, 63; description of the Orange, 221–248; Edison's private, in Llewellyn Park home, 227; men who have worked with Edison in his laboratories, 239–241; the Menlo Park, revisited, 261–262; present state of the Menlo Park, 264–265.

358 INDEX

Lathrop, George Parsons, 343.
Law department of Orange laboratory, 234–235.
Law Gold Indicator, the, 62–63.
Lecture, Edison's first (Boston), 58–60; at Saratoga, on loud-speaking telephone, 77–81; in New York (1879), on experiments with platinum wire, 126–133.
Lefferts, General Marshall, 64.
Legion of Honor degrees conferred on Edison, 285–287.
Leo XIII., Pope, photographed for kinetoscope, 167–168.
Library, in the Orange laboratory, 222; at Llewellyn Park residence, 280–282.
Li Hung Chang and Edison, 330–332.
Llewellyn Park, Edison's residence at, 221, 279–288.
Logue, W. S., 306.
London, news in, of Edison's invention of incandescent light, 99–100; Edison's visit to, 277–278, 296–297.
Loud-speaking telephone, 76–81.
Lowry, Grovernor P., 94, 100, 250; letter of, regarding Edison, 100–102.
Luhr, Charles W., 229–230.
Lumbermen, telephones for, 91–93.

M

Macdonald, Dr. Carlos F., 203.
MacGowan, Frank, 241.
Mackenzie, J. U., 38–39, 44.
Magnetic bridge, the, 186.
Magnetic Dinner, the, 259–260.
Magnetic telephone, the, 75.
Maisonville, Barney, 15–17, 26.
Maisonville, Captain Oliver, 15.
Marconi, 182, 337.
Maxim, Hiram, at Menlo Park, 113.
Medals, Edison's collection of, 284–287.
Megaphone, invention of, 183–184.
Memphis, Edison a telegraph operator in, 50–52.

Menlo Park, Edison locates at, 71–72; illumination with incandescent lamps at, 112–113; New York aldermen at, 113, 118–119; experiments in electrocution at, 203–206; a dinner to Edison at, 260–263; description of present appearance of, 263–266; memories of Edison at, 265; effect on, of removal of laboratory, 266.
Mercury telephone, the, 75.
Microphone, the, 186.
Milan, O., birthplace of Edison, 1–5.
Miller, Lewis, Edison's father-in-law, 288.
Millet, Frank D., use of phonograph by, 163.
Milliken, G. F., 53.
Mimeograph, invention of, 181–182.
Ministers, story of the troublesome, 200–201.
Monkeys, speech of, and phonograph, 159.
Moore, William H., 96, 108.
Motay, Tessie du, 130.
Motograph, the, 178.
Motograph receiver, the, 186.
Mt. Clemens railroad station, noteworthy incidents at, 17, 27, 38–39.
Moving pictures. *See* Kinetoscope.
Musical transmitter, the, 75.

N

Newark, Edison's factory at, 66, 71.
"New Genius of Light, The," 223.
Newspaper, Edison's publication of, when a train-boy, 17–26.
Newspapers, Edison and the, 87–89, 187–189; Edison a student of, 319; Edison's remarks on, 320–321.
Newspaper reporters, 187–190, 192–194, 201–202, 268–269, 296, 309–312, 320–321; experiences with unscientific, 309, 324–325.
New York, Edison's first experiences in, 61–66; central station in, 114–120.

INDEX

New York Edison Illuminating Company, 115.
New York *Herald* building first to adopt incandescent lighting, 120.
Nickel steel the coming metal, 336–337.
Nitro-glycerine, dangerous character of, 199.
Notion books, 249–253.

O

Ocean, telephoning across, impossible, 84–85; wireless telegraphy of the, 337.
Odoroscope, the, 184, 185.
Oil, Edison's suggested use of, in vessels, 334–336.
Old age, a preventive of, 190–191.
Orange, the laboratory at, 221–248.
Orchestra at German court and the phonograph, 149–150.
Ore-milling machinery, number of patents on, 186.
Ore separator, the magnetic, 169–171.
Ott, Fred, 167, 228.
Ott, John F., 232, 233, 240, 315.

P

Paris Exposition (1889), Edison exhibition at, 67, 178–179, 267, 270–272; statue of "New Genius of Light," at, bought by Edison, 223; an impostor impersonates Edison at, 267–270; Edison's visit to, 272–276; Legion of Honor degrees conferred on Edison, 285–286.
Pasteur on Edison and himself, 317.
Patent, specifications of, for incandescent light, 110–112.
Patents, Edison's views concerning, 122, 236; on the phonograph, 138–139; great number of, in America and in foreign countries, 176; large number for one invention, 186; on storage battery, 213; applications for, in connection with the various Edison interests, 235.
Paul Pry, Edison's second paper, 29–30.
Pauncefote, Sir Julian, letter by, 285.
Peanut trick, 30–31.
Pen, the electric, 180–181; invention of a pneumatic, 181.
Phonogram, Edison's first letter in form of a, 153–154; Gladstone's, 156.
Phonograms, Emperor William's, 150; of famous men in collection at Llewellyn Park, 156.
Phonograph, invention of, 134; Edison's account of discovery, 135–137; Kruesi's model of, 137–139; tinfoil discarded for stearin as recorder, 140–141; a forecast of its usefulness by Edison, 141–142; attempted combination of telephone and, 142–143; early predictions of, 143–145; in Germany, 147–151; humorous and other experiments with, 151–153; in England, 153–156; records of famous men, 156; in Thibet and Russia, 157–159; study of monkey and of cat language by, 159–162; the feeble-voiced coster and the, 162–163; artists' use of, 163; large number of patents covering, 186; construction and improvement of, at Orange laboratory, 233–234.
Phonograph box, made in one operation, 233.
Phonograph Experimental Department, Orange laboratory, 233–234.
Phonographic Archives, 150.
Phonographic Temple, Paris Exposition, 272.
Phonograph records, 153–157; Edison's judgment of, 347; performances at Orange for, 347–348; voices suited for, 348; Edison will not lend his voice for, 348–349.

"Phonograph's Salutation," the, 155.
Phonomotor, the, 184.
Photographs, for kinetoscope, 166-169; of Edison, 313-316.
Photography, Edison's researches in, 166.
Platinum light, Edison's, 98-99, 102; Edison's experiments with, 126-133.
Poe, favorite writer of Edison's, 282.
Porter, C. H., engine built by, 115-116.
Port Huron, Edison family at, 10-11.
Portraits of Edison, 292, 323-324.
Poste, Deputy Attorney-General, 207 ff.
Powers, Rev. H. N., "Phonograph's Salutation" by, 155.
Praying wheels supplanted by phonographs, 157-158.
Precision room in Orange laboratory, 233.
Prize-fight story in connection with kinetoscope, 169.

Q

Quadruplex telegraph, the, 68.

R

Randolph, J. F., vii, 223.
Receiver, electro-motographic, 75, 186; the chalk, 178.
Recorders in phonographs, 140-141.
Reid, Whitelaw, 276, 286.
Reis, Philip, 72-73.
Rheostat, the carbon, 185.
Ricalton, James, 96, 108.
Rockwell, Dr. A. D., 203.
Roosevelt, President, comes to Edison's aid at Patent Office, 236-237.
Roys, J. A., 28.
Ruskin, Edison's liking for, 282.
Russia, the phonograph in, 158-159.

S

San Francisco, attempted combination of telephone and phonograph in, 142-143.

Saratoga, Edison's lecture at, 77-81.
"Scratch," a discovery called a, 177.
Scripture, Dr. Edward, 150-151.
Seubel, Philip, 241.
Sextuplex telegraph, 68, 71.
Seymour, James, 241.
Shirt, fake story of the patent, 189-190.
Silver Lake laboratory, 313.
Sims, Gardiner C., engine built by, 117-118.
Sims, W. Scot, 192.
Smith, W. Wiley, 183.
Snow-melting machine, a supposititious, 188.
"Sorcery and Magic," quotation from, 122-123.
Sprague, Frank, 240-241.
Stanley, Mr. and Mrs. H. M., at Orange, 156-157.
Steel, Dreyfus' experiment in melting, 228; nickel, the coming metal, 336-337.
Stephenson, George, compliments young Edison on the *Weekly Herald*, 26.
Stevenson, Conductor Alexander, 26-28.
Stewartsville, N.J., Edison's works at, 171-174.
Stieringer, Luther, descriptive catalogue of Edison's inventions by, 67, 179; quoted, 76-77, 119-120; sketch of career of, 179-180; in the Orange laboratory, 239.
Stock-room in Orange laboratory, 224-225.
Storage battery, Edison's work over the, 213; hard tests of, 214-215; cobalt discovered to be best for making condenser, 215; Edison's statement on use of, in vehicles, 216-217; description of the perfected, 217-218; story of development of the perfected, 218-220.
Switchboards, description of telephone, 90-91.

INDEX

T

Tasimeter, the, 184–185.
Tatum, Dr. Edward, 203.
Telephone, early prophecies of, 72; certain narrow escapes from inventing, 72–73; Bell's and Gray's inventions of, 73–74; Edison's attention aroused and carbon transmitter invented, 74; Edison's inventions of various kinds of, 75; the loud-speaking, 76–81; the first practical, at Centennial Exhibition, 81; first recorded message over, 82; early form of, among Catuquinary Indians, 83–84; impracticable for telephoning across the sea, 84–85; facts respecting the, as it is to-day, 89–93; failure, to date, of combination of the phonograph and, 142–143; number of patents covering, 186.
Telephone experts, tests for, 86–87.
Telephonograph, the, 186.
Tennessee, cobalt from, 215, 216.
Tennyson, phonograph record by, 156.
Tesla, Nikola, in the Orange laboratory, 238–239.
Theatre, the first, lighted by electricity, 120–121.
Thibet, the phonograph in, 157–158.
Thomson, Sir William, 82, 256.
Ticker, Edison's improvement on, 63–64.
Times, London, notices young Edison's *Weekly Herald*, 26.
Torpedo-boat, invention of a, 192.
Torpedo-boats, Edison's views on, 340.
Trains, telegraphing from moving, 182–183.
Transmitter, carbon-button, 74, 81; musical, 75.
Trolley-car, remains of the first, 263–264.
Tyndall, Professor, on the subdivision of the electric light, 100.

U

Underground railway, London, Edison suggests electricity for, 277–278.
Upton, Francis R., 121, 126; an assistant in the Orange laboratory, 239.
Uses of the phonograph, 141–142, 157–163.

V

Vacuum pumps, 186.
Vail, J. H., 239.
Vehicles, use of storage battery in electric, 216–217.
Verne, works of, read by Edison, 282.
Vessels, suggested use of oil in, 334–336.
Vibration, location of, in telephone, 85.
Visitors' Book, Orange laboratory, 349.
Vocal engine, 184.
Voices suited for phonograph records, 348.
Voltaic pile telephone, the, 75.
Vote-recording machine, 53–54.

W

Waldorf-Astoria banquet (1904), 254–259.
Walker, Albert H., 85.
Wallick, John F., 45–47.
Wangemann, A. T. E., vii; with the phonograph in Germany, 147–150; assistant of Edison's at Orange, 233–234.
Ward, Dr. Leslie, 101.
Ward-Leonard, H., 241.
War machines, an interview on, and its results, 192–198.
Waste connected with coal consumption, 350.
Water telephone, the, 75.
Weber, August, 241.
Weekly Herald, Edison's paper when a boy, 17 ff.; copy of, preserved at Glenmont, 17–18, 283; specimen extracts from,

18–26; is complimented by George Stephenson and favorably noticed by London *Times*, 26; eviction of, from train, by Conductor Stevenson, 27; publication of, at home and discontinuance, 29.

William III., Emperor, and the phonograph, 147–151.

Wireless telegraphy, 182, 337.

Wizard of Menlo Park, Edison called, 71–72, 87, 147.

Worry, Edison's views on, 301, 320.

Wright, J. Hood, residence of, first to be lighted by electricity, 121.

X

X-ray machine, story of, in connection with McKinley's assassination, 229–230; a cardsharper's request for, 339.

X-ray room in Orange laboratory, 229.

X-rays, death of C. T. Dally from effects of, 231–232.

Z

Zoëtrope, kinetoscope suggested to Edison by, 165.

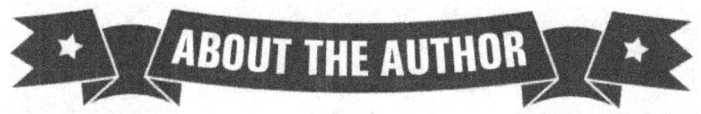

FRANCIS ARTHUR JONES
(1871 - * * * *)

English writer and journalist (b. 3/15 May 1871 in Chester), born Francis Arthur Launcelot Jones; also known as Francis Arthur Jameson.

A native of the English city of Chester, he lost his father, William Jones, at an early age. Francis and his mother, Anne, who was of Irish stock, moved to Devon during the 1880s where Mrs. Jones became a lodging house proprietor. After completing his school education Francis worked as a tutor for a few years, but eventually embarked upon a career as a music writer and journalist for The Strand Magazine. He was also involved in the Young Men's Christian Association (YMCA) at Torquay in Devon.

On 16 January 1893 [N.S.] Jones wrote to Tchaikovsky (in English) explaining that he was working on an article entitled "How Composers Compose" and asked him to send a small fragment of one of his manuscripts, as well as to answer a series of questions for his article. Jones pointed out that he had already contacted a number of composers — including Grieg, Saint-Saëns, Massenet, and Gounod — regarding the same query, and they had all kindly obliged. At the end of his letter Jones promised to forward Tchaikovsky a copy of his article. After receiving Tchaikovsky's detailed and helpful reply, Jones wrote to him again on 27 February [N.S.], apologizing for having to use English again as he was not proficient in French. He thanked the composer for the musical autograph he had sent and asked him to clarify which work it was from . Tchaikovsky replied on 28 February/12 March 1893: "You ask me about where the fragment I sent you is taken from. Unfortunately I've completely forgotten what musical phrase I communicated to you. Please let me know". It seems that Jones, not wishing to trouble the composer further, did not return the autograph to him for clarification, and no more correspondence between the two men has come to light. He had very likely realised that, since Tchaikovsky in his first letter had named The Queen of Spades as his finest work, the fragment must have been taken from that opera.

Jones's article "How Composers Compose" containing the replies of various British and European composers to his questions on the creative process, and illustrated with facsimile reproductions of portions of their manuscripts, finally appeared in two instalments in the February and April 1894 issues of The Strand Magazine. The section on Tchaikovsky appeared at the very end of the second instalment. It began with a warm tribute — "Klin, near Moscow, was the home of one of the busiest of men. It is here that the late Russian composer Tschaïkowsky, lived and worked, devoting the greater part of the day to his art" — and after the concluding paragraph — "Of his own compositions, Tschaïkowsky considered his opera La Dame de Pique the best work he had ever done, an opinion which is shared by many of his admirers" — there appeared a facsimile of the beautifully written quotation from the finale of The Queen of Spades which Tchaikovsky had sent him a year earlier.

After moving to London, Jones emigrated to New York in 1902, where he worked as a journalist for The Strand Magazine and Wide World Magazine — a career which saw him eventually rise to the position of editor and American representative of these two British monthly illustrated publications. While still a junior journalist, Jones found the time to write his first book

— one which reflected his abiding interest in music and his Christian faith: Famous Hymns and their Authors (London, 1902). For this ambitious project he had followed a similar procedure to that of his article "How Composers Compose": he interviewed (often by correspondence) both contemporary British and American hymnists, and also the descendants of the authors of famous hymns from the eighteenth and early-nineteenth century. Moreover, the book contained facsimile reproductions of the opening verses of many of these hymns. Jones dedicated the book to his mother, who had taught him as a child many of the hymns it discusses.

Jones's decision to move to America, even though he still returned to Britain occasionally for short visits, allowed him to realise another dream of his: to meet the inventor Thomas Alva Edison (1847–1931), an idol of his boyhood, about whom he would go on to write a biography: Thomas Alva Edison: Sixty Years of an Inventor's Life (New York / London, 1907). Jones was probably unaware that Tchaikovsky had been among the first to pay tribute to one of Edison's most important inventions: the phonograph (see the Endorsement of Thomas Edison's "Phonograph", written in 1889), but he would certainly have appreciated the connection! In the foreword to the second and revised edition (New York and London, 1924), Jones explained his motivation for writing this book:

This Foreword is in the nature of a confession. Thomas Alva Edison has always possessed a great fascination for me. Even when a boy in an English school I read everything concerning him that I could find. On the wall of my bedroom was placed that striking picture of him by Outcault (I think) which showed the "Wizard" listening to his first phonograph. I saw that portrait long before I ever had an opportunity of listening to a "talking machine," and visualised the inventor as a mortal who lived somewhere on earth, perhaps, but who was seen only by the elect. I thought of him as her Indian subjects are said to have thought of Queen Victoria!

When as a very young man I got my first engagement on a London magazine, and was given an assignment to write an article on Edison, the editor went to some little trouble to tell me who he was. He advised me to look him up in the Metropolitan Library or, better still, to consult the "morgue" of the London Times. I had no need to do either. The article was written without consulting any reference whatever, and the editor was kind enough to say that I "might have been personally acquainted with the inventor".

A couple of years later the publishing firm with which I was associated decided to send a man to America to write articles on this country for the delectation of English readers. I was offered the position. For many reasons I was not very enthusiastic about it, but the thought flashed through my mind: perhaps I shall see Edison! This factor helped me to decide. I hesitated no longer but packed my trunk and took ship for New York.

About a month after my arrival I wrote to Mr. Edison asking for an interview in behalf of my magazine. I did not get an immediate reply and had almost made up my mind that the inventor really was some supernatural being, when a pleasant note came saying that Mr. Edison would be pleased to see me at such and such a time. I remember it was a beautiful spring morning when I arrived in Orange and the apple and pear trees were full of bloom. Everything was so sunny and bright that I felt satisfied that the great event of my life was to take place. I reached the Laboratory about eleven o'clock and knocked at the little office just outside the gates. A workman let me in, and presently Mr. Randolph, the great man's Secretary, appeared and ushered me into the library where he said Mr. Edison would meet me in a few moments.

Left alone I felt what the French call "a great emotion". I know that when the inventor made his appearance at the door my knees knocked together. But he hurried forward with such a genial smile on his face, such a kindly look in his eyes, such a welcome in his outstretched hand, that all my nervousness vanished. I felt as though I were greeting an old friend. We sat and talked for an hour. When the interview was over, he told me that I might come whenever I wished, and that any information he or his associates could give me would be at my service.

MR. EDISON REPLYING TO SOME PUZZLING QUESTIONS.

Francis Arthur Jones (b. 1871)
Interviewing **Thomas Alva Edison** (1847–1931)
for his biography of the American inventor.

That was the first of many visits and each visit increased my admiration for this wonderful man. One cannot speak to Edison for five minutes without realising that he is in the presence of a very unusual personality — a man who is already among the immortals. And yet he laughs and tells amusing stories in a way that is very human and wholly delightful. Born of these intimate talks came a great desire to depict Edison as I knew him for others; and one day I asked him if he would have any objection to my publishing the results of my many interviews in book form. He had none. In fact he gave me full permission to consult everything there was concerning him in the Library and put at my disposal a mass of valuable material. I set to work at once and for many weeks occupied a desk in the Edison library where I was left undisturbed and free to use anything that might prove useful.

I have made this frank personal confession in the first person, to explain why it was that I wrote a Life of Edison. It has been penned because of my intense admiration for him and as a modest tribute to the man who must be regarded as the greatest inventive genius of all times".

There are indications that Francis Arthur Jones may still have been active as a literary agent in New York in the early 1930s, but these are not conclusive and nothing is known to us about his later years.

This section **'ABOUT THE AUTHOR'** uses material from the
Wikipedia article **Francis Arthur Jones**:
http://en.tchaikovsky-research.net/pages/Francis_Arthur_Jones,
Authors History:
http://en.tchaikovsky-research.net/index.php?title=Francis_Arthur_Jones&action=history
which is released under the Creative Commons Attribution-*ShareAlike 3.0*

FEEDBACK

Now that you have read the book ...

Was it interesting?

Did you enjoy what you wanted to read?
Was there any room for improvement?

Let us know at:
http://www.diamondbooks.ca/feedback

Your feedback is highly appreciated.
Thank you!

Would you like to buy a copy of

' THOMAS EDISON '
by Francis Arthur Jones ?

Please visit:
http://www.diamondbooks.ca/books

HUGE SAVINGS ON BULK ORDERS
(10 copies, 20 copies, 50 copies, 100 copies, 500 copies, 1000 copies)

Please send your request at:
http://www.diamondbooks.ca/bulkorder

Would you like to buy a copy of 'GREAT ASTRONOMERS' ?

Original Edition

**Please visit:
http://www.diamondbooks.ca/books**

Would you like to buy a copy of 'FAMOUS CHEMISTS' ?

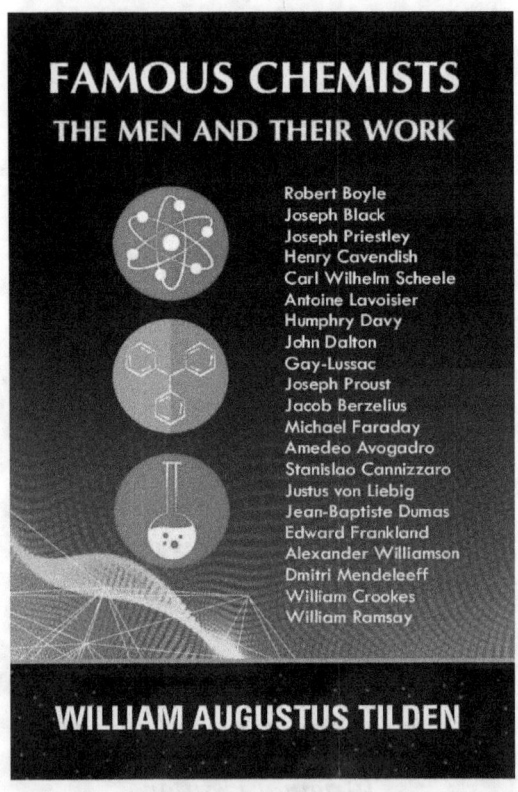

Original Edition

Please visit:
http://www.diamondbooks.ca/books

Would you like to buy a copy of 'CLAUDIUS PTOLEMY'?

Please visit:
http://www.diamondbooks.ca/books

**Would you like to buy a copy of
'NICOLAUS COPERNICUS' ?**

**Please visit:
http://www.diamondbooks.ca/books**

**Would you like to buy a copy of
'JOHANNES KEPLER' ?**

**Please visit:
http://www.diamondbooks.ca/books**

Would you like to buy a copy of 'ISSAC NEWTON' ?

Please visit:
http://www.diamondbooks.ca/books

Would you like to buy a copy of 'GALILEO GALILEI' ?

Please visit:
http://www.diamondbooks.ca/books

Would you like to buy a copy of 'EDMOND HALLEY' ?

Please visit:
http://www.diamondbooks.ca/books

Would you like to buy a copy of 'PIERRE-SIMON LAPLACE' ?

Please visit:
http://www.diamondbooks.ca/books

Would you like to buy a copy of 'JOHN HERSCHEL' ?

Please visit:
http://www.diamondbooks.ca/books

**Would you like to buy a copy of
'WILLIAM PARSONS' ?**

**Please visit:
http://www.diamondbooks.ca/books**

**Would you like to buy a copy of
'THE TRUE BENJAMIN FRANKLIN' ?**

Original Edition

**Please visit:
http://www.diamondbooks.ca/books**

Would you like to buy a copy of 'MICHAEL FARADAY'?

THE BEST LITERARY COLLECTION

MICHAEL FARADAY
MAN OF SCIENCE

Michael Faraday (September 22, 1791 – August 25, 1867)
AN ENGLISH SCIENTIST
(ELECTROMAGNETISM AND ELECTROCHEMISTRY)

WALTER COPELAND JERROLD

Original Edition

Please visit:
http://www.diamondbooks.ca/books

FOR ALL PUBLISHED TITLES

Please visit:
http://www.diamondbooks.ca/books

HUGE SAVINGS ON BULK ORDERS
(10 copies, 20 copies, 50 copies, 100 copies, 500 copies, 1000 copies)

Please send your request at:
http://www.diamondbooks.ca/bulkorder